鈴木隆之

表現空間論

建築／小説／映画の可能性

TAKAYUKI TAKI SUZUKI

Fictive Space :
for Architecture, Literature and Film

論創社

表現空間論
建築／小説／映画の可能性

FICTIVE SPACE :
for Architecture, Literature and Film

To Readers in English

I wrote the text in primarily in Japanese first, though sometimes I wrote in English first. I then translated into both languages. My English has its shortcomings, however, hopefully it reflects the process of my thinking. his book includes some images of art, and a few images of architecture. These images are parts of a whole, and it is advised that the reader look up these sources as well as other various sources mentioned in the book.

Taki

日本語の読者へ

　日本語で読めば理解できるように書いているのは当然のことですが、英語と合わせ読むことで、理解が突然深まることもよくあることです。

　また、特に学生や若い読者は、これから先、英語でのプレゼンテーションを求められる場合も少なからずあるでしょう。

　その時のためにも、日本語と英語とを突き合わせて読むことをお勧めします。

　この本では、言及する建築やアートの作品の図版を多くは掲載していません。

　一点を掲載するより、読者がインターネットで画像検索したほうが、はるかに多くの情報を得られるからです。

　検索する際は、必ず英語で検索すべきです。インターネットは情報の「海」ですが、英語での「海」に比べると、日本語での「海」は湖程度の広さしかありません。

著者より

Fictive Space : for Architecture, Literature and Film　　　　　　　*contents*

To Readers in English　　　　II

Prologue

A Fiction Called "FUTURE"　　　　2

Chapter One

Structural Similarity of Architecture, Literature, Film, and Possibly...

　1.　Description / Construction of Scenery　　6

　2.　Towards Architecture, Literature and Film　　10

　3.　Space for "Possibility"　　12

　4.　Predictable Difficulty　　16

　5.　Crisis of "Future"　　20

　6.　The End of "Growth"　　26

　7.　Fictive "Future"　　32

　8.　Escape from "Realism"　　36

Chapter Two

The Planning behind Literature

　1.　Planning a Novel　　46

　2.　Blueprints of the Novel　　58

　3.　Who is Actually Involved, Protagonist or Author?　　64

iv

表現空間論——建築／小説／映画の可能性　　　　もくじ

日本語の読者へ　　　III

序　章

〈未来〉という名のフィクション　　　3

第1章

建築／小説／映画の構造的類似、あるいは

　1．風景の描写／構築　　　7
　2．建築／小説／映画へ　　　11
　3．「可能性」の空間　　　13
　4．予期される困難　　　17
　5．〈未来〉の危機　　　21
　6．「成長」の終焉　　　27
　7．〈未来〉とフィクション　　　33
　8．リアルからの〈脱出〉　　　37

第2章

文学の計画

　1．小説の計画　　　47
　2．小説の設計図　　　59
　3．主人公と作者あるいは事件　　　65

v

4. Proper Noun, Symbol, Memory — 74

5. The Shape of Reality / Shape in Imagination — 80
—*The Atomic Bomb Dome and the Tower of Babel*

6. Shape and Imagination in Literature — 88

7. An Architect Who Died Young, and His Daughter — 92

8. "The Death of the Author" — 100

9. The Discipline and Phenomenon of Overlapping — 104

10. A Small Crack in Overlapping — 112

11. How to Forget the World — 120

12. Possibility of Lightness in Architecture and Novel — 130

13. Memories of Future — 140

14. About Emotion — 152

15. From Words to Pictures — 160

Chapter Three

Film

1. Moscow —*Four Timelines* — 188

2. The Magic of Film —*"Cutting" and "Editing (Montage)"* — 192

3. Time in Reality / Space in Illusion — 196

4. A City in Your Brain — 198

5. The Camera which Captures Inter-Subjectivity in Space — 202

6. "Future" is Another Name for "Memory" — 210

7. Imagine the Invisible Space — 216

8. Architecture as "Another World" — 222

Chapter Four

Architecture

1. "Another Time" in "Another World" — 230

4. 固有名、シンボル、記憶 75

5. 現実の姿／空想の形態 81
　　——原爆ドームとバベルの塔

6. 文学における「形態」と想像力 89

7. ある早世した建築家とその娘 93

8. 「作者の死」 101

9. 「重ねあわせ」の原理と現象 105

10. 重ね合わせに生じた小さな亀裂 113

11. コマーシャルの言葉と世界 121

12. 〈軽さ〉の可能性——建築において、物語において 131

13. 〈未来〉という名の記憶 141

14. 感情について 153

15. 言葉から映像へ 161

第3章

映　画

1. モスクワ——4つのタイムライン 189

2. 映画の魔術——「カット」と「編集（モンタージュ）」 193

3. リアルな時間／幻想の空間 197

4. 脳内都市 199

5. カメラ、空間の主観性として 203

6. 「未来」とは「記憶」の別の名 211

7. 見えない空間を夢想せよ 217

8. 建築とは「もうひとつの世界」 223

第4章

建　築

1. 「もうひとつの世界」の「もうひとつの時間」 231

2.	"Cutting" and "Editing" in Architecture	234
3.	Hidden Possibilities — *"Expressionism Debate"*	238
4.	The Story of the Formalists	244
5.	Learning from Moscow	252
6.	Formative Design in Literature	258
7.	*Alpine Architecture* and *Terrain of Future*	262
8.	"The Magic Mountain" in Ronchamp	266
9.	Design Architecture in Fiction	268
10.	The Real "Another World" in the Ocean	274
11.	Necessary Conditions for the Future	278
12.	Information, Imagination and the Instant City	286
13.	The Technology of Literature and Space	290

Chapter Five

Future

1.	We Might Have Known from the Beginning	304
2.	Aura and Copy-Paste	308
3.	A Nightmare Called "Identity"	316
4.	How to Draw Your Self-Portrait	326
5.	You Can Do Nothing but Travel	332
6.	What is Possible with Architecture?	336
7.	Once Ideology Tried to Lead	342
8.	Trotsky and "the Eggs"	352

Epilogue

Dedicated to Annie Hall   362

2. 建築空間の「カット」と「編集」 235

3. 埋もれた「可能性」──「表現主義論争」 239

4. フォルマリストたちの「物語」 245

5. モスクワから学ぶこと 253

6. 文学における「造形」の力 259

7. 『アルプス建築』と『未来の地形』 263

8. ロンシャンの「魔の山」 267

9. フィクションで建築を設計せよ 269

10. 現実の「もうひとつの世界」 275

11. 「未来」のための必要条件 279

12. 情報、想像力、インスタント・シティ 287

13. 空間と文学のテクノロジー 291

第5章

未　来

1. 最初からわかっていたはずだった 305

2. アウラとコピペ 309

3. 「アイデンティティ」という悪夢 317

4. 自画像の描きかた 327

5. 「旅」をするしか他にない 333

6. 「建築に何が可能か？」 337

7. かつては「思想」が導こうとした 343

8. トロッキーと卵 353

終章

アニー・ホールのために 363

Fictive Space :
for Architecture, Literature and Film

TAKAYUKI TAKI SUZUKI

———— 鈴木隆之

表現空間論
建築／小説／映画の可能性

Prologue

A Fiction Called "FUTURE"

We can only talk about "future" as fiction.

This applies not only to the distant future, but also to the near future. The architecture that may someday be built is also fiction written down in the form of a blueprint.

Not only SF can picture the "future," but architecture, literature, and film can as well. Future as fantasy sometimes shows a trivialized possibility of the future. Even "realism" involves a fiction called "this world." "Magic realism," which is one of the important devices applied in a novel, tries to build a "magical world" to reveal a fictional part of "this world."

Future not only in the sense of time, but also in the sense of history. After the renaissance, referring to history became synonymous with designing fictive "future" in art and architecture.

Future" is not the destination. It is the power that seeks to stay. In the early period on modernism, poets and architects who named themselves "Futurists" emerged. Meaning that the "future" is the motive of modernism. In the same period, artists called "Expressionists" moved their interests from "object" to "motion." We can feel the power of motion in their paintings.

And "future" never means "hope." The inevitability of the future is

序　章

〈未来〉という名のフィクション

　〈未来〉は、フィクションとしてしか語りえない。

　遠い未来のことだけではない。数年後に建つはずの建築も、実現前には設計図に記されたフィクションである。

　SF小説やSF映画だけではない。ファンタジーとしての未来は、むしろ矮小化された「可能性」に過ぎない。リアリズムですら「この世界」という名のフィクションを含んでいる。小説におけるマジック・リアリズムの手法は、「この世界」のフィクショナルな部分を際立たせるために、奇妙な〈未来〉を構築する。

　時制としての未来だけではない。時には歴史ですら、〈未来〉になる。ルネサンス以降のアートにおいては、歴史を参照することは、〈未来〉をフィクティブ（創作的）に構築することと同義になった。

　〈未来〉は目的地ではない。それは今ここにこそ求められる「力」だ。モダニズムの初期には、「未来派」と自らを任ずる詩人や建築家たちが現れた。それは〈未来〉こそが、モダニズムの原動力だったからだ。同じころ「表現主義」の画家たちは関心を「事物」から「運動」へと移した。彼らの絵画からは、「運動」を引き起こす「力」があふれ出る。

　そして〈未来〉とは「希望」と決して同義ではない。生きるものすべて

always depressing like death which comes for us all... That is why people have been trying to build "fictive future." After modernism, society is losing a drive for motion. The reality of stagnation sometimes makes us distrust the significance of fiction.

But we can never give up imagining "the future." live in a peaceful iteration, and yet we want to escape it.

Today, it is pretty difficult to be affirmative for the coming future. The Global environment is now collapsing. Modernism that has always been accompanied by evolution and development is now closing its role. But we cannot live today if we have no future.

We are losing imagination for "future" after the ending of age for "growth" then sometimes we confuse "reality" with "political correctness." Not only such real issue, not simple future but something lurking between inevitability and fiction, or between iteration and escape. That is what we must find and watch.

Now we begin to see. We are going to read descriptions as example, and walk in spaces where it is present. Then we will dig up the method to express it.

We will see the thing lurking between invitability and fiction after researching how to design fiction.

We move into the realm of literature, film and architecture.

We will certainly come to know them all as "fiction." It will become apparent what binds fiction and reality together.

Finally, we will see the "future."

にとってやがて死が訪れるように、確実性としての未来は常に暗い。だからこそひとは、フィクショナルな〈未来〉を構築しようとしてきた。今、社会は「運動」しようとする「力」を失いつつある。停滞のリアリティが、フィクションの有効性を疑わせる。

　しかし私たちは、〈未来〉を諦めることもできない。私たちは日常の「反復」のなかを生きているが、「反復」からの「脱出」も常に夢見ている。

　いまや〈未来〉を単純に肯定することはできない。地球環境は壊れかけている。進化、発展というフィクションとともにあった「モダニズム」は終わりを告げられた。だが私たちは「未来」なしでは今を生きることもできない。

　私たちが見つめなければいけないのはただ目の前にある現実ではない。単純な未来像でもない。〈成長〉の時代を終えた今、私たちはうまく〈未来〉を思い描くことができなくなり、結果〈現実〉をポリティカル・コレクトネスと混同するようにすらなっている。だが確実性とフィクションとの隙間に、あるいは「反復」と「脱出」との中途に忍び込むもの。私たちはそれを見つめなければならない。それは現在のなかに、予兆として——あるいは記憶として、忍び込んでいる。

　それを見よう。それを見せる記述を読み、それがある空間を歩こう。そしてそれを表現する方法を探り当てよう。

　そのために本書では、フィクションの構築方法を詳細にみる。フィクションと確実性との隙間がどのような形をしているのか、それで浮かび上がるだろう。

　小説と映画、そして建築への旅を始めよう。

　それらはすべて、同じようにフィクションであることがやがて知れるだろう。と同時に、それぞれが現実とどのような関係を取り結んでいるのかも、明らかになる。

　〈未来〉がその時、見えてくるだろう。

〈未来〉という名のフィクション——序　章　　5

Chapter One

Structural Similarity of Architecture, Literature, Film, and Possibly...

1. Description / Construction of Scenery

A train runs through the forest. You sit by the window and look at raindrops as they are on the brink of dropping off their branches. High school students on the train sometimes laugh and talk in high voices but you are not listening. You are only looking at the raindrops. Raindrops silently fall into you and make a dark pond in the bottom of your mind. You are looking up at the forest from the bottom of the pond, and the train is still running.

Glaring outside the window, you ask yourself the following: "What should I do? I took off on this journey because I didn't want to do whatever I was doing. But I know I can still do nothing except look at the raindrops dropping throughout the forest." You assume that it will keep raining until the train arrives at its destination, and that the journey will end before you realize it, having changed nothing.

You will find that the scenery outside of the window begins to change slightly. The raindrops dropping from the branches are dwindling. Instead of raindrops, sunlight begins to fall. The sunlight falls on the

第1章

建築／小説／映画の構造的類似、あるいは

1. 風景の描写／構築

　列車は森のなかを走っている。あなたは窓際の席に座り、木々の隙間か
ら落ちてくる雨粒を眺めている。列車のなかでは登校途中の生徒たちが時
おり嬌声をあげている。だがあなたは聞いていない。ただ、雨粒を眺めて
いる。雨粒はあなたのなかに静かに落ちていき、そこに暗い池をつくり出
す。池の底から森を見上げているようなあなたを乗せて、列車は走り続け
る。

　窓の外を睨みつけながら、あなたは考える。——いったい何をしたらい
いのだろう？　何もかも嫌になって旅に出たのはいいけれど、ただ森から
零れ落ちる雨粒を見つめていて、何ができる？　あなたはこの雨が、終着
駅までずっと降り続けるのだろうと思う。何も変わらぬまま、旅はいつか、
知らぬ間に終わるのだろう、と。

　その時、あなたは気がつく。列車の窓からの風景が、微妙に変化を始め
たことに。森の枝葉の隙間から落ちる雨粒は少しずつ減っている。その代
わりに零れ始めたのは、日の光だ。頼りない光が、隙間から差し始め、そ

7

window of the train and it fades as the raindrops begin to disappear. Trying not to blink, you witness the transformation.

After a few minutes, the rain is gone and the clear light of the morning fills the forest. You are blinded by the light.

You get an inkling that you will remember this moment for the rest of your life. At the moment of death you will surely remember that light.

At that time of the inkling, you might think like one of the following examples:

CASE 1:

"I will write a novel describing this scenery." The idea flickers faintly in your mind. The forest, rain, and the light. The train running through the scenery, and the eyes looking at it through the window. These are memories that will be come back to life in the future. A Novel can depict all of this. Finally, you write the first line of the novel.

CASE 2:

"I will design a work of architecture depicting this scenery." The idea flickers faintly in your mind. The forest, rain, and the light. The train running through the scenery. The architect creates the future from memory. Finally, you draw the first line of the drawing.

Literature and Architecture can co-exist in this sense. The end result, depiction and construction, seem pretty different. But is that really the case?

Is the writing of a novel solely about depicting something? No. To write a novel is to plan a story and to build a world in the story.

Is the designing of architecture truly only about building something from nothing? No. To design architecture is to plan a society and describe a story in the society.

So you should formulate questions like this:

How can I construct a novel?

How can I depict in architecture?

8   Chapter 1———*Structural Similarity of Architecture, Literature, Film, and Possibly...*

の量は雨粒が減るのにつれ増えていく。あなたはそれを、瞬きの時間まで惜しむほどに見つめ続ける。

　木々の隙間から落ちる雨粒はやがて完全に姿を消し、午前の鮮やかな光が、森のなかを満たす。その光にあなたの目は眩む。

　——この風景を、生涯忘れることはない。そうあなたは予感する。

　——やがて死ぬときには、この光のことを思い出すのだろう。

　そしてあなたはこう考えるのかもしれない。

　ケース１。

　この風景を、小説に書こう。あなたの頭のなかに、そんなアイデアが小さく閃く。森と雨と光、そのなかを潜り抜けていく列車、そして列車の窓から雨と光の一滴すら見逃すまいとしている視線。それらは未来によみがえるはずの記憶だ。そのすべてを小説なら描写することができる。あなたはやがて、物語の最初の一行を書き始める。

　ケース２。

　この風景を、やがて建築としてつくり出そう。あなたの頭のなかに、そんなアイデアが小さく閃く。森と雨と光、そのなかを潜り抜けていく列車。建築は記憶をつくり出すはずの未来だ。あなたはやがて、設計図の最初の線を引き始める。

　小説と建築とは、このように始まりを共有することができる。その後の、描写と構築とは、互いに異なる作業のようには見える。だが本当にそうだろうか？

　そもそも、小説を書くことは、ただ描写する作業だろうか？　違う。それは物語を計画し、物語のなかの世界を構築しようとする試みだ。

　あるいは、建築を設計することは、ゼロから構築する作業だろうか？それは社会を計画し、社会のなかの物語を描写しようという試みに近いはずだ。

　だから、問いを立てるとすればむしろこうである。

　小説をいかに構築することができるか？

　建築でいかに描写することができるか？

　　　　　　　　　　建築／小説／映画の構造的類似、あるいは——第１章　　9

You should have begun to think about these questions when you looked at the light shining through the forest.

2. Towards Architecture, Literature and Film

You are watching a movie.

A car is driving along the highway.[1] The highway leads into an underground tunnel. A small circle of light emerges ahead, the hole becomes bigger, before the car finds itself on an elevated road. After a while, the car -the camera once again enters a short period of darkness.

Images of recurring light and dark remind you of the scenery from the train.

The scenery of the raindrops and the sunlight. You remember the first novel that you wrote after getting off the train. All parts of the novel had occurred before you got on the train. You remember the work of architecture you designed after writing the novel. You visualize the sunlight leaking between the branches of the camphor tree in the courtyard, which reaches the wall of the house. Every time a car in the movie runs into darkness, you begin to search your memories. Every time a car gets on an elevated road, another memory comes to mind.

You feel that memory is similar to film. The chronological order dissipates, and the point of view changes. You find that memories are always edited. As a story consists of a lot of edited shots, consciousness consists of edited memories.

A novel is similar to a movie. They are completely similar in terms of narration and perspective. The only difference between them is the ways we vizualize them.

Architecture is similar to a movie. They have a common narrative of visualization. However, most architects are not self-conscious of utilizing this in the process of designing.

10   Chapter 1——*Structural Similarity of Architecture, Literature, Film, and Possibly...*

木々の隙間から落ちてくる光を眺めながら、あなたはこれらの問いについて考え始める。

2．建築／小説／映画へ

あなたは映画を見ている。

車が高速道路を走っている。道は地下に降りトンネルに入る。道の先に光の穴が見え、それはすぐに広がり、次に車は高架の上を走っている。[1] それからまた沈み再び短い闇に入る。

その繰り返しの映像を見ながら、あなたは思いだす。森のなかを走る列車から見たあの雨粒と光の風景を。

あなたの記憶が少し混乱する。あの列車を降りて後に、最初に書いた小説のことを、あなたは覚えている。小説に書かれたことは、すべて列車に乗る前に起こっていた。あなたはその後に設計した建築の風景を思い浮かべる。庭に植えたクスノキの枝葉を通って、建築に光が注いていたのを記憶している。映画のなかの車が暗闇に入るとともに記憶の探索が始まり、高架に上がるたびに別の場面がよみがえる。

記憶は映画に似ている、とあなたは感じる。時系列が入れ替わり、視点も移り変わる。記憶は編集されている、とあなたは気がつく。撮影されたフィルムが編集されてひとつのストーリーとなるように、記憶も編集されて意識に現れる。

小説と映画はかなり近い。記憶の話法としては同じだと言ってもいい。ただ、視覚的に異なる。

建築と映画もかなり近い。視覚の話法としては、共通すると言ってもいい。ただ、建築の設計過程で編集という作業を自覚的にしてきたものは少ない。

建築／小説／映画の構造的類似、あるいは――第1章　*11*

A movie sometimes depicts the future. Motion picture is quite adequate in picturing the imagery of the future. Motion picture often give a fictional landscape to a real city. There is no difference between history and future in motion pictures.

You notice these things while watching a movie. Memories become substantial, they make something happen in the real world, and disappear as ephemeral memories. Looking at such stories and pictures, you consider the possibility of film that can be one of the keys to find the "future" between novel and architecture.

3. Space for "Possibility"

I wrote part 1 and 2 with "you" as the subject of the sentence because you might have had similar thoughts. Anyone can experience space, scenery and memory as I did.

I am one of "you." I have certainly been on a train running through a forest. I have looked at raindrops and sunlight leaking through gaps between the branches. A fairly long time has passed since then.

The first novel[2] I wrote earned an award from "*GUNZO*" literature magazine, and I have been writing novels since then. Now I have my own architect office and a position as a professor at a university.

In 2014, my novel *The Perfect World*[3] was published. The story occurs in the near future, and I wrote it as a Science Fiction movie project.

—Destruction of environment, terrorism, chain of violence caused by false information. The people begin to believe that this world is collapsing. One day, a huge meteor passes by the earth, barely missing. This "event" wakes people up to the reality that the world might come to an end. The demise of the world is inevitable. With the help of fear, one smart guy presented an idea to construct "another world" to the United Nations. The man told them that this constructed world would

映画はしばしば未来を描く。映像というメディアが、未来のイメージを描くのに適しているからだろう。映像は実在する街ですら、フィクショナルな風景に変える。未来と歴史との違いは、映像のなかでは存在しない。

　映画を見ながら、あなたはそんなことを考える。記憶が実体化し、それが何かを引き起こしては、再び記憶として消えていく物語とその映像を見ながら。小説と建築の共通点を考えるとき、そこに「未来」の可能性を見出そうとするなら、映画もまた考察の対象から欠かせないものになる。

3. 「可能性」の空間

　「あなた」を主語に書いてきたのは、あなたにも、こうした思考をする／した可能性があるからだ。空間と風景と記憶について、こうした経験をする可能性は、だれにもある。

　僕もそのひとりだ。確かに僕は学生時代に森を抜ける列車に乗った。車窓から、枝葉を抜け落ちる雨粒と光を眺めていた。あれから長い時間が過ぎた。

　最初の小説を書き、それが新人賞を得[2]たことで、その後も小説を書き続けた。設計事務所を構え、建築を講じる教員にもなった。

　小説『パーフェクト・ワールド[3]』を2014年に上梓した。これは近未来を想定したSF映画のためのストーリーを持つ。

　──環境破壊、テロリズム、偽情報の氾濫による暴力の連鎖。世界はこれらによって壊れかけているとひとびとは感じ始めていた。そんな時、地球の上空を掠めるように巨大隕石が通過する。この「出来事」で不安と恐怖は一気にリアリティを帯びる。世界崩壊はほぼ不可避に違いない。この恐怖を利用して、ある男が国連に、「もうひとつの世界」の建設を提案する。この世界が滅びても、「もうひとつの世界」が生き延びられるように、と。やがて「もうひとつの世界」は実現する。だがそれは、この世界の衰

建築／小説／映画の構造的類似、あるいは──第1章　　*13*

continue forever, even if this world will come to an end. After a few decades, the "Another World" is realized. However this world is undoubtedly stopping to function because of the "Another World." The man knew that this would happen to the world. He is satisfied with the "Another World" that is built as a huge work of architecture that denies "growth." This is the plot.

The first draft was presented by Greg Manos[4] who is a screenplay writer in the United States. Greg got an idea that he would make the story with someone knowledgeable in both architecture and writing, because the movie will be shot in a fictional, huge work of architecture. And he figured that it would be better if the architect and novelist is Japanese, because the huge architecture would be more minimalistic than our world. A Japanese architect must have a good sense of minimal space, supposed Greg. So he found me.

The relationship between Greg and I is that of client and architect. Greg asked me to design "Another World" with the kind of society it was, and the kind people that lived there in mind... And I also designed the story as a novel.

These designs are not applicable in the real world. Architecture in both film, and the novel, are equally fictitious.

Fiction is not the same as fantasy. For example, "Harry Potter" is fantasy. Unlike fantasy, fiction shows a possible future...for today or another day. You can see what it means if you think about a process of designing architecture. The architect presents an idea as one of several possible options. It shows something different from what is right in front of you, and is like peering into "another world." Designing spaces including various possibilities is exactly what fiction should do.

Design architecture as fiction broadens the possibilities of architecture. Also, applying techniques from architecture, might help you to write a

弱を決定的なものにしてしまう。男はそれを、あらかじめ知っていたのだ。男は「もうひとつの世界」に満足している。それが「成長」を拒否する「建築」のなかに実現したことに——そんなプロットだ。

　原案はアメリカの脚本家グレッグ・マノスによる。グレッグは、ひとつの「建築」が主舞台となるこのストーリーを建築と小説の両方を知るものとともにつくり上げたいと考えた。さらに、それが日本人ならばもっといい、とグレッグは思ったという。なぜなら「もうひとつの世界」は、今ある地球上の世界よりも、ずっと小さい。小さい世界について、日本人ならばアイデアを持っているのではないか？　グレッグはそれで僕を探し当てた。

　グレッグと僕との関係は、まさにクライアントと設計者のそれになった。グレッグは「もうひとつの世界」がどのような社会で、どんな人間が住む予定なのかを話す。それを聞いて僕は、その社会の容器としての建築を設計する。そして僕はさらに、その物語を小説として「設計」したわけだ。
　これらの「設計」は、物理的に建設される予定を含まない。映画のなかの建築も、小説も、ともにフィクションだ。
　フィクションはファンタジーとは異なる。ファンタジーとは例えば「ハリー・ポッター」シリーズのような幻想のことだ。それに対してフィクションとは未来の——あるいは現在や過去にもありえたかもしれない——選択肢を描く。建築の設計を考えればそれはよく理解できる。その場所にどのような空間が出現しうるか、可能性は無限にある。建築家はそのうちのひとつの可能性を選択して提示する。それは今目の前にあるものとは異なるもの、つまりは「もうひとつの世界」を見せることになるだろう。多様な可能性を含む空間を構想すること、それがフィクションの役割だ。
　建築をフィクションとしてとらえることは、だから建築の可能性を広げるだろう。そして小説や映画に、建築のような設計手法を応用すれば、新

建築／小説／映画の構造的類似、あるいは——第1章　*15*

new kind of novel, or make a new kind of film.

That is why we are going to research the similarity of architecture, literature, and film.

4. Predictable Difficulty

We can find many examples of research and several essays that analyze architecture, literature and film comparatively.

However, most of the research is focused on architecture and cites described in literature,[5] or to explain architectural concepts by quoting existing literature. Some architects tried to apprehend film from an architectural point of view.[6] Another critic analyzed architecture like it was film.[7] This research teaches us a lot of things, but it is not satisfactory. These only show us a resemblance of a part or a shared appearance of architecture, literature and film. They have never looked at them equally. They have not applied the same perspective across the board, and they have not tried to construct them using the same construction method. It means previous works were useful as critiques, but fell short in the practical realm.

"Architecture is the same as literature,"[8] said Hiroshi Hara.[9] This book owes a lot to Hara's work. Except for Hara's study, there has not been a lot of relevant discussion on the topic.

On the other hand, we can intuitively point out structural similarity between the novel and architecture, and understand it without difficulty. Let's look at the beginning of the novel titled *Snow Country* by Yasunari Kawabata.[10]

> *The train came out of the long tunnel into the snow country. The earth lay white under the night sky.*

> (translated by E. G. Seidensticker)

しい小説や映画が生まれてくるかもしれない。

　建築／小説／映画のあいだの構造的類似について考察しようとするのは、そのためだ。

4．予期される困難

　建築、文学、映画の作品を批評的に比較検討した研究は少なくない。

　しかしそれらの多くは、文学のなかに現れる建築や都市を論じるものであり、あるいは建築空間を文学作品の言葉を引用して説明するものだった[5]。映画を建築的な視点から見ようとする試み[6]、あるいは建築を映画的に解析した本もある[7]。これらの研究が教えるところは多いが、それでも十分ではない。これらは建築と文学あるいは映画の、類似する部分あるいは共有される性質について論じている。つまり建築／文学／映画をまるごと同じ場に引きずり出そうとするものではなかった。同じ見方ですべてを見ていたのではなかったし、同じ方法でそれらを構築しようと試みたのでもなかった。つまり先行する研究の多くは、批評としての力は十分に持っていたかもしれないが、つくり出す力には大きな不足があった。

　建築は文学と全く同じだ[8]、とまで言い切ったのは原広司だ[9]。本書は多く原の論考の影響を受けている。だが原以外によって、そこまで突っ込んだ考察が多くなされているわけではなかった。

　一方で、直感的には、例えば小説と建築の構造的類似は容易に提示できるし、理解も難しくない。

　川端康成の小説『雪国』[10]の冒頭部分を見てみよう。

　　トンネルを抜けると、そこは雪国だった。夜の底が白くなった。

Kawabata is often associated with a school of literature called neo-sensualism (*shin-kankaku-ha*). So we can understand this sentence by sensation more than logic. The original is written in Japanese, but we can clearly feel the sensual scenery in the translation. Or in the translation more so than the original, the structure of space appears clearly.

In this case, Snow Country is architecture. Falling under the same category of architecture is the "Long Tunnel" of the novel's opening lines. A space slightly different from real, everyday space (Snow Country) + the path of entry (Long Tunnel) = architecture. The feeling we get when we read this sentence is similar to the experience we have when we enter a great old temple or a well-designed theater.

The protagonist that emerges from the depths of the darkness that is the tunnel, looks at this space as another world. The protagonist who have had a personal problem in the ordinary world goes into "another world" = goes inside the architecture through a space of transition = "tunnel." The "another world" gives a feeling that something will happen to the protagonist, or the reader by means of a spatial event that is "the earth lay white under the night sky."

Like this, we can intuitively grasp the structural similarity between the novel and architecture. But it is just intuition, and the beginning of a theory. For developing it to the theory of construction, we have to go further than the beginning, and research a lot more details of architecture, literature, and film. It's not enough to think about structural similarity. If we review only structural similarity, we might miss essential differences. "structurally same" doesn't mean "equivalent." Architecture / literature / film have their differences as well as similarities. We need to be careful looking at the difference that might have a concealed logic in it for construction.

As the protagonist in *Snow Country* has a private problem, all of us have problems searching for meaning in life. There is no doubt that the novel

「新感覚派」と呼ばれた川端らしく、この一文は論理的というよりも、感覚的につかみやすい。しかしながら、日本語の感覚がなければ成立しないかと言えば、そんなことはない。むしろ、英語への翻訳を見ると、その空間構造がはっきりと立ち現れる。

ここではつまり、「雪国」こそが建築なのだ。その内部に入る通路＝「長いトンネル」もこの建築の一部だと言ってもいい。日常とは少し違う空間（雪国）＋そこに入り込むための通路（トンネル）＝建築。この書き出し部分が呼び起こす感覚は、古い寺や上質の劇場に入るときの感覚に通底する。

「トンネル」の手前の、夜の底が暗い〈日常の空間〉から来た主人公にとっては、「夜の底が白くなる」空間とは、〈異化された空間〉、わかりやすく言えば〈別世界〉だ。〈日常の空間〉で個人的問題を抱えていた主人公は、「トンネル」という移行空間を経て、〈別世界〉＝建築内部に入り込んだ。〈別世界〉は主人公に対し（あるいは読者にも対し）、そこでやがて何かが起こる予感を与える。「夜の底が白く」なるという、空間的な事象によって。

こうして小説と建築の構造的類似を、直感的に感得することができる。だが、これを一つの理論にするには——特につくるための理論として構築するには、この直感の起点から遥か遠くまでを詳細に見ていく必要がある。そして、構造的類似が取りこぼしているかもしれない両者の本質的な差異についても、注意深く見ていかなければならない。構造的に「全く同じ」だということは、差異がないということを意味するのではない。建築／小説／映画は同じであり、同時に差異がある。その差異にこそ、つくるための理論に必要な、最後の論理が隠されているのかもしれない。

『雪国』の主人公が問題を抱えていたように、僕たちは皆、生きるための問題を抱えている。小説も建築も、その問題に関わっているのは間違い

建築／小説／映画の構造的類似、あるいは——第1章　*19*

and architecture is connected to these issues. But each of them has their specific ways to respond to them. The novel focuses on identity and singularity of the individual problems to reveal universal matters. Architecture directly puts the individual's problems on a space that is universal and abstract. Individuality is lost in space. For example, space in church or temple would show the answer with general intensity for each people who asks faith because of own unique problem.

This difference is by no means small. It is easy to see that this difference is going to bring difficulty in building a theory of construction, however intuitive comprehension of the similarity of literature and architecture is easy.

But that is not the only problem.

It is a much bigger problem than the first one. It might even seem impossible to resolve.

The extinction of the notion of "future."

The expressions of this era are facing this crisis to lose the reason.

5. Crisis of "Future"

Zaha Hadid[11] died in 2016.

She was once selected as an architect to design the *New National Stadium* for the Tokyo Olympics 2020 by winning a competition, but later they cancelled her contract and scrapped the idea. A few months later, she suffered a heart attack in Miami and passed away.

Arata Isozaki[12] wrote a message of condolence for her funeral in which he showed indignation, and called the situation an "assassination of architecture."

Regardless if the word "assassination" is adequate or not, the messy conflict surrounding the Olympic Stadium which ended with a tragedy of

ない。しかし小説と建築とでは、その問題に対する対処のしかたが異なる。小説は個人の問題の固有性にフォーカスすることによって、逆に問題の普遍性を暴き出そうとする。建築は個人の問題をいきなり「空間」という抽象性＝普遍性のなかに置いて、解決しようとする。「空間」においては人間の固有性は、多くの場合、捨象される。宗教を思い浮かべればわかりやすい。信仰するひとびとは個人的な問題を解決したくて聖典という物語を読む。寺院や教会は、それをいきなり空間性に置き換えて、解答を暗示しようとする。

この差異は決して小さくない。そしてその差異が、両者の類似の直感的理解を遥かに超えて、つくる理論の構築に、困難をもたらすだろう。

だが、それだけではない。

予期される困難はもうひとつある。それは最初の困難よりも、ずっと大きい。そしてほとんど解決不能にすら思われる。

〈未来〉という概念そのものの消滅。

この時代の表現は、その危機と向かい合っている。

5. 〈未来〉の危機

ザハ・ハディド[11]は2016年に死んだ。

2020年東京オリンピックのための施設『新国立競技場』の設計者としていったんは選定されたが、のちに設計案は破棄された。それから間もなく、心臓発作のためマイアミで客死する。

磯崎新[12]はザハの葬儀に弔辞を寄せ、これは「建築の暗殺」ともいうべき事態だと憤った。

「暗殺」という言葉が適切かどうかは置くとしても、建築家の突然の死という悲劇とともに終わった「オリンピック・スタジアム騒動」は、「建

建築／小説／映画の構造的類似、あるいは──第1章

sudden death of the architect informed us of what is going on with regards to "architecture and future."

The referees[13] who selected Zaha's design think that architecture should represent the new age with its latest technology. The opposite side thinks that a "new age" is a typical anachronistic idea, or that preservation is the most important factor.[14]

In the end, the Japanese Government terminated the contract with Zaha half-way through because the alleged estimated construction fee, 2.24 billion dollars, would exceed the initial budget of 1.17 billion dollars. They held another competition under unusual circumstances. The organization committee of the Tokyo Olympics 2020 (chairperson: Yoshiro Mori)[15] must have believed that the budget inflation of 900 million dollars would be approved, but they were wrong.

Let's have a look at the 1964 Tokyo Olympics. Almost one-third of the national budget was directed towards architecture, facilities, civil infrastructure and traffic network. Eika Takayama, architect and city planner, charged for disposition of facilities, was so-to-speak in charge of there-construction of Tokyo. He wrote an essay[16] in an architectural magazine with enthusiasm and unquestioning belief in the "future."

The ex-prime minister Mori, and the other committees that still remember the exciting times of 1964 might have thought that the expenses for the Olympics, including the stadium designed by Zaha, would be even more abundant. The national Budget in 2016 is 30 times the budget they had in 1964. They must have presumed that the government would invest more...

But times have changed. The Olympics is not the biggest national event, but just one of several sports games or commercial events. The estimated cost for Zaha's stadium is almost same as the cost of "*Roppongi Hills*" which is a complex developed by a private real estate company. But the government and the people has concluded that the country has no need

築」について、あるいは〈未来〉について今起きつつあることを決定的に知らしめた。

　ザハの建築案を採用した側には、建築は最新のテクノロジーで新しい時代を示すもの、という考えがあり、これに反対する側は「新しい時代」などという概念こそがアナクロニズムだと——つまり保全こそが大切なのだと——論じた。

　結果としてザハ案を実現しようとすれば当初予算1300億円を大幅に上回る（2520億円）という理由で、設計コンペをやり直すという異常事態に至った。東京五輪組織委員会（会長・森喜朗）には、千数百億円程度の予算の膨張くらい何とかなるという目論見があったのだろうが、そのあては外れた。

　1964年の東京オリンピックでは、関連施設から首都圏の交通網整備まで含めて、当時の国家予算の３分の１弱が費やされた。施設の配置計画——というよりもむしろ東京の大改造計画——を担当した高山英華はその成果を、無邪気とすらいえる〈未来〉への信頼とともに書き綴っている。

　64年が持っていた〈未来〉の熱気を記憶する森元首相他委員会の幹部たちからすれば、ザハのものも含め施設関連にかける予算はもっと潤沢にあってしかるべき、という気分だったのかもしれない。2016年の日本の国家予算は1964年の30倍近い。それなのにケチくさいことを、と考える五輪関係者がいたとしても、不思議ではない。

　しかし、時代は大きく変わった。オリンピックは、国家の最大行事ではなく、数あるスポーツ・イベント（あるいは商業イベント）のうちのひとつになった。ザハの、高価だと批判されたスタジアムの見積もり額は、民間開発の複合施設「六本木ヒルズ」の総工費（約2700億円）とさして変わらない。それでも、そんな「高価な夢」を国家が見る必要はないという結

of such an expensive dream.

In a book titled End of *Art / Future of Art*[17] by Heinz Friedrich, an art historian. Art is facing its demise as the "people are uniting for a new common truth." The Olympics and the Stadium is no longer able to be an illusion to unify the people for common significance.

"*PRADA*" and "*MIUMIU*" that were designed by architects Herzog and de Meuron[18] with a rich budget, and the latest technology are situated not so far from the Olympic Stadium. They are modest commercial buildings by a private company. They are highly valued by architects and critics, and are also loved by the people. Architecture by *PRADA*, and not by the nation, is made for the sake of business, and not for the sake of the Olympics, and has essentially nothing to do with "the people uniting for truth." "*PRADA*" is only for personal gain or taste. As brand names serve to fulfill the tastes of the buyer, so does this kind of architecture.

Zaha's overrun plans were severely criticized because people thought innovativeness of architecture was only and issue of taste and hobby. They did not accept the idea of using tax payer money for something like that. *PRADA* is a fashion brand so it stands to reason that they dispense a big budget towards their own taste, and the people agree.

Eventually we will have no sense of communion in the "future." Any art or expression is only valued by the people who share the same tastes.

Now people invest only in their individual future, but not in their communal "future." The "future" has been divided into tiny pieces. We can't find a unified "future" anywhere. The host city for the Olympics is selected 5 to 7 years before it happens. In 1959, Tokyo was chosen to be the host city for the 1964 Olympics. They began to draw pictures of the "future." Even the general population must share a dream of the "future." As it stands now, no one draws such pictures.

It might be troublesome if utopia they draw shows inconvient idea or

24   Chapter 1———*Structural Similarity of Architecture, Literature, Film, and Possibly...*

論を、政府と国民は出した。

『芸術の終焉・芸術の未来』[17]という本で歴史家のハインツ・フリードリヒはこう書いている。「共通なもの、すべての人を統合する真実へ向けての新たな集結」としての芸術は終焉を迎えた、と。オリンピックも、その容器としての建築も、もはや「すべての人を統合する」幻想など持ちえない。

一方、新国立競技場にほど近い青山にある「PRADA」や「MIUMIU」は、ヘルツォーク・アンド・ド・ムーロン[18]によって、やはり潤沢な予算と最新のテクノロジーを駆使してつくられた建築だ。規模はずっと小さく、私企業によって建てられた商業建築である。こちらの建築は建築界では評価が高く、そして一般の人も誰も文句を言わない。国ではなくPRADAが、オリンピックではなくその商品のためにつくった建築は、〈すべての人を統合する真実〉などとはもとより無縁である。ブランド品の購入はひとの趣味や趣向による。その容器としての建築も、趣味や趣向を満たすことを最初の目的とするだろう。

ザハの「新国立競技場」案が批判されたのは、建築の新しさなどは趣味の問題なのだから、そんなことに税金を投入すべきではない、と考えられたからだ。「PRADA」は最初から趣味のものなのだから、私企業が金をかけるのは結構なことだと、同じ思考回路は結論する。

もはや共有されるべき〈未来〉などない。だからあらゆる表現は、たまたま趣向を同じくする人にのみ価値を持つ。

ひとが投資をするのは、それぞれの未来に対してであって、共有される〈未来〉に向けてではない。〈未来〉は今や細分化され、統合された〈未来〉などない。オリンピックは実施の５〜７年前に開催地が決まる。64年オリンピックは、59年に東京開催が決まり、そこから都市の未来図が急ピッチで描かれた。今は誰もそんな未来図を描いたりはしない。

ユートピアを描いてその理想が間違っていたら困るし、ディストピアを

建築／小説／映画の構造的類似、あるいは――第1章

dystopia harms someone. They fear to picture the future and choose to follow just political correctness. Can tiny broken pieces made to cater to tastes still be called the "future"? In modernism in the twentieth century, "future" must have worked to unify various classes and the disparate masses. "Future" to win a war, "future" to establish economic growth, or "future" to realize peace.

Look around you. There's no "future" like that.

But we need to carefully ask ourselves. Is it definitely true that the "future" has come to an end?

6. The End of "Growth"

Shinji Miyadai,[19] a sociologist, commented in a discussion[20] with Shin Isozaki and Riken Yamamoto.[21] "An architect can no longer contribute any more to the design base substance or the linchpin of the social system" he said. He suggests that it "can be accepted as entertainment but no more than that."

Miyadai analyzes the reason why. In today's society, what should be controlled is not physical activities, but informational activities." Therefore "not physical activities but psychological tastes have come to frame a topology which defines distance." Like a web-site on the internet, "authorities no longer depend on real space." We are seeing "how everything can work without real space." So "what kind of spaces have to be designed has no significant meaning."

Real space is now not only losing its meaning, but the "future" is also collapsing in real space.

Narihiro Kato[22] discusses the case of the "future" disappearing in Fukushima.[23]

26   Chapter 1——*Structural Similarity of Architecture, Literature, Film, and Possibly...*

描いてだれかを傷つけてもまずい。それで未来を描くことを恐れ、ポリティカル・コレクトの枠内にとどまることを最優先する。細かく砕けた未来は、果たしてまだ〈未来〉と呼ぶにふさわしいのだろうか？　かつて〈未来〉とは、さまざまな階層や異質な集団を統合する役割を担っていたはずだ。それが20世紀のモダニズムにおける〈未来〉だった。戦争に勝つという〈未来〉、経済成長を成し遂げるという〈未来〉、あるいは平和を実現させるという〈未来〉。

　今、そのような未来はない。

　だが本当に、〈未来〉そのものが、終焉を迎えているのだろうか？

6.「成長」の終焉

　宮台真司[19]は、磯崎新[20]や山本理顕[21]との鼎談でこう発言している。「建築家が、システムの基体や基軸にかかる設計にかかわることはもうできない」のだと。そうである以上、建築家の提案は「娯楽的な思いつき以上の意味を持たなくなる」。

　なぜか。宮台はこう分析する。現代社会において制御されるべきものは「狭義の身体挙動ではなく、コミュニケーションになった」。したがって「物理的な身体挙動ではなく、趣味こそが、距離を定義するようなトポロジー（位相空間）になった」。インターネット上のウェブ・サイトがそうであるように、「権力が空間に依存しなくなった」現代は、いわば「脱空間化しつつある」ともいえ、「その結果、空間をどう設計するかなどということを考えても、意味を持ちにくくなってきている」のだ、と。

　リアルな空間が、その意味を失いかけている。いや、失われようとしているのは意味だけではない。〈未来〉が、リアルな場所において崩壊を始めた。

　加藤典洋[22]は、フクシマで崩壊を始めた〈未来〉について論じている。[23]

Kato researched the insurance plans for nuclear plants.

Nuclear plants are by law only allowed to work if they are insured against severe accidents. But after the Fukushima incident, all insurance companies have renounced their contracts with any nuclear plant under Tokyo Electric Power Co. Ltd. The indemnity must be much higher than the risk the company takes. So after the Fukushima incident, Tokyo Electric Power Co. should be unable to run any nuclear power plant, but they have never announced it because they made another regulation with the Japanese Government. They agreed that Tokyo Electric Power Co. deposits huge sums of money, and that the Government will cover the expenses if a severe accident occurs.

Kato says that Insurance is a system made for calculating the "future." In the future, if any accident happens, the insurance insures the future. Hence to be denied insurance means to have no future.

Kato says that the insurance system of today was first designed in the Industrial Revolution era. The investment in the future creates a rapid increase of production, but it can never deny the possibility of failure or an accident. It needs a system called insurance. The system ceases to work after the severe accidents of the latest technology caused by modernism. The technology that should create the "future" is now forsaken by the system that should ensure the "future."

Still someone insist that we absolutely need nuclear power plants for ensuring growth in the economy and society. People cannot easily give up the idea of "growth" that modernism dreamed of.

People have do not doubt the economy, and society has never stopped growing. They have lost any image of not growing society. Actually in Europe, since ancient Rome until medieval times, population and production had been virtually the same size. In Japan, for about 260 years in the *Edo* era, various indexes of society increased a little, basically

加藤は原子力発電所にかけられる保険について調べていく。

　原発は事故に備えて多額の保険をかけない限り、運転は認められない。ところが、福島の事故以来、保険会社は東京電力の原発について保険契約を拒否した。原発の過酷事故の場合、保証規模は「想定」をはるかに超えることが判明したからだ。したがって、東電は今後原発を運転できないはずだが、そんな話は聞こえてこない。なぜなら東電は保険の代わりに、巨額の供託金を政府に預け、それが事故の際には保険代わりに支払われるという仕組みを考えだしたのだ。

　加藤は言う。保険とは、「未来」を仮想して作られたシステムだ。未来に何か事故があっても、保険があることによって、さらにその先の未来が保証される。だから「保険がかけられない」ということは、「未来」がないと認定されることにも等しい。

　現代の保険システムは、産業革命期に現れたと加藤は述べている。未来への投資は生産の急激な拡大を生み出すだろうが、失敗や事故の可能性も否定できない。それが保険というシステムを必要とし、生み出した。そのシステムが、同じモダニズムの生み出した最新技術の過酷事故によって、機能しなくなるという事態が生じたのだ。「未来」を創出するはずの技術が、「未来」を保証するシステムから見放された、といってもいい。

　それでもなお、社会あるいは経済の「成長」のために、原発は必要だと主張するひとたちも少なくない。「成長」という、これも「近代」が生み出した概念から、ひとは容易には離れることができない。

　社会や経済は常に成長し続けるものだと、ひとびとは信じ込んだ。それが常識になった。実際のところはヨーロッパでは、古代ローマから中世で、人口も様々な生産量もさして増えていない。日本でも、江戸時代の260年間、社会の様々な指標は微増こそすれ、さして変化はない。江戸時代の人びとに、「経済の成長」や「見たこともない未来」という概念はなかった

建築／小説／映画の構造的類似、あるいは――第1章　　*29*

there was no change. People in the *Edo* era probably didn't have ideas about the "growth of the economy" or "the unforeseen future."

Modernism, or should I say the Industrial Revolution, had changed everything. People began to believe that their society must grow and change within the next five or ten years, which is a lot shorter period than the 260 years of the *Edo* era.

Politicians and entrepreneurs continue to say, "We need more growth!" But we are beginning to feel that it's impossible for our world to keep growing any more. Of course, it's still possible to feed the economy with more efficient production, and financial engineering. On the other hand, considering the global environment, having only one earth is not enough to sustain the average American-lifestyle for all the people in the world which keep increasing, according to the WWF [24] White Paper. How can they claim to be innocent, and still continue to advocate this endless growth?

We have an event named "EXPO" that can show you an illusion of a bright "future." In 1968 in Japan, we had the biggest EXPO in Osaka. The *Shinkansen* super-express had been built just before the Tokyo Olympics and appeared in the Osaka EXPO. It was exactly the time when the word "growth" had real power. Kenzo Tange [25] designed as the head of a team for *Festival Square* and Taro Okamoto, [26] and made a sculpture named "Tower of Sun" that cut through the roof of *Festival Square*. They apparently believed in the future.

Seven years later, in 1975, the Ocean EXPO was held in Okinawa. Kiyonori Kikutake [27] realized his idea about a city on the Ocean as a huge work of architecture named *Aqua Polis*. He experienced the end of World War II, and when he was 17 years old he became an architect aspiring for the "future." His projects always included a lot of ideas for the "future," which shows in the images. But in the mid 70's, the theme "future" began to fade. *Aqua Polis* changed natural scenery and devastated the environment of Okinawa. [28] Finally, the life cycle cost of the

に違いない。

　近代が——産業革命が——すべてを変えた。江戸時代の260年の比ではない。5年後、10年後には、経済は成長し社会は必ず変わっているはずだと、ひとは信じ始めたのだ。

　今でも政治家たちや経済界のひとたちは主張し続けている。「成長せよ」と。だが、成長し続けることはもう無理だと、すでに多くのひとが感じている。生産効率を上げ、金融の操作をすれば、数値上の経済成長は当面できるかもしれない。しかし増え続ける地球上の人口のすべてのひとびとに今日のアメリカ市民なみの生活水準を与えるためには、地球が何個あっても足りないことは既に明らかになっている（WWF、環境白書）。な[24]ぜ、そんな時代に、無邪気に（あるいは無邪気なふりをして）「成長」を唱え続けることができるのだろうか？
　成長がもたらすはずの「明るい未来」を幻視させるイベントとして、「万博」がある。1970年の日本万国博覧会（大阪万博）は、日本における代表的な万博だ。東京オリンピック開幕直前に開通された東海道新幹線が、今度は人を東から西へと運ぶ。「成長」という言葉が存分に力を発揮していた時代だ。丹下健三が『お祭り広場』の設計を指揮し、岡本太郎が広場[25]の屋根を突き破る『太陽の塔』をつくった。彼らはあからさまに〈未来〉[26]を信じていた。

　そのわずか7年後、1975年に、沖縄海洋博覧会が開かれる。建築家の菊竹清訓は、ここで海上都市計画案『アクアポリス』を実現させてみせた。[27]終戦を17歳の少年時に迎えた菊竹は、徹底して〈未来〉志向の建築家だった。新しい都市の姿を見たくてしかたがなかった。だが75年の日本では、すでに〈未来〉は色褪せ始めていた。『アクアポリス』は、景観を変更し、自然環境を破壊し、コスト・サイクルは破綻して建築の機能は停止した。[28]この「未来都市」はやがて、鉄くずとして売られるために、海上を引きずられていく。

　　　　　　　　　　　建築／小説／映画の構造的類似、あるいは——第1章　　*31*

architecture collapsed, so it was essentially dead. Later, the "City of the Future" was towed on the ocean to be sold as iron scrap.

What "architecture" means began to change in the end of twentieth century. Until then, "future" was something like the DNA embedded in "architecture." Now it's gone.

The Japanese society cannot help shrinking with the downsizing population. In the next 30 years, it's predicted that hundreds of cities will lose all their residents. How does the picture of the future look like for "a city for 3 million people" by Le Corbusier[29] Could it work in such a downsizing society?

The "future" has come to end in the real world. It has brought a serious crisis to the economy, society, and the issues of city and architecture. Despite this situation, few architects seriously think about the loss of the "future." They can believe that there is great merit in the word "hobby" if they pretend not to see the problem.

7. Fictive "Future"

There is not only a problem with real architecture, but also with the novel, which at first glance does not seem to be economically relevant.

In modern Japan, from the Meiji era to the Showa era, (around 1870-1970) why did people feel the need to write and read novels?

Kojin Karatani discusses this issue in his book, *The End of Modern Literature*[30]. In the process of establishing the modern country that is a nation state, private suffering or pain can be directly connected to a problem of the nation state. Karatani wrote:

> *"The novel can be a base for a community of shared sympathy, an imaginary sympathy that forms the basis of the nation state. Through the novel, Intellectual class and working class or more various classes can be*

進歩する社会を前提としていた「建築」の概念も、20世紀末には変質していたのだ。それまで〈未来〉は「建築」のDNAに組み込まれていると思われていた。それが消えた。

　この先数十年の間に、数百の地方都市の消滅が予測される日本の縮小する社会で、ル・コルビュジェの「三百万人の都市」[29]のような未来像が役に立つはずもない。

　リアルな空間における〈未来〉の終焉。それは経済や社会、それに連なる都市や建築に決定的な危機をもたらしている。にもかかわらず、そのことを直視する者は多くない。見ないふりをしていれば、「趣味」にも大きな意味があると思えてくるのだろう。

7. 〈未来〉とフィクション

　リアルな空間の問題に限られるのではない。小説のような、一見経済的活動とは無縁のように見える表現ジャンルでも、事の本質は変わらない。

　近代日本、つまり明治から昭和期にかけて、なぜひとは、小説を書き、そして読んだのか？

　柄谷行人[30]は、著書『近代文学の終わり』のなかで、こんなふうに論じている。近代国家の成立過程においては、個人の苦悩がそのまま社会や国家＝nation stateの問題になり得た。そして近代文学＝小説について、こう書く。

　　小説は、「共感」の共同体、つまり想像の共同体としてのネーションの基盤になります。小説が知識人と大衆、あるいは、様々な社会的階層を「共感」に拠って同一的たらしめ、ネーションを形成するので

建築／小説／映画の構造的類似、あるいは──第1章　　*33*

united and identified with sympathy, and then a nation would appear involving all of these classes."

(translated by Suzuki)

As Karatani said, Natsume Soseki[31] found modern European literature and discovered a concept of individuality that had not existed in Japan before its modernization. Natsume was shocked by the concept, and began to write novels about how it would take form in Japan, how it might struggle to integrate into the collectivist body. Kenji Nakagami,[32] another novelist, made his debut in the pre-modern scene, and later seized the opportunity to de-construct narrative story. Karatani critiqued Jean Paul Sartre.[33] Sartre was a standout philosopher, which helped him be a good novelist. But Karatani argues that times like that have already passed.

"Literature is a project of adolescence," said Masashi Miura[34] in a book titled *The End of Adolescence*.[35] A boy or a girl must suffer pain to their spirit when they grow up to be adults. They lived in a small world during childhood, relating only to their parents or siblings. But while they are teenagers, they are thrown into a big world and expected to understand both the system and the meaning behind it. They are forced to adapt. The contradiction, and anger materializing then and there become the motif of the novel. And the motif belongs not only to the individual but to the generation. We can say that it's a story of growth that comes to the new generation when they are thrown into the old world.

Is it possible to write such novels in a society that essentially binds you to growth? Karatani declared that modern literature had ended because it is a historical inevitability. He wrote:

"I'll never tell the novelist to reclaim "literature." Once modern

す。

　確かに、夏目漱石[31]は、ヨーロッパの近代文学と出会い、そこに「個人」という概念を見出して衝撃を受け、その後それが日本のなかでどのように形成されていくかを、小説として——自らの苦悩かつ日本という「共同体」の問題として——記した。あるいは中上健次[32]は、前近代的な物語に出自を見出し、それを一挙に脱物語的な小説のなかに置き換えた。

　個人の苦悩は「共同体」と直結し、その表現としての小説は様々な表現のなかで特権的な地位を占めることができた。柄谷は、サルトルを引き合[33]いに論じている。サルトルが他の哲学者から抜きん出た存在たり得たのは、彼が「小説家」だったからだ、と。だが、柄谷はこうも言う。そんな時代は、もう終わった。

　文学とは青春のプロジェクトだった。そう言ったのは、三浦雅士だ[34]（『青春の終焉』[35]）。ひとは、成長期に大きな苦悩に出会う。それまで親との関係くらいしかなかった子どもが、十代の10年間で、次々により大きな世界との出会いのなかに放り出され、それを理解し、適応を半ば強制される。そこに生まれる齟齬や苦悩こそが、小説のモチーフになった。そしてそれは個人を超えて、ジェネレーションの問題に連なった。それはいわば、新しい世代が、旧世界との出会いのなかにいきなり放り出されて感じ取る「成長」の物語だ。

　だが、「成長」を本質的に諦めざるをえない社会のなかで、そのような小説が、ありうるだろうか？

　柄谷行人は、近代文学はもう終わったのだ、それは時代の必然なのだと断じている。そしてこう念を押す。

　　　　私は、作家に「文学」をとりもどせといったりしません。近代小説

literature had come to an end, the modern novel became mere entertainment, and sentimental story-telling which permeate the Japanese canon. This might even be a good thing. Write an exciting story and sell it all over the world as as the Manga artists do. Actually, I know quite a few writers that write a good mystery novel. On the other hand, I believe that writers who can do nothing but write vulgar stories must stop pretending to uphold pure literature.[36]"

(translated by Suzuki)

8. Escape from "Realism"

We can substitute "architecture" for the "novel" in the argument by Karatani. It will mean the same. Architecture, literature, film or any other art is losing its common base. This crisis can be summed up in the following points.

a) In a society ending its growth, suffering or hope would enter and endless loop. It would not make the essential change needed. Newness comes to only mean superficial novelty. Any art forsaking to meet essential change must become vulgar expression.

b) A city ending growth does not need spatial expansion. It means that the frontier for expression is vanishing, because the frontier existed to tackle the problems of its age. The architectural experiments in the Tokyo Olympics of 1964, and literature and film as a medium of opposition became impossible.

c) Modern literature came to have a special value by describing physical reality and the real scenery of cities. Architecture and film has done the same thing. But now sites on the internet are becoming a main space for communication instead of real place. How can this kind of a virtual site without physical reality make literature?

が終わったら、日本の歴史的文脈でいえば、「読本」や「人情本」に
なるのが当然です。それでよいではないか。せいぜいうまく書いて、
世界的商品を作りなさい。マンガがそうであるように。実際、それが
できるような作家はミステリー系などにけっこういますよ。一方、純
文学と称して、日本でしか読むにたえないような通俗的作品を書いて
いる作家が、偉そうなことを言うべきではない。[36]

8. リアルからの〈脱出〉

　柄谷の主張のなかの「文学」あるいは「小説」の語のかわりに、「建
築」の語を代入しても全く意味は変わらない。建築も文学も、あるいは映
画など様々な表現ジャンルも、共通の地盤を失いかけている。
　この危機を、次の3点に要約してみる。

①成長を終える社会では、苦悩も希望も、ただ繰り返しのループの中
　に入るだろう。それは本質的な変化と出会わない。新しさは表面的
　なものだけになる。本質的な変化を断念する表現は、趣味あるいは
　「通俗的作品」にならざるを得ない。
②成長を終える都市は、空間の物理的拡張を必要としない。それは表
　現にとってのフロンティアの消滅である。なぜならフロンティアに
　こそ時代の問題は凝縮して存在した。64年オリンピックにおけるよ
　うな建築も、こうした「開発」に対抗的な文学や映画も、同時に消
　滅する。
③近代文学は身体性と都市風景を描くことによって成立してきた。そ
　れは建築や映画においても同じである。だがコミュニケーションの
　「場所」がインターネットやスマホのアプリなどに移行するとき、
　身体性も都市風景も消えてしまう。身体性の消えた場所で、どんな
　表現が可能だというのだろう?

建築／小説／映画の構造的類似、あるいは──第1章

We once need to recognize that the "future" is gone.

"Growth" is just one illusion attributed to an era called "modern times." We need to remember the fact that "innovativeness," "spatial expanding" and "physical reality" is fading.

At the same time, we always have to keep another truth in our mind.

The "future" is nothing but a fiction.

Fiction can never be restricted by spatial expansion or physical reality. In fiction, you can be free to picture innovativeness and to see the scenery from any place where your imagination would not be restricted.

What if we could escape from "reality" and travel to "fiction"? We know that the "dream" means nothing to us in the real world. The shared illusion has totally lost generality. As the evidence, insurance is now invalid as a "future."

Meanwhile, we can picture various "futures" as another possibility. It will be different from the dream of the nation state. It will be separated from the shared illusion of the majority. The people should nevertheless not be be categorized into trivial subsets of taste or hobby. But we should find "fiction" that is free from illusion or taste.

"Fiction" is a structural future that can be uncoupled from the real future. That is why "fiction" can present another possibility for the real world. In modernism, the future had too much realty so that people put excess illusion into it. We need to drag such illusions away from the real future.

Now we have a starting point. We look at structures of fiction at the point where we escaped from the real future. Later, we will learn that we should have been looking for the structural "future." The structural "future" is not so simple as what the Tokyo Olympics had, and not so effective for economic growth. It might change ideas of "growth," "scenery" or "physical reality." It will also reveal another possibility.

38　　Chapter 1————*Structural Similarity of Architecture, Literature, Film, and Possibly...*

私たちは一旦、リアルな〈未来〉の消滅を認めざるを得ない。

　成長は「近代」という一時代が得た幻想にすぎない。「新しさ」「物理的拡張」「身体性」が消えていく様子を、心に刻まなくてはならない。

　だが一方で、このことも思い出さなければならない。

　〈未来〉とは、常にフィクションである。

　フィクションは物理的な拡張や身体性から自由でありうる。自由な場所から、「新しさ」を思い、「風景」を見つめることができる。

　私たちは一旦、リアルから脱出し、フィクションに赴けばいい。リアルな社会において共有されるべき「夢」などは消えた。共同幻想は、今や普遍性を持ちえない。リアルな〈未来〉に備えての「保険」は無効だ。

　だが、リアルとは別の可能性としての〈未来〉は、いかようにも描きうる。それはかつて国家が見たような夢とは異なる。多くの人々に共有された幻想ではない。かといって、直ちに一部の人たちのためだけの趣味・趣向にカテゴライズされない。むしろ、幻想や趣味から自由なフィクションが、あるのではないか？

　フィクションとは、構造的な〈未来〉であって、それは《リアルな未来》からいったん切り離される。だからこそ、リアルな社会に、別の可能性を提示し得る。近代においては、〈未来〉があまりにリアルな感覚を持ちえたがゆえに、ひとは過剰な幻想をそこに重ねた。そうした幻想を、〈未来〉から一旦引き剝がさなければならない。

　いま私たちは出発点を見つけた。フィクションの構造を《リアルな未来》から脱出した地点から、検討してみよう。じきに明らかになるだろうが、我々はもともと、そのような構造的な〈未来〉こそを求めていたはずだ。構造的な未来は、「オリンピック1964」のようにわかりやすくはなく、経済的な効果も持たない。ひょっとして、「成長」も「風景」も「身体性」も、大きくその意味を変えるかもしれない。そしてさらに、別の可能性が浮かび上がるだろう。

建築／小説／映画の構造的類似、あるいは──第1章　　*39*

What "future" can we design instead of the lost future?

This book will answer this fundamental question.

First, we're going to discuss the "planning of fiction."

＊ notes

1   *Solaris* is a movie, directed by Andrei Tarkovsky, 1972.

2   *Portrait in Number*, Awarded by Kodansha Publishing, 1987. A book published in 1988.

3   RONSO Publishing, 2014.

4   Guy Manos, movie director, is his brother.

5   For example, *Literature in Urban Space*, Chikuma Shobo Publishing, 1982, by Ai Maeda.

6   *Architectural Movie : Material Suspense*, LIXIL Publishing, 2013, by Ryoji Suzuki.

7   *Architecture Like Movie / Movie Like Architecture,* Shunjusha Publishing, 2009, by Taro Igarashi.

8   Magazine *Eureka,* March, 1983, featuring "Architecture in Illusion."

9   Architect, Honorary Professor of University of Tokyo.

10   Novelist, 1899-1972. Nobel Prize Winner, 1968.

11   Architect. 1950-2016. Born in Iraq. Designing architecture over the world with based in UK.

12   Architect. Born in 1931. He discovered Zaha's talent as a referee of architectural competition *Hong Kong Peak*, 1982.

13   Tadao Ando, Chair of referees, architect, born in 1941, mentioned this drift.

14   Fumihiko Maki, architect, born in 1928, mentioned this drift.

15   Politician, ex-prime minister. Born in 1937.

**「失われた未来」に対し、僕たちはどんな「別の未来」を設計すること
ができるのか？**

本書は、そのような根源的な問いに応答する。

最初に、「フィクションの計画」を検討してみよう。

◈注

1　アンドレイ・タルコフスキー監督の映画『惑星ソラリス』（ソビエト連邦、19
72年）にそのシーンがある。

2　第30回群像新人文学賞受賞（1987年）。単行本は、『ポートレイト・イン・ナ
ンバー』現代企画室、1988年

3　論創社、2014年

4　弟は映画監督のGuy Manos（1959〜）

5　例えば、前田愛『都市空間のなかの文学』筑摩書房、1982年

6　例えば、鈴木了二『建築映画 マテリアル・サスペンス』LIXIL出版、2013
年

7　例えば、五十嵐太郎『映画的建築／建築的映画』春秋社、2009年

8　雑誌『ユリイカ』1983年3月号「特集・幻想の建築」

9　建築家、東京大学名誉教授。1936年生まれ。

10　小説家。1899〜1972。1968年ノーベル文学賞受賞。

11　建築家。イラク生まれ。1950〜2016。イギリスに拠点を置いて活動。

12　建築家、1931年生まれ。建築コンペ『香港ピーク』（1982年）で審査委員長を
務め、当時まだ無名だったザハ・ハディドを見出した。

13　例えば、このコンペの審査委員長・安藤忠雄〈建築家、1941年生まれ〉はそ
の旨の発言をしている。

14　例えば、槇文彦（建築家、1928年生まれ）はその旨の発言をしている。

15　政治家、元首相。1937年生まれ。

16　『新建築』1964年10月号「オリンピック東京大会における総合施設計画」（高
山英華、加藤隆）。これによると、インフラ整備も含めた関連計画で、およそ

建築／小説／映画の構造的類似、あるいは——第1章

16 Magazine *SHINKENCHIKU Japan Architect*, October, 1964. According to the essay, 1 trillion and 10 billion Yen were expensed for projects for Olympic. National Budget of Japan in 1964 was 3 trillion and 660 billion Yen. In 2016, National Budget. For comparison, In 2016, it is 96 trillion and 700 billion Yen.

17 Original German title is *Ende Der Kunst? Zukunft der Kunst.*

18 Architects unit by Jacques Herzog and Pierre de Meuron. Both of them were born in 1950 in Switzerland.

19 Born in 1959. Active critic for current situation.

20 *A City We Want To Live In,* Heibonsha Publishing, 2006.

21 Architect. Born in 1945.

22 Literature Critic. Born in 1949.

23 *What if human being will not continue forever?*, Shinchosha Publishing, 2014.

24 World Wildlife Fund. One of the biggest international NGO for conservation of the environment.

25 Architect. 1913-2005. Representative work; *Hiroshima Peace Center.*

26 Artist. 1911-1996. Involved with Avant Garde Art movement abroad.

27 Architect. One of school of "Metabolism." Representative work; *OEDO Museum.*

28 Even if *Aqua Polis* itself didn't, exploration for it surely did.

29 Architect in France. 1887-1965. Representative works; *Le Savoir, Chapelle Notre-Dame du Haut.*

30 Kojin Karatani is a Philosopher. Born in 1941. Published in English; *The Origins of Modern Japanese Literature* (Duke University Press) and *Architecture as Metaphor* (MIT Press).

31 Novelist. 1867-1916.

32 Novelist. 1946-1992. Books in English; *Snakelust* and *The Cape : And Other Stories from the Japanese Ghetto.,*

１兆800億円が使われた。当時の日本の国家予算は約３兆6600億円。ちなみに、2016年の日本の国家予算は96兆7000億円。

17　勁草書房、1989年

18　Jacques HerzogとPierre de Meuronによる建築家ユニット。ふたりとも1950年スイス生まれ。

19　社会学者。1959年生まれ。主な著書に、『終わりなき日常を生きろ——オウム完全克服マニュアル』（筑摩書房、1995年）、『野獣系でいこう!!』（朝日新聞社、1999年）など。

20　建築家。1945年生まれ。

21　山本理研編『私たちが住みたい都市』平凡社、2006年

22　文芸批評家。1948年生まれ。著書に『アメリカの影』（河出書房新社、1985年）、『敗戦後論』（講談社、1997年）など。

23　『人類が永遠に続くのではないとしたら』新潮社、2014年

24　World Wildlife Fund 世界最大規模の自然環境保護団体である国際的NGO。

25　建築家。1913年〜2005年。代表作に『広島ピースセンター』『代々木国立競技場』など。

26　芸術家。1911年〜1996年。海外の近代芸術前衛とも深くかかわる。

27　建築家。1928〜2011。「メタボリズム」提唱者の一人。主な作品に『大江戸博物館』など。

28　『アクアポリス』そのものではなくても、そのための周辺開発は環境を破壊した。

29　建築家。フランス。1887〜1965　『サヴォア邸』『ロンシャンの教会』など。

30　思想家。1941年生まれ。著書に『マルクスその可能性の中心』（講談社、1978年）、『日本近代文学の起源』（講談社、1980年）など。

31　小説家。1867〜1916　『吾輩は猫である』『こころ』など。

32　小説家。1946〜1992　『枯木灘』『異族』など。

33　哲学者、小説家。フランス。1905〜1980　『存在と無』（哲学）、『嘔吐』（小説）など。

34　編集者、評論家。1946年生まれ。

35　講談社、2001年

建築／小説／映画の構造的類似、あるいは——第1章

33 Philosopher, Novelist. France. *L'Etre et le Néant* (philosophy), *La Nausée* (novel).

34 Editor, Critic. Born in 1946.

35 Kodansha Publishing, 2001.

36 *The End of Modern Literature,* Inscription Publishing, 2005.

36　『近代文学の終わり』インスクリプト、2005年

Chapter Two

The Planning behind Literature

1. Planning a Novel

"Go to chapter 57," If such an indication is written when you get to the end of Chapter 2, what do you do?

The Argentinian Julio Cortazar's novel *Hopscotch* has a strange structure. The first section of the novel has 56 chapters. Naturally you begin to read chapter 1 at first, then 2, 3, 4, 5... All the way to chapter 56. You can read it normally like this, but you could also read it a different way. At the end of every chapter there is a "go to chapter xx." So you read chapter xx, and the indication "go back to chapter x" in the first section. If you follow the indication by Cortazar, you will jump over some chapters, go back, and then jump over some again.

Following the first section of 56 chapters is a section with 99 chapters Cortazar terms "expendable chapters." The 99 chapters explain the art, characters and more, which appear in the first section. If you go with the usual route, you read the story first, and then the explanation termed "expendable"; but if you follow the instructions you go back and forth between the sections.

第2章

文学の計画

1. 小説の計画

　「第57章へ進め」。こんな指示が、小説の第2章を読み終えたところに著者によって記されていたら、どうしようか？

　フリオ・コルタサルの小説『石蹴り遊び』は奇妙な構成を持つ。56章からなるこの小説の第1部を巻頭からページを繰っていけば、それは当然のことながら1章、2章、3章……と進んでいってやがて第56章に至る。もちろん、この本もそうして読んでいくことができる。しかし別の読み方も示されている。ある章の章末には「＊章に行け」という指示がある。それで＊章を読むと、その次には「☆章へ行け」と。コルタサルが各章末に記した指示に従って読むと、ページをジャンプし、戻り、またジャンプして、読んでいくことになる。

　56章の「本編」の後には99の章（expendable chapterと呼ばれる）があり、こちらには、「本編」中に現れた様々なアート作品や、登場人物についての「解説」が記される。ページ順に読むのなら、「本編」を読み終えた後でこの「expendable」の「解説」を読むことになるが、各章末の指示（table of instructions）に従えば、「本編」と「解説」とを行きつ戻りつ、しかも時系列によらない物語展開を見ることになる。

47

Thus, *Hopscotch* contains three stories: Oliveira, a guy from Argentina who meets a prostitute; Oliveira's life in Buenos Aires; and "the expendable chapters."

Hopscotch reminds me of my own first novel *Portrait in Number*,[2] published in *GUNZO* magazine in 1987. *Rayuela* (the original title of *Hopscotch*) was published in 1963, and the English version in 1966. It means just I had not read a preceding novel.

Portrait in Number doesn't indicate that the reader should jump over chapters. The protagonist who is a student at a university in Kyoto drew 36 self-portraits when he was a high school student. He gave titles to his 36 drawings which were just No.1, No.2, No.3...all the way to No.36 in chronological order. The protagonist sometimes recalls memories of his high school, and the memories are told as an explanation of the self-portraits. What the self-portraits tell us is not their chronological order, but the connection the "now" has with our memory, and how we call it forth by its number.

Here we illustrate these two novels schematically.

[fig. 1-2] (p. 182)

You can clearly see the similarity of these two novels. They have different stories, aesthetics and descriptions, but structurally they are very close to each other.

Similarity of structures doesn't mean that the works are similar. For example, detective novels have so many various stories, but many of them have a common structure that is to "seek and find." A mysterious case happens, a protagonist seeks the secret and finally discovers the truth. It is a basic structure for detective stories. Few people would say that Raymond Chandler[3] and Agatha Christie[4] are similar simply because their stories have a "seek and find" structure.

Yet no one would misconstrue that *A Wild Sheep Chase*[5] written by

48   Chapter 2——*The Planning behind Literature*

物語は３つの話から成る。ブエノスアイレス出身の主人公オリベイラが
パリで娼婦ルシアと出会う話。ブエノスアイレスでの話。そしてその他
諸々。

　この小説を読んだ時、僕は自分の最初の小説『ポートレイト・イン・ナ
ンバー[3]』を思い返さずにいられなかった。とはいえ、『ポートレイト・イ
ン・ナンバー』を『群像』誌で発表したのが1987年、『石蹴り遊び』の原
著は1963年、英語版が1966年刊行だから、先行する小説を僕が知らなかっ
ただけだ。

　『ポートレイト・イン・ナンバー』のほうには、章をジャンプさせて読
ませるような「指示」はない。京都で「今」を過ごす大学生の主人公は、
「過去（高校時代）」に36枚の「自画像」を描いていて、描いた順にナン
バー１から36までの番号をつけ、それがそのまま絵のタイトルになってい
る。主人公は今を生きるなかで時に記憶を呼び起こし、それは「自画像」
の「解説」として語られる。語られる「自画像」は番号順ではなく、
「今」起きていることと関連がある記憶として、その都度適当な「ナン
バー」の「自画像」が呼び出される。

　ふたつの小説を図式化してみよう。

[fig. 1-2]（p. 182参照）

　こうしてみれば、ふたつの小説の構造的類似は明らかだろう。むろん、
書かれている内容も、感覚も、記述も、両者においてはすべて異なる。た
だ構造的に類似する。

　構造的な類似というのは、作品の性質の類似ということを意味しない。
例えば探偵小説には無数のヴァラエティがあるが、多くがSeek and Find
という共通の構造を持つ。事件が起こり、秘密を探して、最後に真実を見
つける、という構造だ。似たような構造をもつからといって、チャンド
ラー[4]とアガザ・クリスティ[5]の小説を似ているというものはほとんどいない。

　まして、このSeek and Findの構造が意図的に用いられた村上春樹[6]の初

文学の計画──第2章　　*49*

Murakami Haruki[6] in his early period is a detective story because of the "seek and find" structure in it.

In *A Wild Sheep Chase*, the protagonist one day notices that his friend called "mouse" is missing. And he finds a picture the friend must have left, which is a sheep with a star branded on his hip. He sets out to find the truth. Murakami himself explained that he wrote this novel with the structure of *The Long Good-Bye*, a detective novel by Chandler in mind.

Murakami clearly spends a lot of time on the structure of his novels, and this is especially true for his longer works. Other than *A Wild Sheep Chase, Colorless Tsukuru Tazaki and His Years of Pilgrimage*[7] also has a structure similar to a detective story, *Hard-Boiled Wonderland and the End of the World*[8] and *1Q84*[9] contain stories about parallel worlds.

As you know, what I refer to as "structure" is a term in "structuralism" from mostly French philosophy and cultural study from the mid-twentieth century. To put it simply, "structure" is a "spatially schematized or to be schematized relationship." "Seek and find," as we have seen, is also a correct schematization that is "something is hidden somewhere, seek and find it." It's same as Levi Straus,[10] who drew spatial description for relations between relatives, and Saussure,[11] who schematized semiotics and meaning.

We have seen a lot of research about architecture and cities within structuralism, most of all from Christopher Alexander[12] who made early and noteworthy progress with his research. In his essay titled *Notes on the Synthesis of Form, A City is Not a Tree*,[13] Alexander criticizes modernism's utilization of the "tree structure." You get into a modern city by the railway or the freeway, then through one of the boulevards, and at last one of the small streets [fig. 3] (p. 182). As you can see in [fig. 3], the point A on a small branch —a place on a small street— cannot connect with another point B on another small branch without going back to the freeway or boulevard. It once looked like a very systematic and functional

50   Chapter 2———*The Planning behind Literature*

期作『羊をめぐる冒険』[7]を探偵小説と読み紛うものもいないだろう。

　この小説では、星形の斑紋のある羊の秘密と、行方不明になった友人「鼠」とを探す「僕」が、やがてそれらの真実を探り当てる。この小説について、村上春樹自身が、レイモンド・チャンドラーの探偵小説『長いお別れ』の物語構造を下敷きにした旨述べている。

　村上春樹は、特に長編小説の場合、構造に自覚的な作家だ。上記の他、『色彩を持たない多崎つくると、彼の巡礼の年』[8]も探偵小説の構造に近いし、『世界の終わりとハードボイルド・ワンダーランド』[9]や『1Q84』[10]はいわゆるパラレル・ワールドの構造を持つ。

　ここで使っている「構造」という語は、あらためて言うまでもないが、20世紀半ば過ぎに主としてフランスで起こった構造主義からきている。構造とは、簡単に言えば、「空間的に図式化された、あるいはされうる関係」だ。先の「Seek and Find」にしても、「空間上のどこかにあるものを探し、見つける」という図式化をしている。それはレヴィ・ストロース[11]が親族の関係を空間的に記述し、ソシュール[12]が記号と意味の関係を図式化して見せたのと同じだ。

　建築・都市の領域でも構造主義的な分析はよく見られるが、いち早くそれを徹底して成果を得たのはクリストファー・アレクサンダーだろう。『形の合成に関するノート／都市はツリーではない』[13]という論文においてアレクサンダーは、「樹木」のような構造になりがちな都市計画を批判した。近代の都市は、幹線道路から大通りへ、大通りから狭い道へと単純に枝分かれしていく構造をもつ [fig. 3]（p. 182参照）。この場合、ある小枝の先の点（狭い道上の場所）Ａと、別の点（別の狭い道上の場所）Ｂとは、分岐をさかのぼり、（幹線道路）まで遡らないと互いに結びつかない。これは一見よく整理された機能的な都市構造に見える。実際の経験からしても、駅から自宅に辿り着くまで、私たちは大通りから小道へと歩くのだから、

structure of a city. Actually, when you go back to your house you get off at the station or exit from a freeway, then you get on a boulevard, and arrive at your street with your house. So far the "tree structure" seems to correctly express the structure of a city. But Alexander claims that a "tree structure" is different in function and imagery on a structural level. Point A and B in a city are connected by multiple paths for the purpose of function and imagery, and he insisted that we need to plan a city according to such complicated paths. Consequently, he presented his idea of a "semilattice structure" [fig. 4] (p. 182) instead of a "tree structure."

Kojin Karatani points out in his book *Architecture as Metaphor*,[14] that the "semilattice structure" is very similar to the "rhizome structure" presented by Gilles Deleuze and Felix Guattari. Karatani discusses formalization[15] as the problem of pure structuralization and the intent of formality in "architecture" as the result. Karatani does not express interest for real architecture in this book. That is why his structures of actual architecture and cities can be an effective idea, especially when we find similarity among them in formal thought and logic. Formal thought and logic can be structures for any art or expression.

Hiroshi Hara asserts that literature and architecture are one and the same thing when it comes to structures.[16] Hara explains this by quoting a poem titled *Listening*, by Shuntaro Tanikawa:[17]

> *I listen / to yesterday 's / raindrops / I listen*
>
> *(omission)*
>
> *I listen / to my daughter's / sobbing / ten years ago / I listen*
>
> *I listen / to a farmers' / hiccuping / a hundred years ago / I listen*
>
> *(omission)*
>
> *I listen / to a fawn's crying /one hundred thousand years ago*
>
> *to the rustling of fern / a million years ago*
>
> *to an avalanche / ten million years ago*

正しく都市を表しているように思える。だがアレクサンダーは、都市の構造は機能的にもあるいはイメージ的にも、トリー構造とは異なると主張する。都市のなかの地点ＡとＢとは、機能的にもイメージ的にも、複数の経路によって結ばれているし、またはそう計画すべきだというのだ。そうしてアレクサンダーはツリー構造とは異なるセミ・ラティス構造を提示する [fig. 4]（p. 182参照）。

　柄谷行人は『隠喩としての建築[14]』のなかで、このセミ・ラティス構造が、現代思想の分野でドゥルーズとガタリが提示したリゾーム構造[15]と似ていることを指摘した。柄谷が同著で論じようとしたのは形式化[16]、言わば純粋なる構造化という問題であり、形式への意志としての「建築」である。つまり柄谷は実物としての建築に関心を表明しているわけではない。にもかかわらず、いやだからこそ、実際の建築や都市の構造が、思考あるいは論理の形式と共通することの有効性が見えてくる。思考あるいは論理の形式はすべての表現ジャンルの構造になりうるからだ。

　原広司は、構造において、文学と建築とはまったく同じだと断言する[17]。原は谷川俊太郎の詩『みみをすます[18]』を引く。

　この詩は「みみをすます／きのうのあまだれに／みみをすます」と始まる。
　「めをつむり／みみをすます／ハイヒールのこつこつ／ながぐつのどたどた」「うみをわたってきた／みしらぬくにの／ふるいうたに／みみをすます」そしてやがて「みみをすます／じゅうねんまえの／むすめの／すすりなきに」「ひゃくねんまえのひゃくしょうの／しゃっくりに」「せんねんまえの／いざりの／いのりに」「いちまんねんまえの／あかんぼの／あくびに」「じゅうまんねんまえの／こじかのなきごえに／ひゃくまんねんま

文学の計画──第２章　　*53*

to star's whispering / a hundred million years ago / to the roaring of the
universe / a trillion years ago I listen

(omission)

I listen / to roadside / pebbles / I listen / to a feeby groaning computer / I
listen / to my neighbor's / muttering / I listen
somewhere a guitar is being strummed / somewhere a dish breaks
somewhere a-e-i-o- u / to the now I at the bottom of the dine I listen

(omission)

I listen / to a brook' s / still- unheard / murmuring / of tomorrow flowing
/ into today / I listen

(translated by William I. Elliott and Kazuo Kawamura)

Hara discusses the following:

> The sound at the present, the sound of ten years ago, something that
> happened a hundred years ago, and the sound of a hundred billion years
> ago, are all sounds I hear simultaneously. "Simultaneously" means that
> the difference in time is disappearing and becoming space. At this moment
> as you perform the physical act of listening, space makes its appearance.

Let us revisit the structures of *Hopscotch* and *Portrait in Number*. [fig. 1]
(p. 182) is a two-dimensional space in which time is drawn in. Episodes,
"expendables" and "self-portraits" are spread across space. We can follow
them in chronological order, but we can also ignore it. *Portrait in Number*
has a structure similar of an art museum. A story of the present is shown
in the main hall, and many paintings of self-portraits are exhibited in tens
of isolated exhibition rooms around the hall [fig. 5] (p. 183).

This can be described as a semilattice structure. It is not only *Hopscotch*
and *Portrait in Number* which have a narrative consisting of one main
stream. Various streams flow randomly everywhere. The semi-lattice is a

えの／しだのそよぎに／せんまんねんまえの／なだれに／いちおくねんまえの／ほしのささやきに／いっちょうねんまえの／うちゅうのとどろきに／みみをすます」。

原は次のように論じる。

　　……現在聞いている音、それから十年前の音、それから百年前のこと、ずっと行きまして一億年前の音も同時に聞こえてくるわけです。同時に（傍点原文）とは、時間が消えていって、時間が空間化する。このとき、身体的な出来事である耳をすますことによって、空間が出現してくるのです。

　もう一度『石蹴り遊び』や『ポートレイト・イン・ナンバー』の構造を振り返ってみよう。[fig. 1]（p. 182参照）は、2次元空間に記述された時間の図である。エピソードや「自画像」は空間上にばらまかれ、それらを時系列的にたどることもできるが、時系列を無視してめぐることもできる。『ポートレイト・イン・ナンバー』は美術館の空間構造に似ている。メイン・ホールに「現在」の物語が流れ、隣接したいくつもの独立した展示室に「自画像」が展示されているようなものだ [fig. 5]（p. 183参照）。
　またこれは、セミ・ラティス構造としても記述できる。『石蹴り遊び』『ポートレイト・イン・ナンバー』の両者とも、大きな流れが一つしかない物語というのではない。複数の流れが、同時に進行する。さらに『石蹴り

文学の計画──第2章　　*55*

more intricate structure [fig. 6] (p. 183). Both of the aforementioned novels were designed to be able to be read in such a manner.

[fig. 5] and [fig. 6] reminds us of a certain architecture, "*Kanazawa 21*[st] *Century Art Museum*" designed by Team SANAA lead by Kazuyo Sejima.[18] Boxes in various sizes are put separately from each other in a large, flattened cylinder. The boxes are exhibition rooms, and the space between the boxes and the cylinders is communal and public. Visitors walk between the boxes and can enter any box randomly. These novels and works of architecture are not the same just because they have a similar structure, but now we have been able to confirm how structures of the novel and of architecture can be overlapped.

Georges Perec's[19] novel *Life: A User's Manual*[20] apparently has more of the same structure we find in architecture. It begins like this:

Chapter One

On the Stairs

YES, IT COULD begin this way, right here, just like that, in a rather slow and ponderous way, in this neutral place that belongs to all and to none, where people pass by almost without seeing each other, where the life of the building regularly and distantly resounds.

(omission)

The inhabitants of a single building live a few inches from each other, they are separated by a mere partition wall, they share the same spaces repeated along each corridor, they perform the same movements at the same times, turning on a tap, flushing the water closet, switching on a light, laying the table, a few dozen simultaneous existences repeated from story to story, from building to building, from street to street.

Chapter 2——*The Planning behind Literature*

遊び』において次に読むべき章の選択可能性を増やしたり、『ポートレイト・イン・ナンバー』において自画像の順番を入れ替え可能にすれば、構造はさらに複雑なセミ・ラティス構造になる [fig. 6]（p. 183参照）。そして両者とも、そのような構造として読むことが可能なように、計画されている。

　ところで、[fig. 5] と [fig. 6] から思い起こすことができる建築がある。妹島和世が率いるSANNA設計の「金沢21世紀美術館」だ。大きな平べったい円筒のなかに幾つもの箱が鏤められていて、箱が展示室、それ以外が公共空間（交通空間）となっている。箱のあいだを縫うようにしてひとは進み、任意の箱に順不同に入ることができる空間構造を持つ。むろん、構造が似ているからといって直ちにそれらを同一に論じることはできない。これについては後に詳述するが、ここでは、小説と建築の構造が類似する可能性を確認しておきたい。

　フランスの作家ジョルジュ・ペレックによる小説『人生使用法』には、よりあからさまに建築と同じ構造がある。その第1章は次のように始まる。

第1章；階段で

　そう、それはこうして、ここで、こんなふうに、少々重々しく、ゆっくりと始まってもいいだろう。みんなのものであり、また誰のものでもない中性的な場所、ひとびとがほとんど見交わすこともなく擦れ違う、遠い、規則的な建物の生活が反響するこの場所で。
（中略）
　同じ建物の住人たちは互いにわずか数センチを隔てて生活しており、彼らを切り離しているのは仕切り壁一枚だけで、階ごとに反復されている同じ空間を共有し、水道の栓をひねったり、水洗を流したり、明かりを点けたり、食事の用意をしたり、おなじ時におなじ動作をしているのであり、それは階ごと、建物ごと、通りごとに反復される、同時進行のいく十もの生活なのだ。

Perec describes "the inhabitants of a single building." "They are separated" and sometimes "share the same spaces." It's a story about "simultaneous existences repeated from story to story." The stories are not related with each other as the stories aren't. It doesn't have a trunk the same way a story has, just various details of things and people recorded down. Perec writes the prologue as if he tries to hint at how you should read his novel, or how he wrote it, as we can see below.

> "...the art of jigsaw puzzles seems of little substance, easily exhausted, wholly dealt with by a basic introduction to Gestalt: the perceived object —we may be dealing with a perceptual act, the acquisition of a skill, a physiological system, or, as in the present case, a wooden jigsaw puzzle —is not a sum of elements to be distinguished from each other and analysed discretely, but a pattern, that is to say a form, a structure"

Perec shows "a form, a structure" by designing various rooms as elements. Perec designs his novel just like he plans his apartment.

2. Blueprints of the Novel

In the last page of the novel, Perec draws a cross section of the apartment.

The building has 9 stories and a basement. The cross section is not so well designed as an architectural shape, but it is not intended to. A form is described in this novel, which is of a world as uncompleted jigsaw puzzle of various lives got into an apartment. Perec seems disinterested in the actual space design, but at the same time he cannot stop himself from describing the the inhabitants lives. Just like Hiroshi Hara explains

この小説は「同じ建物の住人」、つまりあるアパートメントの様々な部屋とその住人たちを描いている。それらは「同時進行の幾重もの生活」ではあるが、互いに何ら関連があるわけではない。つまり、太い幹のような物語があるのではなく、様々な事物と人物が、記録のように詳細に描かれる。作者ペレックは、この小説の読みかたのヒント（あるいは書くときの方法）を示唆するように、第1章に先立つ「序」にこんなことを記している。

　　ジグソー・パズルの技巧というものは、はじめは束の間の、取るに足りない技巧、ゲシュタルト理論のちょっとした授業にすっぱり収まってしまうような技巧に見える。極めるべき目的は——問題が知覚行為、見習い奉公、生物学の体系、あるいはわれわれの場合がそれだが木でできたジグソー・パズルのいずれであっても——まずもって切り離し分析しなければならない諸要素の集合なのではなくて、ある総体、つまりある形態、構造なのだ。

「人生使用法」は、「諸要素」としての部屋を作り出しながら、総体としての「ある形態」を浮かび上がらせようとする。まさに、アパートメント建築の計画をするように、ペレックは小説を書いている。

2．小説の設計図

　ペレックはこの小説の巻末に、舞台となったアパートメントの「建物断面図」を書いている。

　地下1階地上9階で、階段の両脇に居室がある。メゾネット・タイプの部屋もある。だが、建築的に見ればそれほど面白い「断面図」ではない。ペレックが描き出そうとしたのは建築の「形」ではない。様々な人間の生の形が、アパートメントという一つのパズルのなかに組み込まれ、その結果浮かび上がる世界の「形態」こそが、この小説に描かれたものだ。ペレックはそれぞれの部屋の住人の生の時間を同時に描きながら——原広司

in "*Time in Spatial Scheme.*"

How does space differ in literature and architecture? The layout of the apartment in *Life: a User's Manual* had to be typical and undistinguished, of the type normally found in Paris. He had to describe how such characterless spaces changed according to the inhabitants' life. A pre-designed space, like an architect's work might never have fit in the jigsaw puzzle. So, does it mean that space in the novel has a different nature than the space in architecture?

Now we are referring to another novel: *La Carte et Territoire* by Michel Houellebecq.[21]

Carte means map, and *territoire* means territory. Jed, the protagonist, is an artist, painter, and photographer. He magnifies Michelin maps, and takes pictures of them. A place that is "only homogeneous green expanse" begins to develop, "bright red, colorful patterns of mesh made by local roads, 'landscape', 'symbols indicating places with good visibility,' woods, lakes, streets, mountain paths." Jed titles these works **Maps are more Interesting than Territories.** Thus, maps become art works to be traded in an art market.

Jed's father, Jean Pierre is an architect who used to try to find the next style of Le Corbusier, but actually works with the planning of resort areas in accordance with developers. Jean Pierre realizes that he is nearing his end, so one day he tells Jed that he is seriously devoted to a utopian idea by William Morris.[22] He says that he want to faithfully recreate a nest of swallows by learning from a real nest. However, no swallow ever makes an abode from a recreated nest.

Another day, Jed visits the house of a novelist named Houellebecq, the writer of this novel!

Jed presented a portrait of Houellebecq he has painted. Houellebecq

60   Chapter 2———*The Planning behind Literature*

の言葉を借りるなら「時間の空間化」を行いながら、実際の空間にはさして興味がないようにすら見える。少なくとも、建築家が空間に抱くような興味は。

　小説に描かれる空間が、建築のそれとは異なるように感じられるのは、驚くべきことではない。『人生使用法』に描かれるアパートメントはパリ市内のどこにでもあるようなものである必要があり、特徴のある空間などはむしろ「ジグソー・パズル」の妨げになるだろう。では、文学のなかの空間は、建築の空間とは確かに異質なのだろうか？

　ミシェル・ウェルベックの『地図と領土』[22]という小説がある。空間に関するふたつの言葉がタイトルになったこの小説を少し読んでみよう。

　主人公ジェドは画家であり写真家でもある。ミシュランの地図を写真に撮り、それを大きく引き伸ばして作品にしている。衛星写真だと「緑のペースト状のほぼ均一な拡がりにすぎなかった」場所が、地図では「県道や、色鮮やかな街道の網の目、〈眺望〉〈眺めのいい場所を示すマーク〉、森、湖、峠を魅惑的に展開して」いる。ジェドはこの作品群にこうタイトルをつける、**「地図は領土よりも興味深い」**。こうして地図は美術作品となり、作品は美術市場で売買される。

　ジェドの父親のジャン＝ピエールは建築家で、かつてはル・コルビュジェの次の新しい建築を目指していたが、結局はデベロッパーに言われるがままリゾート開発に携わった。病で死期を悟ったジャンは、ある日ジェドに、自分が若いころウイリアム・モリスのユートピア的な思想に深く傾倒[23]していたことを語る。そして最近では、ツバメの巣をツバメの作り方を忠実に真似して作ったが、ツバメはそこには住もうとはしない、とも言った。

　別の日、ジェドは作家のウェルベック（この小説の作者！）を自宅に訪ねる。

　ジェドが自ら描いたウェルベックの肖像画をプレゼントすると、ウェル

文学の計画──第2章　*61*

tells him about the life of William Morris, as well as gossiping that Morris's wife had an affair with Rossetti, who is an artist and a friend of Morris. Houellebecq tells Jed, "The model of a community that William Morris proposed cannot become a utopia at all in the world where people like William Morris live." Jed feels as though he is leaving a world that, in truth, he had never belonged to.

Not long after, Houellebecq is murdered.

A few days later, the police show a photograph of the murder scene to Jed. It looks like an abstract painting by Jackson Pollock to him.

The police find that the murderer killed Houellebecq to get a portrait by Jed because of its estimated economic value.

Jean Pierre dies. Jed finds Jean Pierre's last drawing and thinks to himself, "My father never gave up designing a house for swallows."

"Maps and Territories" in the title can be replaced by Jed's picture and the house for a swallow in the story.

Although Jed admits that there is a beauty in abstract paintings and pictures of Michelin maps, or even the murder of the auther, he cannot believe that he certainly belongs to a world that is portrayed by maps and photographs. His father once found utopia in a nest of swallows, but no one will ever live there if the utopia is realized. Houellebecq, writing this story, was killed in the middle of the story, therefore Jed and Jean Pierre completely lose touch with the world that is the real world outside of the novel.

Now we witness a crisis that novel, architecture and the entire spectrum of today's art is facing a bigger problem than the difference between literature and architecture. Everything is being reduced to semiotic and economic value. As I wrote in the prologue, any art cannot avoid being reduced to "taste" or "hobby." And of course we cannot revive the idea

62   Chapter 2——— *The Planning behind Literature*

ベックはジェドに、ウイリアム・モリスについて詳しく教える。モリスの
妻ジェーンが芸術家仲間のロセッティと不貞を働いていたことも含めて。
ウェルベックは言う、「ウイリアム・モリスが提案した社会のモデルは、
誰もがウイリアム・モリスのような人の住む世界では少しもユートピア的
ではなかっただろう」と。ウェルベックの家から車を走らせて帰る途中、
ジェドは感じる。「これまでも決して本当に属していたわけではないこの
世界から、自分が今やたち去りつつある」と。

　程なく、ウェルベックは何者かに殺される。

　後日、ウェルベック殺害現場の写真を見たジェドは、それをまるでジャ
クソン・ポロックの描いた抽象画のようだと思う。

　ウェルベックを殺したのは、ジェドが描いた肖像画の経済的価値を見込
んだ者であったことが、やがてわかる。

　ジャン＝ピエールが死ぬ。ジェドはジャンが最後に描いたデッサンを見
て思う。「父はツバメのための家を作るという望みを最後まで決して捨て
なかったのだ」。

　タイトルの「地図と領土」という対比は、本文内の言葉に置き換えれば、
ジェドの作品とツバメの家、ということになると思う。

　ジェドはミシュランの地図に、あるいは作者の殺害現場の写真にすら抽
象絵画の美しさを認めながら、その地図や写真が示しているはずの世界に
は「本当に属してはいなかった」と感じている。建築家の父ジャンはユー
トピアをツバメの巣に見るが、それを作ってもそこに住むものはいない。
作者ウェルベックが途中で殺されることによって、その作中人物であるは
ずのジェドとジャンは決定的に世界〈小説の外部〉とのつながりを絶たれ
る。

　ここで感じられるのは、小説の空間と建築のそれとの違いというよりも、
小説や建築あるいはアートも含めて今日の表現が直面している危機だ。す
べてが記号化し経済価値にのみ転換していく。それならばこの本の序章に
記したように、すべてが「趣味」化していくしかない。かといってウイリ
アム・モリスの理想に帰ることもできない——建築家がつくるツバメの巣

文学の計画——第2章　　*63*

of William Morris, because no one would live in a house for swallows designed by architects.

In this novel, the author appears in the story and is killed. It is the most characteristic point in the structure of the novel [fig. 7] (p. 183). Not only the author or characters in the story, but every person was born into the world to build his or her world. It might however, not feel like reality to belong to the world, and it will finally pass away. This novel topologically shows the crisis man faces today. There are no architectural works, but serious problems architects should consider are described in this novel.

3. Who is Actually Involved, Protagonist or Author?

In *Map and Territory*, the author writing the story appears as one of the characters. These kinds of techniques might look a little tricky but they are actually not so rare, especially in the post-modern novel. *Sabbatical* by John Barth[23] shows us another technique utilizing the author himself. Characters in this novel read and harshly criticize books written by John Barth. A text different from the main story is generated. The structure becomes multi-layered, and the layers begin to conflict. These techniques release novels from tale that is seemingly has a simple "tree structure," so the technique can be called "deconstruction."

Novels are not a simple effusion of the emotion of authors put to writing. They are not tales reflecting moral values. Novelists have been designing complicated structures to describe multi-layered relations between the world and man, and it was especially prominent during and after the post-modernist movement.

It didn't begin with the post-modern movement however. *The Life and Opinions of Tristram Shandy, Gentleman*[24], written in eighteenth-century England and reputed as one of the origins of the modern novel, already had the techniques necessary for surpassing simple tales. The protagonist

64   Chapter 2——*The Planning behind Literature*

には誰も住まない。

　この小説を構造的に見た時、その最大の特徴は、作者が作中に現れ、そして殺されるというところだろう [fig. 7]（p. 183参照）。作家や作中人物のみならず、ひとは誰も世界に生み出され、あるいは自分の世界をつくり、しかしそこに真に属した実感もなく、やがて消えていく。この小説は人間の危機を空間的に表している。この小説に建築家の「作品」は現れないが、小説自体に現代建築が提示すべき問題が現れている。

3．　主人公と作者あるいは事件

　『地図と領土』では作者が物語中に現れる。こうした手法はトリッキーにも見えるが、特にポスト・モダンの小説においては珍しくない。例えばジョン・バース『サバティカル──あるロマンス』[24]では、少し違ったやり方で作者自身を利用する。この小説の登場人物は作者の著作を読みそれを批評する。それらがすべてメインのストーリーとは別のテクストを成し、構造は重層化し錯綜する。こうした試みはツリー構造のような単純な構造になりがちな物語を言わば「脱物語」化する。

　小説は作者の感情のストレートな吐露ではない。あるいは単純な価値観（例えば勧善懲悪のような）を示すものでもない。世界と人間との複層的な関係を描くために、特にポスト・モダン以降の作家は複雑な構造を「設計」してきた。

　ただ実のところそれはポスト・モダンに始まったことでもない。近代小説の起源のひとつとも評される『トリストラム・シャンディ』[25]が書かれたのは18世紀のイギリスだが、ここにはすでに、単純な物語には決して回収され得ない工夫がなされている。主人公は自分が生まれる前の様子を見て

tells a story of before he was born as if he was there, and had seen everything. Sometimes he expresses his emotions not with words, but a line graph or just a page painted black. The modern novel as a description of a complex "stream of consciousness," not as a tale, began there.

However, in some novels, authors have deep relation with the works.

Kenzaburō Ōe wrote a novel titled *A Personal Matter*, a few years after his debut. Thereafter, his novels have become reflective of his personal experience. But it is so different from a simple effusion. Moreover, its method should be called "grotesque realism" or "magical realism."[25] In one of his works titled *The Game of Contemporaneity*,[26] he describes the real landscape of a valley in Shikoku where he supposedly was born and grew up, and wove it together with a mythological story from the valley. Its structure is complicated but clear.

Hiroshi Hara analyzed three novels, *Silent Cry*, *The Game of Contemporaneity* (not translated) and *Letters to Years of Nostalgia* (translated into French; *Lettres aux années de nostalgie*), which Kenzaburo Ōe wrote with scenes in a village in a valley in Shikoku island where Ōe grew up, and described as the following.[27]

> *We signify two happenings, for example, as Γ_1 and Γ_2, and situation in the valley as ϕ. We signify a situation after Γ_1 as $\Gamma_{1\phi}$, and another situation after Γ_2 as $\Gamma_2\Gamma_{1\phi}$. Generally, if a history is described as $\Gamma_2\Gamma_{1\phi}$, we should say $\Gamma_2\Gamma_{1\phi} \neq \Gamma_1\Gamma_{2\phi}$. It means <we can never be back in the history> or, commonly said, <It is no use crying over spilled milk.> On the other hand, someone says <history repeats itself.> If both historical processes of Γ_1 and Γ_2 are same, it is described as $\Gamma_2\Gamma_{1\phi} = \Gamma_1\Gamma_{2\phi}$. <Results would be same whatever you do> can be described as < $\Gamma_2\Gamma_{1\phi} = \Gamma_1\Gamma_{2\phi}$ though $\Gamma_1 \neq \Gamma_2$.> If it is so, Γ_1 and Γ_2 are <commutative.>*
>
> (Note : Γ means 'operator' in mathematics. Quantum mechanics treats operation of differentials or integration as general 'operator' so that classical mechanics by

きたように語り、気分の起伏をグラフで表して、時にはそれをページまるまる黒く塗りつぶして表現する。物語ではなく、複雑な「意識の流れ」を表現するものとしての近代小説がここで始まった。

　小説の場合、作家と作品との関係は深い。
　大江健三郎はデビューして数年後に『個人的体験』[26]という小説を書き、それ以降、自身の経験を色濃く反映した作風となった。とは言えその手法はグロテスク・リアリズムあるいはマジック・リアリズム[27]と呼ばれるものに近い。例えば『同時代ゲーム』[28]は、大江の生まれ故郷と思われる四国のリアルな谷の地形に、神話的な物語を重ねあわせたもので、その構造は複雑だが明快だ。

　原広司は、大江が四国の谷を舞台として描いた三つの小説『万延元年のフットボール』『同時代ゲーム』『懐かしい年への手紙』を分析し、次のように書いている。[29]

　　　ふたつの出来事Γ_1、Γ_2があるとし、谷間の状態をϕであらわす。Γ_1が起こったあとの状態を$\Gamma_1\phi$で示し、さらにΓ_2が起こった後の状態を$\Gamma_2\Gamma_1\phi$とあらわす。一般に、歴史が$\Gamma_2\Gamma_1\phi$ならば、$\Gamma_2\Gamma_1\phi \neq \Gamma_1\Gamma_2\phi$であると考えられる。これは、〈歴史はひきもどすことができない〉であるとか、もっと俗に言えば、〈覆水盆に返らず〉とか言われる。ところが一方、〈歴史は繰り返す〉とも言われる。Γ_1、Γ_2の歴史過程が同じなら、$\Gamma_2\Gamma_1\phi = \Gamma_1\Gamma_2\phi$であり、〈何をしても結果は同じ〉だとすれば、$\Gamma_1 \neq \Gamma_2$でも、$\Gamma_2\Gamma_1\phi = \Gamma_1\Gamma_2\phi$になるのである。このとき、$\Gamma_1$と$\Gamma_2$は〈可換である〉といわれる（補注：数学では$\Gamma_1$、$\Gamma_2$のことを演算子と呼び、量子力学は微分や積分などの操作を演算子一般の要素に組みこみ、ニュートンやマクスウエルの古典力学をより一般化した）。

Newton or Maxwell have been generalized.)

In the novels by Kenzaburo Ōe, the history in the valley can be signified as $\Gamma n\, \Gamma_{n-1}... \Gamma i... \Gamma_{1\phi}$, but for characters facing the protagonist "I," it appears to be interpreted as it is $= \Gamma_i\, \Gamma_{n-1}... \Gamma_i... \Gamma_{1\phi}$, or $= \Gamma_n\, \Gamma_{n-1}... \Gamma_n... \Gamma_{1\phi}$, or $= \Gamma_i\, \Gamma_{n-1}... \Gamma_n... \Gamma_{1\phi}$. Happenings in the novels begin to have <commutativity>. Jorge Luis Borges regulated the <commutativity> as singular and general phenomenon in the world. Nevertheless, Kenzaburo Ōe described in the three novels that <commutativity> is one of attributes of the valley and simultaneously means death of the protagonist. Ōe, in other words, described <commutativity> of time as 2° (*). Ōe found a structure in a space in the valley that is the origin of the same form of the three novels (*note by Suzuki; "2°" indicates one of common patterns appeared in the three novels, which Hara pointed out. Hara wrote this. <2° Characters facing "I" in the novels, "Taka", "my young sister" and "bro Gee", are close relative for "I," and they once get out of the valley in forest and come back there to end the story with their death.>).

(translated by Suzuki)

We can read Hara's analysis including mathematical description as a logic that explains relation between unique experience proper to an author and the novel though it is actually critic for the same pattern found in three novels by Ōe. Unique experience must have a structure as <there is no use crying over spilled milk> and can be translated into a novel with given <commutativity.> Also happenings in *Hopscotch* and *Portrait in Number* were given <commutativity> in the stories, as we have seen.

Otherwise, Kojin Karatani wrote a critic titled *A Phase in the Novel* for Kenji Nakagami's novel, *Makeup*,[28] which is a kind of "I" novel.

Two lines are there in Makeup. One is for a protagonist, big guy working

Chapter 2——— *The Planning behind Literature*

さて大江健三郎によれば$\Gamma_n \Gamma_{n-1} \cdots \Gamma_i \cdots \Gamma_\phi$が谷間の歴史であるが、あたかも$= \Gamma_i \Gamma_{n-1} \cdots \Gamma_i \cdots \Gamma_\phi$あるいは$= \Gamma_n \Gamma_{n-1} \cdots \Gamma_n \cdots \Gamma_\phi$あるいはまた$= \Gamma_i \Gamma_{n-1} \cdots \Gamma_n \cdots \Gamma_\phi$であると解釈できるように、「僕」に向きあった主人公に出来事がおこる。出来事のあいだに可換の性質が生じるのである。ボルヘスはこの可換性を、世界の特異であるが一般的な現象として規定した。しかるに大江健三郎は、彼の3部作を通じて、次のように描出した。可換性は谷間の属性ではあるもののそれは直ちに主人公の「死」を意味するのだと。言い換えれば時間の可換性を、2゜（＊）として記述した。3部作の同型性の原因、谷間の空間を構造化したのである（＊引用者注：「2゜」とは、原によるこの3部作の共通の性質のひとつであり、原はこう書いている。〈2゜「僕」と向かい合っている主要な人物、それぞれの小説において「鷹」、「妹」、「ギー兄さん」は「僕」の近親者であり、「森のなかの谷間」から一度はその外に出るが、帰還し、作品は彼らの「死」によって完結する。〉）。

　この数学的な記述を含む分析は、大江健三郎の「3部作」を対象としたものではあるが、作家あるいは誰かの固有の経験と、小説との関係を示したものであるとも読める。固有の経験は「覆水盆に返らず」の構造を持つが、それは「可換」の構造を与えられることによって、小説になる。1－1で例にあげた『石蹴り遊び』『ポートレイト・イン・ナンバー』も、その小説内において、出来事には可換性が与えられている。

　一方、中上健次の小説の「私小説」的な性質について柄谷行人は、中上の『化粧』の解説に『「小説」の位相』と題して、こう書いている。

　　（前略）『化粧』には二つの系列がある。一方に東京で労働しており、

in Tokyo, who comes back to his hometown Shingu after the divorce because of his violence. Another line is for another big guy rambling in deep forest in Kumano in unspecified age. We can say Nakagami tried to connect space in real in former line and space in narrative folklore in another line. He began to write with modern consciousness and in modern space, processes to reduce it then reached space in narrative folklore. (omission)

These lines to be called polar opposites can be easily found in literature before Nakagami. In the history of literature, one of them has appeared as naturalism or "I"-novel, another one has appeared as narrative tales or mythology. These lines seem to be antagonistic to each other. Critics see, in the dominant idea in general, that novel became poor because the former line suffocate the latter line. So someone advocates restoration of narrative tale. But I don't think such a banal idea is valid especially for Nakagami's works. He had these antagonistic lines inside him and envisage novel as something transcend the polar oppsites.

(translated by Suzuki)

We cannot see Kenji Nakagami and Kenzaburo Ōe in the same vision but find something both of them have in common. They create their own novel with throwing their proper experience into another tale.

Personal experience and novel are strongly related but totally different with each other.

But still we can say that the relationship between the personal experiences of a novelist and his works are close and direct, compared to the relationship between an architect and his works.

In Japanese literature after World War II, we popularized a genre called the "I-novel." An author becomes "I" as a protagonist, and "I" directly narrate his/her actual experience and emotion, like a kind of confession. The "I-novel" genre follows "Naturalism"[29] or "Realism,"[30] but it's difficult to

再三の暴力沙汰のために妻子に別居させられ、郷里の"新宮"に戻ってきた「大男」がいる。他方で、"熊野"の山中を彷徨し、どの時代ともいえないような空間に生きている「大男」がいる。中上は、いってみれば、前者のようなリアリスティックな空間と後者のような民俗学的な空間をつなごうとしている。彼は、前者、すなわち近代的な意識及び空間の側から出発し、それを還元することによって後者に至るという手続きを取っている。（中略）

　両極的といってよいこの二系列は、むろん、中上健次以前からあったものである。文学史的に見れば、一方は、自然主義的あるいは私小説的であり、他方は、古代からの物語や伝承である。両者は、ふつう完全に対立するものとみなされている。今日では、前者が後者を抑圧したことが小説を貧しくしたというのが、むしろ支配的な見解である。そこで「物語」の復権が唱えられる。しかし、中上にかんしていえば、そうした凡庸な見解はまったく妥当しない。彼はそうした両極を所有し、かつそれらを超えたところに「小説」を考えていた。

　中上健次は大江健三郎とは異質ではあるが、共通しているところもある。つまり、固有の経験を「両極」の一つとして所有しながら、それを別の「物語」とぶつけることで、「小説」を生み出している。

　固有の経験と、小説とはこのように、強い関係を持ちながらも、大きく異なる。

　それでもやはり、作家自身の経験と作品との関係は、とても近く、直接的だ。建築家とその作品との関係に比べれば。

　私小説というジャンルがある。作家自身が主人公として、一人称の語りでその経験をそれへの心情も含めて描くもので、いわば告白に近い。自然主義あるいはリアリズムの流れをくむが、日本の近代文学のみに現れたもので、否定的に批評するものも多い。だが今でも『私小説的』なものは少

文学の計画──第2章　　*71*

find the same style of "I-novel" in countries except Japan. Not so few critics have a negative opinion of the "I-novel," but even today such novels are written, and some of them are highly appraised, and do sell. Readers might believe that the "reality" surrounding our lives can interweave the minds of readers and authors. We can say that it is a bit similar to blogs on the internet which have attracted a large readership.

Meanwhile, it is difficult for us to get a picture of "I-architecture." How is it possible to make a close relationship between the "I" and the works of architecture in the same way Houellbecq and Ōe did in their novels?

In France, there is a work of architecture called the *Ideal Palace of Postman Cheval*. It has not received adequate credit in the history of architecture, but is nonetheless conserved as an important work of architecture by the French government. Its planning and construction took almost 30 years through the late nineteenth century to the early twentieth century.

Cheval was a postman his entire life, and a complete amateur when it comes to architecture. His design sources for the shape of *The Palace* were only his memories and impressions of architecture he had seen in pictures or has imagined. Materials for The Palace were stone, wood, or otherwise limited to what he could get his hands on. Finally, *The Palace* emerged as a strange work of architecture looking like a random mixture of deformed styles of all eras and cultures. The mixture and deformity of the work was a result of nothing other than Cheval's memories and emotions.

If we could find "I-architecture," would it not be something along the lines of the *Ideal Palace of Postman Cheval*? It's difficult to comprehend or appreciate this palace without knowing about Chevel's real life and emotions which made this work of architecture. It is the same process in which a reader tries to understand an "I-novel" through researching the novelist's real life and emotions.

Chapter 2——*The Planning behind Literature*

なからず書かれ、時に高い評価を受け、そして売れる。身近にある「リアル」こそが、作者と自分がつながる、あるいは重なるように感じさせてくれるからかも知れない。それはインターネット上の人気「ブロガー」が多くの読者を集めるのに似ている。

　他方、建築には「私建築」は、なかなか存在しない。ミシェル・ウェルベックや大江健三郎的な意味での作者と作品の近さですら、建築では、はたしてありうるのかどうか？
　フランスに『シュヴァルの理想宮』あるいは『郵便夫の家』と呼ばれる建築がある。正統な建築史のなかには現れないが、フランス政府から重要建築物に指定され保存されている。19世紀の終わりから20世紀のはじめにかけて、30年以上の年月をかけて、郵便夫シュヴァルによって構想・建設されたものだ。

　シュヴァルは生涯郵便夫であって、建築の素人だった。形態は、シュヴァルの頭のなかにある建築の記憶──実際に見たものや写真が残した印象──のみに基づいた。材料は、郵便配達の折に見つけた石など、これまたシュヴァル自身がその好みによって手に入れられるものに限られた。その結果、古今東西の建築様式がドロドロに変形し混合したような建築が出来上がった。その変形と混合は、シュヴァルという作者の記憶と感性のみが行った。

　「私建築」というものをもし探すなら、このシュヴァルの『理想宮』のようなものを言うのだろうか。確かにこれは、シュヴァルその人の『人生』と結び付けられて語られるし、そうしなければ理解も評価も難しい。それは「私小説」を読むものが、その作家の実生活や感情とともにその作品を理解しようとするのに似ている。

文学の計画──第2章　　73

On the other hand, architecture generally doesn't need such a personal story. We know the private story of Frank Lloyd Wright.[31] He had a love affair with a client's wife and eloped, putting his career in architecture on-hold. Then his lover was killed by his maid. His life was a great deal more scandalous than the average "I-novelist," and a lot of people know about it. But we never care for such a story when we see his architectural works. The story would affect nothing in comprehending his works. It's possible to make a chronological table on his life and works, but it would just end up as something a historian would record.

Is it the case that architecture does not relate to the individuals mind or issues?

We will consider it some more by comparing Japanese haiku,[32] the shortest style of poem, to modern architecture, even if the comparison is slightly odd.

4. Proper Noun, Symbol, Memory

Narrow Road to the North by the haiku poet Matsuo Basho, is a book every Japanese person knows. To make haiku of the northern landscapes of Japan, he journeyed north by foot, utilizing spatial structure. The first chapter begins: "The months and days are the travelers of eternity. The years that come and go also voyagers."[33] This famous sentence represents the idea that "time can be translated into space" by Hiroshi Hara. Now let's read one of the haiku from the book.

> *They sowed a whole field,*
> *And only then did I leave*
> *Saigyo's[34] willow tree.*

(translated by Donald Keene)

だが普通の建築の場合はそうではない。フランク・ロイド・ライトはクライアントの妻と不倫関係に陥り、挙句駆け落ちして、その後しばらくキャリアの中断を余儀なくされた。さらには使用人にその愛人を殺されるという悲劇にあう。「私小説」作家顔負けの私生活で、誰もがそんなストーリーを知っているが、ライトの建築を見るときそんなことを思い出すものはいないし、思い出したとしても空間の鑑賞に一抹の影響も与えない。むろんライトの生の歩みを作品と対照し、あわせて論じることはできるだろうが、それはただ歴史家の仕事だ。

　それでは、建築にはやはり、個人的な心理や課題は関連し得ないのだろうか?
　少し突飛な比較だが、俳句と現代建築[31]を合わせ見ながら、この問題を掘り下げることにする。

4. 固有名、シンボル、記憶

　松尾芭蕉の『奥の細道』は、日本語を母語とするものなら知らないものはいない。風景を句に詠むために東北への道を歩むという、それだけで既に空間的な試みだ。「月日は百代の過客にして、行かふ年も又旅人也」という有名な序文も、原広司の言う「時間の空間化」が現れていて、構造的に建築に近い。さてこの本のなかに、次のような俳句がある。

　田一枚　植ゑて立ち去る　柳かな

This haiku feels just like space in architecture to me.

It means that "Time as an entire rice-field has been sown; it has passed me by while I was getting lost in thought." This is one example of how time is translated into space. The course of time is shown with the changing of the landscape which transforms from a big body of water into a scenery of green shoots. Basho felt that the point of "change" was under "Saigyo's willow," which had a specific meaning for Basho. If we can define architecture as something which gives meaning to a place, and transforms the landscape, we would have to conclude that this haiku is architecture.

We look once again at the difference between architecture and literature. This "willow tree" is not just a plain old tree. Saigyo, a waka[35] poet Basho respected, had written a waka about the willow. The waka was first published in the *Kokinshū, A Collection of Ancient and Modern Japanese Poetry, 905*. The waka reads:

> *In the shade of a willow*
> *Where a crystal stream flows*
> *Alongside the road*
> *I thought I would spend a moment,*
> *But I could not leave the spot*

(translated by Donald Keene)

The proper name Saigyo was figuratively carved on the willow, or the place, and was of immense importance to Basho. Saigyo's poem (=existing space) overlaps with Basho's poem, (=new space) and create intensity.

Modern art would never attribute any meaning to proper names. For example, painters drew stories of specific people who had proper names like Jesus or Mary before the Renaissance, then people or landscapes

Chapter 2——*The Planning behind Literature*

この俳句は、建築の空間そのもののように、僕には感じられる。

　内容は、「柳の下で物思いにふけって、ふと気がつくと、目の前の田で、田植えが終わるほどの時間がたってしまっていた」というものだ。ここでも時間の空間化が行われている。時間の経過は、風景の変化〈＝ただ水だけが広がっていたはずの場所が、緑色の苗が一面に点在する風景へと変貌する〉によって示される。そして芭蕉がその変化を感じるのは、ある「柳」の下という、他のどことも異なる場所においてである。建築とは、ある場所に意味を与えるもの、そしてそこにおける風景を変化させるものである、もしそう定義しうるのなら、この句は建築そのものというしか他にない。

　しかし、ここでまた、文学と建築との差異が生じる。

　この「柳」は、ただの柳ではない。芭蕉が敬愛する歌人・西行が読んだゆかりの柳という「意味」[32]を持つ。古今集[33]に収められたその歌[34]は

　　道のべに清水流るる柳かげ
　　しばしとてこそ立ちどまりつれ

というものだ。

　柳（という場所）には西行という固有名が刻まれていて、そしてその固有名はほかでもない作者の芭蕉にとってこそ最大の意味を持つ。西行の歌（既存の空間）に重ね合わされることで芭蕉の句（新しい空間）に強度が生まれる。

　固有名に、モダンアートは意味を認めない。例えば絵画は、かつてジーザスやマリアなど固有名を持つ者の物語ばかりを描いたが、やがて対象を無名のひとや風景に移し、ついには対象そのものを消去して抽象画に至っ

文学の計画──第2章　*77*

that had no onomastic stories became the object of interest, and at last, they erased real objects from the painting, and abstract paintings became popularized. It is not an important issue who the *Weeping Woman*[36] is. Andy Warhol[37] knew enough about this particular history of modern art, but still selected Mick Jagger[38] and Marilyn Monroe[39] as objects of his paintings. He used general and banal impressions of their names. "Marilyn Monroe" is a stage name that works for the impression, but her real name would bear no meaning to Warhol and his audience. These attitudes towards proper names were inherited by Yasumasa Morimura[40] through his appropriations, or by Takashi Murakami[41] through his sculptures.

Architecture, as well as music, intrinsically has no object to be drawn, and as such they have been thoroughly excluding proper names and denying symbolism, which is especially true in the case of modernism. Symbolism is for example a quality of the obelisk, where it sometimes takes on the meaning of a historical person or an event. Modern architecture rejected to connect with anything outside of its own field. It insisted that architecture should only follow the necessities such as function or mathematical beauty. Before long, simple symbolic assumptions such as "Japanese houses should have Japanese tile-roofs" was denied, and an international style was established. It was also what economics and industrial technology requested. Symbolism does not contribute anything to efficiency.

Some architects and critics expressed dissent towards this simple anti-symbolism. Among them were Robert Venturi[42], an architectural theorist, and Rem Koolhaas[43], a leading architect. To roughly summarize their argument, a form (shape) is not a simple representation of function, but has an ambiguous relationship with diverse factors in actual architecture or cities. Venturi says that the building shaped like a duck in Las Vegas fulfills a symbolic role in the city. On the other hand, Koolhaas says, the minimal shape of modern skyscrapers in New York would tell us nothing

78   Chapter 2———*The Planning behind Literature*

た。『泣く女』[35]が誰であるかは重要ではない。アンディ・ウォーホル[36]は現代絵画のそうした性質を逆手に取るようにミック・ジャガー[37]やマリリン・モンロー[38]を題材に選んだが、それはそうした名前がもたらす普遍的かつ陳腐なイメージを利用したに過ぎない。マリリン・モンローは芸名でそのイメージのために重要だが、本名はウォーホルや鑑賞者にとって意味がない。固有名へのこうした態度は森村泰昌[39]のなりすまし・シリーズや村上隆[40]のフィギュア・シリーズなどの現代アートにつながっていく。

　建築は音楽と同様にもともと絵画のような「描く対象」を持たないから、余計に「固有名排除」の傾向は徹底している。特にモダニズムにおいて、シンボリズムは否定された。シンボリズムとは、例えばオベリスクが持っていたもので、歴史的な人物や事件という「意味」を強いてくる。近代建築はそうした〈建築形式の外部〉との結びつきを拒否したのだ。建築は建築に内在する必然性、例えば機能や数学的な美にのみに従うべきだと主張した。やがて、「日本だから日本的な瓦屋根」というような素朴なシンボリズムも否定され、いわゆるインターナショナル・スタイルが生まれた。これは経済や工業技術からの要請でもあった。シンボリズムは効率に寄与しない。

　これに対して異を唱えたのが、ポスト・モダンの建築理論家ロバート・ヴェンチューリ[41]であり、現代建築をリードする建築家レム・コールハース[42]だ。彼らの言うところを乱暴に要約すると[43]、実際の建築や都市においては、形態は機能と単純に一対一対応をするようなものではなく、もっと多くの要素と多義的な関係を持つ。ラスベガスのアヒルの形をした建物は、その形態が都市のなかで十分にその象徴的役割を果たしている（ヴェンチューリ）。逆に、ミニマルな形態の高層ビルでは、機能は外部からは読み取れぬものになり、それによってむしろただの象徴に成り下がっている（コー

about their function, so they became no more than simple symbols. Actually, it was easy to regard WTC twin towers as a symbol of American capitalism or globalism which were attacked by a terrorist organization in the 9/11 incident. We can presume that was why terrorists chose those buildings as their target. Someone who says it's ridiculous to design hambarger restaurant with the shape of hambarger might accept Italian restaurant designed with mediterranean-taste even if it is in Kyoto or Beijing.

The meaning and symbolism that shape can convey is more complex and contradictive than words.

Furthermore, shape has a lot of potential power.
Where does this power come from?

5. The Shape of Reality / Shape in Imagination
—The Atomic Bomb Dome and the Tower of Babel

We would say "willow" exists in the Haiku poem. It doesn't mean it exists as real material. So we have no sensor to clearly see it in the detail. We only imagine it as a fictive shape.

We can read such a description about fictive shape of city and architecture in a novel *Invisible City* by Italo Calvino.

> *you can say that four aluminum towers rise from its walls flanking seven gates with spring-operated drawbridges that span the moat whose water feeds four green canals which cross the city, dividing it into nine quarters, each with three hundred houses and seven hundred chimneys. And bearing in mind that the nubile girls of each quarter marry youths of other quarters and their parents exchange the goods that each family holds in monopoly —bergamot, sturgeon roe, astrolabes, amethysts —you*

ルハース）。実際、例えば「9.11」のテロ攻撃で破壊されたWTCツイン・タワーを、アメリカ資本主義の（あるいはグローバリズムの）象徴であったと読み取ることは可能だった（だからこそ攻撃対象にされた）。ハンバーガーの形をしたハンバーガーショップの建物を嘲笑する者でも、地中海沿岸風デザインのイタリア料理店は普通に受け入れてしまうかもしれない、たとえそれが京都や北京にあったとしても。

　オベリスクや凱旋門、あるいは装飾的な様式に特別の、そして固有の意味や象徴性があるとは、論理的に言って考えない。形態が示しうる意味や象徴性は、言葉のそれよりもずっと複雑で、時に対立的だ。
　それでもなお、形態は力を持ちうる。
　一体それは、どこからきているのだろうか？

5．現実の姿／空想の形態——原爆ドームとバベルの塔

「柳」は俳句のなかに存在していると、私たちは言うだろう。だがそう言う時、その存在とは、リアルな物質として存在するという意味ではない。したがって私たちはその「柳」を物質として、細部まではっきりと観察する知覚を持たない。それはいわばフィクティブな形態として想像される。
　イタロ・カルヴィーノの小説『見えない都市』[44]には、都市や建築の奇妙な形態の描写があふれている。

　　（前略）その城壁からは四つのアルミニウムづくりの塔がそびえ、その傍らに寄りそう七つの門は濠をまたぐバネ仕掛けのはね橋をそなえ、その濠はまた市内を貫いてこれを九つの街区に分つ四条の掘割に緑の色あざやかな水を注ぎ、その街区の各々は三百戸の家と七百本の煙突をかぞえ、さらにまたそれぞれの街区の娘はほかの区内の若者と結婚し、その家族はそれぞれに特許専売といたしております商品、すなわちベルガモット香やチョウザメの卵、測天儀、紫水晶をたがいに

文学の計画——第2章　*81*

can then work from these facts until you learn everything you wish about the city in the past, present, and future.

(translated by William Weaver)

We can find double or triple devices for fictive description in the novel. This novel is a kind of parody of *Travels of Marco Polo*. *Travels of Marco Polo* was written in a style of reports in real but we know it contains a lot of fiction. Calvino made it more fictive with a system of novel.

Description in the novel is also ambiguous. It describes materials and life of people there but we cannot figure if it exists now or only in history.

Calvino uses ambiguity between words and images that the words create. Reader must feel frustrated because we cannot clearly see but only in imagination.

The power of fictive shape including ambiguity is important.

Calvino described another invisible city like this.

The city does not consist of this, but of relationships between the measurements of its space and the events of its past: the height of a lamppost and the distance from the ground of a hanged usurper's swaying feet; the line strung from the lamppost to the railing opposite and the festoons that decorate the course of the queen's nuptial procession; the height of that railing and the leap of the adulterer who climbed over it at dawn; (omission) The city, however, does not tell its past, but contains it like the lines of a hand, written in the corners of the streets, the gratings of the windows, the banisters of the steps, the antennae of the lightning rods, the poles of the flags, every segment marked in turn with scratches, indentations, scrolls.

Chapter 2——*The Planning behind Literature*

交換いたしておりますことどもを勘考し、これらをもとに計算いたしますならば、この町の過去現在未来にいたるまでの事柄を望むがままに知ることができると申し上げるか。

　この小説は、二重、三重にフィクティブの力がかかっている。まず、それはマルコ・ポーロの『東方見聞録』のある種のパロディである。『東方見聞録』は「見聞」の報告すなわちリアルなものとしての体裁をとるが、実のところはかなりフィクティブなものであったことが知られている。それをカルヴィーノはさらに小説という仕組みでフィクティブなものにした。

　描写も、先に引いたように、物の描写をしていたかと思うと人々の暮らしの話になり、またそこで今起きていることなのかそれとも歴史なのかも判然としない。

　カルヴィーノは、さらに言葉とそれがつくりだすイメージとの間の曖昧さを利用している。読者は、そのフィクティブな都市の姿を想像しながらも、はっきりとは細部が見えないもどかしさを感じるしかない。

　だが重要なのは、その曖昧さの全ても含めての、フィクティブな形態の力である。

　別の「見えない都市」は次のように描写される。

　　空間の寸法と過去のさまざまな出来事とのあいだの関係によりその都市（まち）はつくりあげられているのでございます。街灯の地面からの距離と吊し首になった簒奪者のたれさがった両足、その街灯から正面の手すりまで張り渡された縄と女王御婚儀の行列の道順を覆う花綵、その手すりの高さと暁にそれをのり越える姦夫の跳躍（中略）

　　しかし都市（まち）は自らの過去を語らず、ただあたかも掌の線のように、歩道の縁（へり）、窓の格子、階段の手すり、避雷針、旗竿などのありとあらゆる線分と、またさらにその上にしるされたひっかき傷、のこぎりの痕、のみの刻み目、打った凹みといったなかに書きこまれているままに秘めておるのでございます。

文学の計画——第2章　83

The shape of the city and architecture have been certainly curved the unique happenings on it but don't tell it by itself.

Fictive shape found in novels can exist in real.

Nobody would doubt the symbolic nature of the Hiroshima Peace Memorial, the Atomic Bomb Dome. Not because of the historical value inscribed in it, nor the nuclear warhead, or the mushroom cloud, but the shape of the dome can tell us something.

In Hiroshima, there are actually dozens of atomic-bombed buildings[44] still in existence today[45]. Every one of these buildings that were bombed contains the memory and history of the war. Even so, the Atomic Bomb Dome has the strongest symbolic value of them all. The symbolic value stems from the shape and the location. It does not stem from the way it has been conserved, or anything else.

Partially destroyed buildings are not rare to come across, but no other work of architecture than the Atomic Bomb Dome has its steel arches which supports the dome, half destroyed and melted. On the other hand, these melted steel arches evoke a gracious apparition of the dome before it was destroyed by the atomic bomb. A small river runs in front of the Dome. This river has a strong symbolic value, especially for Japanese people because a river sometimes signifies a border between the living and the dead.

The "Atomic Bomb Dome" was obviously not constructed with its current name and shape in mind. It was designed as the "Products Exhibition Hall of Hiroshima[46]," by Jan Letzel, a Czech architect. Before World War II, a lot of architects were invited from Europe to contribute in the modernization of Japan. A work of architecture designed by a European architect for the sake of modernizing Japan, was caught up in the war,, and destroyed by an ultramodern weapon from the United States of America. The entire history of modern Japan is embedded in its shape.

Chapter 2——*The Planning behind Literature*

固有の出来事を刻み込まれてしかしそれを自ら語ることはない都市と建築の形態。

　こうしたフィクティブな形態は、リアルにも存在する。

　広島の原爆ドームの象徴性を疑うものはいないだろう。それはそこに、歴史を記した記念碑が埋め込まれているからではない。ただその形態が、語るのだ。

　実際、広島市内には、原爆ドーム以外にも「被爆建物」[45]は今も幾つもある。どの被爆建物にも記憶が染み込み歴史的な意味があるが[46]、原爆ドームはそれらから抜きん出て強い象徴性を持つ。保存のされかたなどにも理由はあるが、大きいのはその形態と場所の力だ。

　戦争や災害で半壊した建築の姿は珍しくない。だが、半球形を成す鉄骨がむき出しになり、半分が溶けたような建築は世界にふたつとない。ドームの名残は破壊前の優雅な姿を思い込ませる。その目の前を川が流れる。これもまた、特に日本人にとっては、象徴的な力を持つ。

　原爆ドームは無論、その名前、その形になるように設計されたわけではない。チェコの建築家、ヤン・レツルが、「広島県物産陳列館」として設計した[47]。第2次世界大戦前、多くのいわゆる「お雇い外国人」建築家たちがヨーロッパから日本に招かれた。日本の近代化のためにヨーロッパの建築家が設計した建物が、その急速な近代化のゆえに戦争に巻き込まれ、やがてアメリカの超近代兵器によって破壊される。日本の近代史が、その形態に、まるごと埋め込まれている。

文学の計画──第2章　85

The symbolic value will never be lost, no matter how few people are able to extract meaning from the shape. It would gain even more value by invoking polysemic interpretation, including possible misinterpretations. We can certainly feel the value in the shape itself, if we compare it to an epigraph consisting of no more than boring signs conveying information.

You might be trying to conjure a picture of the "Atomic Bomb Dome" in your mind when reading this chapter. The shape does not manifest itself with physical sufficiency, even if you confirm its shape by looking at photos. And still, the shape keeps its value. Why does it?

Because shape is an imagined idea before it is a physical form.

This might sound like a bold hypothesis, but it is not. By looking at a few examples, you will understand that it is true. Imagine the shape of the Tower of Babel. The story of the tower of Babel is written in the Book of Genesis in the Old Testament. Many an artist has drawn its shape, and novelists and poets written about it. The Tower of Babel will forever and always only have an imaginary or fictive shape because nobody has actually seen it. However imaginary or fictive it might be, who would ever say that the shape of the Tower of Babel has no value?

Unlike the Atomic Bomb Dome, the Tower of Babel might have never existed. Hence, only in our mind, can we see the shape that is obscured by a veil drawn over by imagination. Nevertheless, its engraved meaning and value are several times greater than the Atomic Bomb Dome. You cannot see the details, you cannot touch the material, but you can feel its value from the shape appearing under the veil of imagination.

Imaginary drawings by Ledoux,[47] Lequeu,[48] Archigram[49] and Zaha Hadid at her early days, successfully captured the value of the architectural shape as the story of the Tower of Babel did. History of drawings for unbuilt architecture has been presenting the possibility of imaginary shape.

そこまでの意味を形態から直ちに読み取るものは稀かもしれない。それでも、その象徴的な力が無効になることはない。むしろ多義的な読み——誤読の可能性も含めて——を喚起することで、それはさらに強度を得る。正確な意味を伝達するが退屈な記号でしかない碑文に比べれば、その強度は明らかだ。

あなたはこれを読みながら、今、「原爆ドーム」の「形態」とはどのようなものであったか、思い出そうとしているかもしれない。写真で確認したとしても「形態」はいまだ十分に物理的なものにはならない。そしてだからと言って「形態」の力が減じるわけではない。それはなぜか？

なぜなら、「形態」とは、物理的なものである以前に、想像上のものであるからだ。

大胆な仮説の類に聞こえるかもしれない。だが例を挙げて考えてみれば、それは単純な真実だとすぐにわかる。たとえば「バベルの塔」の形態を思い起こしてみればいい。旧訳聖書の創世記に最初の記述があらわれ、その後多くの画家がその記述をもとにその姿を描いたが、もとより見た者はいないので、それは常に、そして永遠に想像的な形態にしかならない。しかしだからといって、バベルの塔には形態としての力がないと、いったい誰が考えるだろうか？

バベルの塔は原爆ドームと違って、ひょっとしたら一度も地球上に存在しなかったのかもしれない。したがって我々は、バベルの塔という名前に接するとき、空想がのがれられないあの曖昧さとともにその形態を頭の中で見るしかない。それでもそれは、原爆ドームに刻まれた歴史の、何十倍もの意味と力を埋め込まれている。たとえ細部は見えず、手で触れる感覚を得られなくとも、想像上に曖昧に現れるその姿は、やはり十分すぎる形態の力を持つ。

ルドゥー[48]やルクー[49]、あるいはアーキグラムや初期のザハ・ハディド[50]の、想像的な建築のドローイングは、バベルの塔がしたようにして、建築的な形態の力を獲得した。アンビルド、すなわち建たない建築のために描かれたドローイングの歴史が、この空想の形態の力を守り続けている。

文学の計画──第2章　*87*

The Atomic Bomb Dome still stands in Hiroshima, unlike the tower from the Old Statement, it is a shape formed by the power of reality. However, it is certain that the stories told of the Atomic Bomb Dome is also generating a power of imagination. The value of the real shape of the Atomic Bomb Dome is exactly like the value of an imaginary shape of architecture.

6. Shape and Imagination in Literature

Imaginative power made manifest.

The imaginative value of shape. In that sense, the "willow" in the haiku by Basho, as mentioned earlier, has value as a shape.

Nobody who ever reads this haiku has seen the shape of this "willow." It can only be imagined. We imagine it through a reference point, but that doesn't mean that we envision it without thinking. We form the imaginary shape of the "willow" in our imagination by superimposing the willow of our memory to the imagery in Saigyo's waka and Basho's haiku.

At first, we would only have a blurred vision of the willow's figure. It has a space where a traveler can stand under the branches. The space is in a specific context for Basho, and by knowing that, we come to sympathize with it. Just as we form an imaginary shape of the Tower of Babel the more we come to know the story from the Book of Genesis, we can have our own imaginary shape of a "willow" that is different from the others. Just as we do for the Tower of Babel, where the pictures and the ruins speak to us.

We are not discussing the significance of knowledge or education behind literature works. This is not only limited to haiku and poetry, but also to any art works before modernism which required people to have knowledge and education for appreciating them. It would be hard for

88   Chapter 2———*The Planning behind Literature*

原爆ドームは現実に今も広島に建っている。原爆ドームは、旧約聖書の
なかに記述された「物語」とは異なり、現実の力によって造形された「現
実」だ。それでも原爆ドームの語る「物語」が想像としての力を発し続け
ていることは確かだ。原爆ドームのリアルな形態の力は、建築の想像的な
形態の力そのものなのだ。

6．文学における「形態」と想像力

　「形態」の持つ想像的な力。その意味で、芭蕉の先の俳句における
「柳」も、「形態」としての力を持つ。

　この俳句を詠むものは、だれもその「柳」を現実には見ていない。私た
ちはただ、想像するしかない。ただしそれは、ただ何も考えずに夢想する
ということを意味しない。西行の和歌と、芭蕉の俳句と、私たちが見たこ
とのある柳を重ね合わせて、柳の想像的な形態を心のなかで造形していく
のだ。

　最初に見えるのは、道端にたっている柳の木のぼんやりとした姿だけだ。
その下に旅人を佇ませる空間がある。柳の前には水田の風景が広がる。芭
蕉にはその柳が特別の文脈のなかにあり、私たちはそれを読み、知る過程
で、芭蕉の柳を共有していく。創世記の物語を知る過程で、バベルの塔の
想像的形態を、頭の中で形成していくように。柳の想像的な形態は、ひと
それぞれによって異なるだろう。それもバベルの塔でも同じことだ。バベ
ルの塔には物語をもとにした絵や、遺跡と語られる場所が残っているとは
いえ。
　今ここで論じているのは、作品の背後にあるものについての知識や教養
の重要性ではない。確かに、俳句や詩歌に限らず、モダン以前のアートは、
作品の外部にある文脈や思想についての教養や知識を鑑賞者に求めた。キ
リスト教や古代ギリシャの思想への理解がなければ、ルネサンスに至るま

文学の計画──第2章　*89*

people to discuss the history of art leading up to the Renaissance, if they didn't understand Christianity or ancient Greek philosophy. Knowledge is also important when we try to understand Basho's "willow," but that is not what I am arguing. What we need to consider right now are the possibilities of imagination.

We recognize something beyond what we register through optical nerve signals. Referring to our memories and reasoning, we recognize it iconographically. Immanuel Kant[50] called it "Einbildungskraft," which is imagination. In *The Imaginary*, Jean-Paul Sartre[51] argues that this power can produce something and shape it. That is what we are discussing when we talk about the possibility of imagination.

When we read a haiku, we only absorb seventeen syllables. We recognize and appreciate what seventeen syllables can produce, and shape it with the ability of memory and presumption, the einbildungskraft. Our ability of imagination can catch the memory and feeling of Basho. After we catch it, we can imagine our "willow" once again based on Basho's "willow." Sartre referred to these abilities as "L'imaginaire."

The personal experience of authors or fictive characters which appeared in literature works were put into a general schema[52] to be commonly realized by many people. A general scheme that architecture produces shapes personal and prior experience through imagination.

As *Narrow Road to the North* does, the author would write with his/her inherent experience, so that the architect could make it into architecture. Imagination in the process would work not only for the inherent experience, but also for any other meaning or comprehension that the inherent things evoke. Inherent identity and generality become the reason and the result of each other through the imagination.

での芸術史を考えることは難しい。芭蕉の「柳」についても同様なことは言えるが、それが論点ではない。ここで考えたいのは、あくまでも想像力の問題である。

　人間は、視神経がとらえたものをそのまま認識するのではない。それを記憶や推理の能力によって、初めて図像として認識する。そうした能力は、カントが構想力＝イマジネーション[51][52]とよんだもののことだ。またその能力は、その時に視神経がとらえているものではない何ものかを構想し、産出することができる。それはサルトルがその著書『想像力の問題』[53]で論じていたことにもつながる。この章で論じているのも、そうした想像力の問題についてに他ならない。
　俳句を詠むとき、私たちの感覚がとらえるのはたった17の文字だけだ。それを記憶や推理の能力で、つまりカントの言う構想力で、認識し、鑑賞する。この構想力が、芭蕉の個人的な記憶や感覚をとらえる。私たちはそれをとらえたのちに、芭蕉にとっての「柳」を、私たちにとっての「柳」として想像しなおすことができる。それがサルトルの言う想像力である。

　文学に現れる作者あるいは作中人物の個人的な経験は、その想像力によって普遍的な図式[54]に落とし込まれることで、多くの読者に共有される。建築で構想される普遍的な図式は、やはり想像力によって、個人の固有の経験を造形する。
　『奥の細道』がそうであるように、作者は固有の経験を文章にし、建築家は固有の事件を建築化することができる。その時働く想像力は、その固有の経験や事件だけではなく、それが喚起するあらゆる意味や解釈に向けても働く。固有性と普遍性は、この想像力によって、互いがその理由になり結果にもなるのだ。

文学の計画——第2章

7. An Architect Who Died Young, and His Daughter

In order to be able to think about the relation between imagination and shape more precisely, I will show you a work of architecture I designed, and the essay I wrote about it.

The work of architecture titled *EXCES*[53], a house with a tutoring school for kids, was built in Kyoto in 1998 [fig. 8-10] (p. 184). The essay reflecting on the process of designing it was published in a magazine in 2009[54]. I have transcribed it here with a few modifications.

> *3K was an elementary school girl when I was designing this house. She has already graduated from university, and has become a businesswoman. Sadly, she is not always at home, because she needs to live in the dormitory which the company provides. She is only at home for a few days a year. It is a sad thing when the protagonist is mostly absent from the story. Someday, it might happen that she breaks out of the story, and becomes independent.*
>
> *There is a room with an oval cross-section in this house. K grew up in this room. The room that looks like it's floating above the living room has two windows. One of them faces out towards the town, and the other one faces her mother's room across an empty space. K must have had special scenery coming through her windows, which were different from what K's classmates must have seen in their teenage years.*
>
> *There once was an architect called Seiichi Nakano in Kyoto. Today, only a few people know his name, for he died too young. He was born in 1953 and lived only for 32 years. Way too short for an architect because of the difficulty involved in getting a chance to design a real project at such a young age. Nevertheless, he left us some impressive works that were published as a book titled Architecture of Life: Works by Seiichi Nakano, by Graphic Publishing. K is the daughter of this architect.*

92   Chapter 2——*The Planning behind Literature*

7．ある早世した建築家とその娘

想像力と形態の関係についてさらに詳細に見るために、僕自身がかつて設計した建築と、それについて書いたエッセイを紹介したい。

『*EXCES*[55]』というタイトルのその建築は1998年に京都に建った [fig. 8-10]（p. 184参照）。その設計過程を振り返ったエッセイは2009年に『本の窓』という雑誌に掲載された。そのエッセイを多少修正して、そのまま書きう[56]つす。

　設計を始めたころには小学生だったKちゃんが、今では大学を出て社会人だ。とても残念なことに、会社の寮に住んでいて、あまり帰って来られないのだという。この家の物語の主人公は、不在がちなのだ。大人になった彼女は、この物語の外部へと、やがて本格的に巣立っていくのかもしれない。

　この家には、卵型の断面をもつ部屋がある。Kちゃんはこの部屋で育ち、大人になった。リビングの上に浮かぶようにしてあるその部屋は、一方に街を眺める窓が、他方に吹抜けを通して母の部屋と対面する窓を持つ。Kちゃんは窓の外に、きっとほかの十代の子たちが見るのとはちょっと違う、特別な風景を持っていたはずだ。

　かつて中野誠一という建築家がいた。今この名を知るものは多くはないだろう。中野はあまりにも早く死んだからだ。1953年に生まれ、32年間生きた。若くして実作の機会に恵まれるのは稀な建築家の世界で、その生はあまりにも短すぎる。それでもいくつかの印象に残る建築作品を残し、それらはグラフィック社から『生の建築・中野誠一作品集』と題されて刊行もされた。Kちゃんは、この建築家の、娘さんだ。

I first heard his name as we went to Kyoto University at around the same time. Sadanori Maeda, who was my classmate, studied under him. "He burns for architecture in a way that amazes me," Maeda often used to say. "I tremble at the thought of having to become as passionate as he." Studying under the tutelage of Nakano must have made Maeda a great architect.

I had no personal acquaintance with Nakano, but I have heard a lot of similar legends about him. So I was at a loss for words, and felt unworthy of the honor, when Mrs. Nakano gave me the chance to design a house for her and her daughter. It felt like the 'God of architecture' had given me a mission. It was fate.

I'm not sure if K remembers her father very well or not. Nakano died when K was a baby, so it might be safe to say that K has little to no memory of her father. I guess that the architecture designed by her father is all that she has of him. And I suppose that for Nakano as well, his architecture, and his daughter are all the traces left of him.

I decided, in the beginning of my planning, that I would design a space dedicated to the sky for K's room.
Entering the house, climbing the stairs, passing by mom's office, arriving in the living room where you look up to see K's room floating in the air. The shape of the room will attract people like a magnet. So to say, I tried to cast a K's room as the protagonist of the house.

Whether you view K's room from the inside or the outside, it is the main feature of this house. I don't believe in heaven or hell, but if I'm wrong, and Nakano's soul is wandering this plane, it will easily find its way to K's room.

僕は中野誠一の名を、存命中から知っていた。京都大学建築学科の、先輩に当たるひとだからだ。当時の僕の同級生で、今建築家として活躍する前田紀貞は、学生時代に中野の事務所で修行していた。それはもう建築に対して厳しくて、といつも前田はこぼしていた。「オレもこんなに建築に真剣に向き合わなくてはいけないのかと思うと、ぞっとするよ」そう言っていた前田が、今建築の第一線で活躍しているのは、間違いなく中野誠一の薫陶のおかげに違いない。

　面識こそないものの、そのように身近に伝説を聞いていた僕に、中野夫人のYさんが、一粒種のKちゃんと暮らすための住宅を設計する機会が巡ってきたのは、身に余る幸運としか言いようがなかった。いや、幸運という言いかたは不謹慎かもしれない。この使命を覚悟を持って引き受けよと、建築の神様が——あるいはただの運命が——僕に命じたように感じたのだ。

　Kちゃんに、お父さんとしての中野誠一の記憶がどれほどあるのか、僕は知らない。普通に考えれば、生後間もなく他界したお父さんの記憶は、Kちゃんにはほとんどないだろう。Kちゃんにとっては、お父さんが残した建築が、お父さんのすべてかもしれない。そして、父であった中野誠一にとっても、その生の痕跡は、建築と、Kちゃんであったに違いない。

　Kちゃんの部屋を、空に捧げられた空間のようにつくろう——設計の初期の段階で、僕の気持はそう固まった。

　家に入り、階段を上り、母の仕事の場を経由して、家族室に至り、そこで上を見上げると、そこにはKちゃんの部屋が浮かんでいる。Kちゃんの部屋が、磁力のような力を発して、この家で暮らすもの、訪れるものを誘う。そのようにして、僕はKちゃんの空間を、この家の物語の主人公に据えようと試みたのだ。

　Kちゃんの部屋は、家のなかから見ても、外から見ても、象徴的に、この住宅の特徴として見てとれるだろう。僕は死後の世界や、天国を信じるものではない。だがもし僕の思い違いで、中野誠一の魂がどこかに存在し、この世界を見下ろしているとしたら、それは必ずや、容

文学の計画——第2章　　95

K's space exists in between the sky and her mother. This specific point is not same as any other point, and it is the center, beginning, and destination of the story that Nakano left behind.

I have never talked about this with K. I have also not written about it in any other outlet, so it is quite plausible that she does not know how I feel. On the other hand, I believe she must have noticed that she is the protagonist of the house, because of her symbolic place, looking at the scenery of the town, and towards her mother through the windows.

At the moment, K is living somewhere else. But still the protagonist has her space in the house. As she will in the future.

The protagonist of the space has an oval cross-section. Why exactly this shape? There are a number of reasons. The abstract shape, like it's floating on waves, which sets it apart from the other parts of the house, and the same visual from the upper or lower level, K's space wrapped by curved face, and so on. Having this many reasons, one can still question how I can pick just one shape, and thereby exclude all the other possibilities. Can this reason exist which settles only on one unique shape? In mathematics, the solution is sometimes unspecified.

You might think that a solution (=shape) would be automatically derived by an algorithm or parametricism. But actually, any shape (=any solution) can be applied by simply changing the program or selection of the parameter.

Hence in EXCES, I thought that I'd design a shape with an ambiguous reason so that people might think, "What is this shape?" or "What a mysterious shape."

Generally, architects want a reason as to why the shape is the way it is. For example, we know from a famous thesis in modernism that "form follows function." Animals certainly appear that way. The shape of the machine does too. It only makes sense that architecture should follow.

易にKちゃんの部屋を見つけ出すに違いない。

　Kちゃんの空間は、空と母親の姿との間に、孤高の一点として、位置している。この、世界の他のどこでもない一点が、中野誠一が残した物語の中心、起点、あるいは目的地になる。

　僕はこんな話を、これまでKちゃんにしたことはない。ほかのメディア上にも、あまり書いたことはないから、Kちゃんはこんな設計者の勝手な思い込みは知らないかもしれない。だけど僕は思っている。空に浮かんだ、あんなに象徴的な空間のなかにいて、そして窓の向こうの、街の風景やお母さんの様子を見ていて、自分がひとつの物語の主人公であることを、Kちゃんが気付かなかったはずがない。

　今、Kちゃんはこの家を離れて暮らしている。しかし空間としての主人公は今もここにある。これからもずっと。

　空間としての主人公は、卵形の断面をもつ。なぜこの形なのか？象徴的な形態、瓦屋根の波の上に浮かぶような感覚、建物のほかの部分とは異なる形、上から見ても下から見ても同じに見える、卵型という柔らかい曲面でKちゃんの空間をつくりたかったから——しかしそれにしても、これらの理由から、なぜこの形が決定されうるのか？この形以外の形の可能性を排除してまで。そもそも、形態を一意に導き出す根拠などというものはあるだろうか？　数学の用語でいえば、解はしばしば一意には定まらない。

　アルゴリズムあるいはパラメトリシズムにおいては、解（形態）が自動的に導き出されるように見えるかもしれないが、実際はプログラムやパラメーターの選び方で形態（解）はいかようにも変わりうる。

　だから、『EXCES』においては、僕はむしろ造形の根拠がはっきりとはわからないものをつくろうとした。あの形は一体何だろう、不思議な物体だな、と思わせるようなものを。

　建築家は、形態に、そのデザインの根拠を求めたがる。たとえば「形態は機能に従う（form follows function）」という近代建築のテーゼがあった。動物の形には、確かに機能的な理由があるように見える。機械はまさにそうだ。ならば建築も、というわけだ。

文学の計画——第2章　*97*

Regretfully, architecture has a lot less function than an animal or a machine. It lacks in function to design the space. Take for instance, the height of a ceiling. A lower one would be more functional, (efficient, economic) but on the other hand, a higher one makes it breathe.

I don't deny the relationship between shape and function. No one can deny that architecture is strongly related to function and program. Function will give a possibility of various shapes —although not specified shapes— to architecture.

Hence, I believe that something mysterious which transcends rational thought attributes something vital to architecture.

Jumping ahead, we are going to look at why Raskolnikov[55] murdered his elderly landlady. Who can clearly uncover the full scope of the murder beyond doubt? Readers of Crime and Punishment[56] differ in their explanations. If it was obvious, I don't think it would have been read for generations. Raskolnikov as well as Dostoyevsky[57] felt the mysteriousness of the murder. The kind of gravity which make a story begin and progress.

I thought I had found the method to design architecture in the same way as you write a novel when EXCES was completed. However, it was just a fragment of a much bigger whole.

The characters in this house have a lot of memories: The memories of a deceased architect and father, of K growing up here, and the time between the past and the future. I wrote this story of space, with K as the protagonist.

People who knew Seiichi Nakano will read the story with his memory in mind, and the people who didn't know him, will just imagine the story,

だが、残念ながら建築は、動物や機械に比べると、機能の数があまりに少ない。一意に形態を決定するほどの機能が充満していない。たとえば天井の高さは低いほうが機能的（効率的、経済的）だが、高いほうが気分はいい。

　機能と形態との関係を否定するつもりはない。建築は機能やプログラムと密接な関係を持つべきだし、そこからさまざまな——一意ではない——形態も生まれえる。

　にもかかわらず、いやだからこそ、僕はこう思うのだ。合理的な思考の末になお残る不可思議さ、それこそが建築を生きた物語にするのではないかと。

　ちょっと飛躍してみよう。ラスコーリニコフ[57]はなぜ金貸しの老婆を殺害したのか？　その理由を、『罪と罰』[58]の読者は様々に説明できるだろう。だがそれが合理的に説明し尽くされることはあるだろうか？

　もし説明がついているのなら、あの小説が長く読み継がれることはないはずだ。ラスコーリニコフにも、つまりは作者ドストエフスキー[59]にも、説明できない不可思議な感触が、『罪と罰』の殺人にはあった。そしてその不可思議な感触が持つ引力によって、物語は始まり、進んでいく。卵型の断面を持つKちゃんの部屋は、そのような不可思議な感触を与えるはずのものだ。その感触を遠くから眺め、ある時は近づき、入りさえすることで、物語は始まり、進んでいく。

　『EXCES』の設計の時に、建築を小説のように設計するという方法を、僕はようやく探り出したのだという気がしている。それはまだ、方法の端緒というべきものだったとは思うのだが。

　この住宅の登場人物たちには、物語があった。死んだ建築家＝父という記憶、これから成長していくKちゃん、そしてその未来と過去とに間に挟まれた今という物語が。僕はその物語を、Kちゃんを主人公に据えて、空間で描写してみたのだ。

　中野誠一を知るものはその記憶にしたがってこの物語を読み、知らぬものはただ京都の空に浮かぶこの形態の外観から、物語を想像する

文学の計画——第2章　　99

inspired by the shape. EXCES must have evoked various ways of reading it, as the novel has various modes of comprehension.

This architecture is a kind of novel titled EXCES, which I wrote. However, it's not completely the same as a novel of course. K is not a protagonist that I created, but a person living in the real world. So I want to someday pose her the question which I could never ask a protagonist in a novel:

"What did it feel like to live in this house?"

8. "The Death of the Author"

Who is a "protagonist" in the general sense? Is it a character reflecting what the author is thinking? Can a protagonist appear in architecture in the same way as in literature? To be able to consider these questions, we should read a critique of literature.

In an essay titled The *Death of the Author*[58], Roland Barthes[59] described a character in a novel as the following:

—Who is speaking in this way? [...] Is it the man Balzac, endowed by his personal experience with a philosophy of Woman? Is it the author Balzac, professing certain "literary" ideas of femininity? Is it universal wisdom? Or romantic psychology? It will always be impossible to know, for the good reason that all writing is itself this special voice, consisting of several indiscernible voices, and that literature is precisely the invention of this voice, to which we cannot assign a specific origin: literature is that neuter, that composite, that oblique into which every subject escapes, the trap where all identity is lost, beginning with the very identity of the body that writes.

Probably this has always been the case: once an action is recounted, for

だろう。小説にただひとつの解釈など無いように、この建築も、多様な読みかたを誘発してきたはずだ。

　僕にとってはこの建築は、「EXCES」というタイトルで書いた小説に他ならない。だけど、もちろん小説とは違うこともある。それはKちゃんが、僕がつくり出した主人公などではもちろんなく、現実を生きている人間だということだ。だから僕は、小説の主人公には決して実際には答えを求めえない問いを、いつかKちゃんにしてみたいと思っている。

　この空間を生きてきて、どんな感じだった？

8.「作者の死」

　だがいったい、主人公とはだれのことだろう？　それは作家の思いを埋め込まれた人物のことだろうか？　建築においても、彼らは小説と同様に出現可能なのだろうか？　それを考えるにはまず、文学への批評から見ることにしよう。

　ロラン・バルトは『作者の死』と題したエッセイで、バルザックの小説中の、ある登場人物についての語りを取り上げ、こう書いている

　　……しかし、こう語っているのは誰か？　（中略）この小説の主人公か？　（中略）バルザック個人か？　作者バルザックか？　万人共通の思慮分別か？　ロマン主義的な心理学か？　それを知ることは永久に不可能であろう。というのも、まさにエクリチュールは、あらゆる声、あらゆる起源を破壊するからである。エクリチュールとは、われわれの主体が逃げ去ってしまう、あの中性的なもの、混成的なもの、間接的なものであり、書いている肉体の自己同一性そのものをはじめとして、あらゆる自己同一性がそこでは失われることになる、黒くて白いものなのである。

（中略）ある事実が、もはや現実に直接働きかけるためにではなく、

文学の計画──第2章　*101*

intransitive ends, and no longer in order to act directly upon reality —
that is, finally external to any function but the very exercise of the symbol
—this disjunction occurs, the voice loses its origin, the author enters his
own death, writing[60] begins.

(translated by Richard Howard)

Barthes intends to criticize literary critics who confuse a work with the author. In this novel by Balzac, there is no speech. Nevertheless, some critics want to construe the line as the author's talking in order to analyze and criticize his life. Barthes says that such criticism is invalid.

—Let us return to Balzac's sentence: no one (that is, no "person") utters it:
its source, its voice is not to be located; and yet it is perfectly read. This is
because the true locus of writing is reading.

Like Barthes wrote, meaning is generated at a 'locus' where a novel is read, then the writing (=écriture) becomes a kind of reality at the locus. It's the same for haiku, or any other poem. A reader reads Saigyo's waka, and remembers it through Basho, so that in the locus, the reader looks at rice fields spread in front of Basho's eyes.

Barthes' intention was to criticize the critics, but we can still apply his theory to literature. A novelist can project himself to one of the characters he creates. The self can be divided into multiple characters. However, the novelist needs to be a reader of his own sentences as soon as they have been put to paper. The novelist needs to get into the 'écriture,' where his own speech has disappeared. He can continue to write the novel only if he re-constructs the écriture as the reader.

We can also apply it to architecture. An architect can write a story, create characters and make assumptions of what's going on. Architects imagine

102   Chapter 2——*The Planning behind Literature*

自動的な目的のために物語られるやいなや、つまり要するに象徴の行
使そのものを除き、すべての機能が停止するやいなや、ただちにこう
した断絶が生じ、声がその起源を失い、作者が自分自身の死を迎え、
エクリチュールが始まるのである。

(傍点原文)

　バルトのここでの意図は、作品と、作者の世界とをしばしば混同する批
評家たちへの批判にある。バルザックの小説において、実際にはいかなる
《人格》も、「語って」いるわけではない。にもかかわらず、ある種の批評
家はそれを作者の声だと捉えたがり、そして作者の人格の調査や批判を始
める。バルトはそれは無効だとし、こう論じる。

　　バルザックの「文の声は、エクリチュールの本当の場ではない。本
　　当の場は、読書である」。

(傍点原文)

　確かに小説は（あるいは俳句も）、意味が生成するのはそれが読まれた場
においてであって、そこにおいてのみある種の「現実」になる。芭蕉の心
に浮かぶ西行の和歌をよむのは読者であり、したがって芭蕉の眼前に広が
る田を見るのもまた読者だ。

　バルトの趣旨は批評家への批判だと先に書いたが、これを小説家の方法
論に応用することも可能だろう。小説家は自らの姿を登場人物の誰かひと
りに投影することもできるし、分解して複数の人物に託すこともできる。
ただし、小説家は書いた次の瞬間には、自らの小説の読者になる。読者と
して、自らの声の消えたエクリチュールに入り込まなければならない。読
者としてエクリチュールを組み直すことによってのみ、小説を書き続ける
ことができる。
　こうした関係は建築にもまったく同様に当てはまる。建築家は、小説家
のように物語を書き、登場人物をつくりだして、そこで起こる出来事を仮

文学の計画──第2章　　*103*

a locus for these things. The field would be transformed into shapes of space, if it were to become the way *EXCES* was designed. People who have an experience with the space would 'read' stories of it. The way this is going, the architect will disappear like the *Death of the Author* to leave 'écriture' as a designed locus.

Architecture and the novel appear as a locus of the story in the same way. The difference might be that the characters become equal to the readers (people who have an experience of the spaces) in architecture. I don't think there is such a big difference any more. Characters in architecture are also a kind of fiction that the architect creates through assuming what experience people will have with the space.

We can see these kind of relationships between the 'characters' and those 'who experience it' in film, but we will come back to that later...

9. The Discipline and Phenomenon of Overlapping

I'm going to spatially imagine "the true locus" which Barthes mentioned.

Jose Saramago[61] wrote a novel titled *The Year of the Death of Ricardo Reis*.[62] 1935, Lisbon. A medical doctor whose name is Ricardo Reis comes back from Brazil to his home country of Portugal. He had gotten word that his friend, a poet named Fernando Pessoa had died. Reis visits his grave, as well as places that remind him of Pessoa. Then he begins to talk and walk with his ghost.

In reality, there was a poet named Fernando Pessoa in Portugal, 1888~1935. He was not so famous before he died, but his poetry became highly regarded after his death. Well, what about Ricardo Reis—did he exist? If he did, he was not a doctor, but a poet. More exactly, Reis is the man, Fernando Pessoa.

Takiko Okamura, who translated the novel into Japanese, explained it

想する。建築家はそれらが起こりうる「場」を構想するだろう。そして「場」は空間の形態に変換され、やがて建築になる。先に例に上げた『EXCES』がまさにそうであったように。空間を経験するものは、その物語を「読む」だろう。その瞬間に建築家は消える。設計された「場」というエクリチュールを残して。

　建築と小説とはこうして同じように物語の「場」として現れる。相違点は、建築の場合、「登場人物」＝「空間を経験するもの（読者）」となるところだろうか。いや、それも相違点とまでは言えない。建築の「登場人物」は「空間を経験するもの」に基づいて建築家が仮想する、ある種のフィクションだからだ。

　「登場人物」と「経験するもの」とのこうした関係は、映画のなかでも現れるが、それは後述することにしよう。

9.「重ねあわせ」の原理と現象

　バルトの言う「エクリチュールの本当の場」というのを、空間的にイメージしてみたい。

　ジョゼ・サラマーゴ[63]の小説に『リカルド・レイスの死の年[64]』がある。

　舞台はポルトガルの首都、リスボン、1935年。リカルド・レイスという医師が、詩人フェルナンド・ペソアの死を知り、ブラジルから帰国する。レイスはペソアの墓を始めとして、ペソアの記憶に係る場所を歩きまわり、やがてペソアの亡霊とも会話や散歩をともにするようになる。

　フェルナンド・ペソアという詩人はポルトガルに実在した（1888〜1935）。生前には一部を除いて一般にその名が知られることはなかったが、没後に高い評価を得たという。他方のリカルド・レイスはというと、これも実在したというべきか、どうか。少なくとも、レイスは実在の医師ではなかった。レイスもまた詩人だった、というよりも、ペソアそのひとだった。

　訳者の岡村多希子の解説によれば、ペソアは詩作にあたって本名の「ペ

文学の計画——第2章　*105*

like this. Pessoa used three synonyms: Reis, Álvaro de Campos, and Alberto Caeiro. Other than that, he used Pessoa, his autonym. Okamura wrote the following: "According to the explanation by Pessoa himself, a synonym is a name of another character than the man of the autonym, who has an independent life. It is a kind of a literary mechanism designed to express various philosophies and different aspects of the life and art of one poet, Fernando Pessoa." She continues, "I can see each poet distinctly, as their different synonyms have their own specific style and écriture when I read their poem. Who would confuse Reis's works with Campos's works?"

Ricardo Reis, is older than Pessoa, a medical doctor, classicist, traditionalist, and political royalist. He is indeed an independent sort of character.

In this novel, the poet, as one of his synonyms, visit the dead poet with the autonym, himself. Saramago, who is also a reader of 'their' poems describes the 'poets.' The world of each poet overlaps the other poets' world, and all the layers make up "Fernando Pessoa." Saramago is looking at these layers through another layer called history. All of the layers cover the city, Lisbon. The structure can be drawn like this: [fig. 11] (p. 185).

Lisbon itself consists of a lot of mosaics, and multiple layers. It has land figures, history, uneven distribution of wealth, areas for people to live, and dead people [fig. 12] (p. 185).

Various characters appear in this novel. Two of them act out important roles whose name come from the odes Reis wrote. This idea makes the structure more complicated [fig. 13] (p. 185).

As I have already written, or as Barthes said, we don't need to consider a character as a real person, even if the name is the same as the real person's name. In the front page of the novel, Saramago quoted these words from Pessoa:

ソア」以外に、「リカルド・レイス」「アルヴァロ・デ・カンポス」「アルベルト・カイデロ」という３つの「異名」を用いたという。岡村はこう書いている。異名とは、「ペソア自身の説明によれば、本名者の人格とは別の人格、人生をもった人物の名前であり、ペン・ネームや別名とはちがう、要するにフェルナンド・ペソアという一個の詩人のうちに宿る人生、芸術などについての多様な価値観、側面を表現するものとして考え出された文学装置である」。「異名者たちの作品を読むと、各人それぞれに独特の特徴的スタイル、エクリチュールがあり、たとえばレイスの作品とカンボスの作品を混同するようなことはあり得ない」。

　ペソアが造形したリカルド・レイスという人物は、ペソアより一歳年長で、医師。古典主義者、伝統主義者であり、政治的には王党主義者だった。確かにレイスは独立した人格を持つ。
　つまりこの小説は、死んだ詩人のもとに、別人格としての詩人自身が訪ねてくるという形式になっている。そして異名者も含めたこれらの詩人たちを、その詩の読者であるサラマーゴが描いているのだ。詩人たちの世界は互いに重なりあって層を成し、その全体でペソアという人間をなしているとも言える。作者サラマーゴはその重なりあう層全体を見ている。その向こうには歴史という層があり、これら全体はリスボンという都市の上に乗る。構造的には、[fig. 11]（p. 185参照）のようになるだろうか。
　また、都市リスボン自体も、多数のモザイクや、層によって形成されている。地形があり、歴史があり、貧富があり、生活の区域があり、そして死者の領域もある [fig. 12]（p. 185参照）。
　この長い小説にはさまざまな登場人物がいるが、重要な役割を果たすふたりの女性の名前は、リカルド・レイスの詩（頌歌）に出てくる名だという。これを考えると構造はさらに複雑になる [fig. 13]（p. 185参照）。
　むろん、既に述べてきたように（あるいはバルトが言うように）、実在の人物が登場してきたからといって、それを現実の人物だと考える必要はない。サラマーゴ自身、この小説の冒頭に、フェルナンド・ペソアの次の言葉を引いている。

文学の計画──第２章　*107*

—If they were to tell me that is absurd to speak thus of someone who never existed, I should reply that I have no proof that Lisbon ever existed, or I who am writing, or any other thing wherever it might be.

What used to exist and has ceased to exist, and what has never existed, both concepts can exist in the novel. They become layers, and sometimes compositions of mosaics which make up the figure of Lisbon. Lisbon as an écriture, as Saramago wrote, "Here the sea ends and the earth begins."

Hiroshi Hara presented the idea of "multi-layered structure," which is important for spatial structure. Hara is an architect, and a well-known professor who researched a lot of villages and cities over the world. He says that the overlapping which creates a "multi-layered structure," appears in landscapes of various villages. He wrote the following in his book titled *A Hundred Things Villages Taught*[63].

—The overlapping creates a "multi-layered structure." The centripetal form of a village is a specific example of "multi-layered structure" which can be easily found in Japanese traditional houses, and surrounding landscapes. They can also be found as tatami-rooms, engawa (a kind of veranda), court, outside walls, tiled roofs, trees, mountains, haze, and sky which are also representative "multi-layered structure" which form sceneries.

The overlapping is also an aspect of the phenomenon of consciousness. Our consciousness can overlap memories as "scenic schemes" of several events at the same time. We sometimes feel a sense of nostalgia even if it's our first time visiting an overseas village, because it has a structure similar to other villages which we remember. But more importantly many villages were built according to the discipline of overlapping which fits the phenomenon of consciousness.

(translated by Suzuki)

108   Chapter 2———*The Planning behind Literature*

存在したこともない人についてこんなふうに語るのはばかげていると
言われたら、僕は答える。書いているこの僕や、その他どんなものも、
どこかしらにかつて存在していたことを証明できるわけではない、と。

　かつて存在し今は存在しないものも、かつても今も想像のうちにしか存
在しなかったものも、この小説のなかのリスボンには存在する。層を成し、
モザイク状に組み合わさって、「リスボン」の地形をつくり上げる。サラ
マーゴが「ここで海が終わり、陸がはじまる」と書き始めるエクリチュー
ルとしての「リスボン」に。
　原広司は、空間構造の重要なひとつとして「多層構造」をあげている。
原は建築家であるとともに、世界の多くの集落や都市を調査・研究したこ
とでも知られている。原によれば、「多層構造」をつくり出す「重ね合
せ」が様々な集落の風景に現れているのだという。『集落の教え100[65]』で、
原はこう書いている。

　　重ね合せを直接的に構造化すると、多層構造になる。求心的な集落
　形態は、多層構造の最もわかりやすい具体例である。日本の住居にお
　ける座敷、縁側、ぬれ縁、庭さき、塀、隣家のいらか、森、山、かす
　み、空といった借景のとり方も、景観形成上の多層構造の代表例であ
　る。

　　重ね合せは、意識の現象の特徴でもある。私たちの意識は、同時に
　幾つかの事象の〈情景図式〉としての記憶を重ねあわせることができ
　る。たとえ初めて接する海外の集落であっても懐かしさを感じるのは、
　私たちが記憶している集落の組立てに似ているからでもあるが、それ
　以上に、意識の現象に符合する重ね合わせの原理に依拠して多くの集
　落がつくられているからである。

　　　　　　　　　　　　　　　　　　　　　　　　　　　　（傍点原著）

文学の計画──第2章　*109*

"Multi-layered structure" and "overlapping" as Hara explained them, can be shown in [fig. 11-13].

The depiction of Lisbon in the novel is beautiful. Hara describes the condition of the villages he visited Lisbon, which appear in Saramago's writing. Ricardo Reis have a lot of walks with Fernando Pessoa, who is already dead.

—*Ricardo Reis crosses the park to take a look at the city, the castle with its walls in ruins, the terraced houses collapsing along the slopes, the whitish sun beating on the wet rooftops. Silence descends on the city, every sound is muffled, Lisbon seems made of absorbent cotton, soaked, dripping. Below, on a platform, are several gallant patriots, some box shrubs, a few Roman heads out of place…*

—*The pavement was wet and slippery, and the train lines gleamed all the way up the Rue do Alecrim. Who knows what star or kite holds them at the point, where, as the textbook informs us, parallel lines meet at infinity. It must be truly vast to inhabit so many things, dimensions, straight and curved lines, intersections, the tram that go up these tracks and the passengers inside the trams, the light in the eyes of every passenger, the echo of words, the inaudible friction of thoughts. A whistling up at a window as if giving a signal, Well then, are you coming down or not...*

—*A little further along the rain comes back. One umbrella shelters both of them, and although Fernando Pessoa has nothing to fear from this water, his huddling gesture was that of one who has still not completely forgotten life...*

原の言う多層構造、重ね合わせは、[fig. 11-13]に示した『リカルド・レイスの死の年』の構造そのものだと言えるだろう。

　この小説に描かれるリスボンの街は、美しい。原が世界に訪ねた集落の様相が、サラマーゴの書くリスボンにも立ち現れる。リカルド・レイスと、レイスよりも先んじて死んだレイス自身＝フェルナンド・ペソアは、何度もリスボンの街をさまよい歩く。

　　リカルド・レイスは公園を横切り、町を、城塞とその崩れた城壁を、斜面を滑り落ちそうな家並を一望する。白っぽい太陽が濡れた屋根に照りつけ、町の上に沈黙が下り、すべての音が無音のうちに押し殺される、リスボンは雫のしたたり落ちる綿から成っているかのよう、下方の大地には、いくつかの愛国的勇士の胸像、柘植の木々、ローマ風の頭部の彫刻がある。（後略）

　　歩道は濡れて滑りやすくなっている、市電のレールがアレクリン通りを上へとまっ直ぐに光っている、平行線が交わるところと学校が教える無限のあの点にはどんな星や凪があるのだろうか、かくも多くのものが、あらゆる大きさのあらゆるものが入るのだから、無限とは広大無辺でなければならない、平行直線、単純直線、曲線、交点、これらの線路を上る電車、そのなかにいる乗客、乗客ひとりひとりの目の輝き、言葉の反響、思考の聞こえるか聞こえないかの摩擦音、信号のように窓に向けられる口笛、それで、下りるのかい下りないのかい、まだ早いよ、上の方で声が答える。（後略）

　　リカルド・レイスがサバテイロス通りを下っていると、フェルナンド・ペソアが見える。（中略）フェルナンド・ペソアは微笑み、こんにちはと言い、リカルド・レイスも同じように答え、ふたりでテレイロ・ド・バソの方に向かう、ちょっと行くと、雨が降りはじめる、フェルナンド・ペソアがその雨に濡れることはありえないながらも、ふたりは傘の下に入る、それは、生をまだ完全には忘れていないもの

文学の計画──第2章　*III*

Here we can see another example of "multi-layered structure." Both synchronic and diachronic: I and another I, the urban and nature, life and death, they are represented with overlapping layering. This brings to mind the sentence from Hara's *A Hundred Things Villages Tught* us to "live with the dead."

> —*A village in Bali has small towers built for the purpose of deifying their ancestors... A village consists of some small buildings and a kiosk in the center. A man dying is moved to the kiosk to have a view of the surrounding buildings = the world the man has lived in. Then the spirit of the man moves to one of the small towers.*
>
> *The dwelling in Bali is an outstanding example which shows the relation between death and home. There are villages in South America where dead people are buried under the floor of the house. These villages tell us to "live with the dead."*

Novel and architectural space does not only share structural resemblance, but also regarding the texture of life and death. Ricardo Reis lives with his dead selves, Jose Saramago lives with their dead.

10. A Small Crack in Overlapping

Not only beautiful or sad harmony emerges from the overlapping. Sometimes a gap arises between layers grows, cracks, and brings forth a crisis of collapse.

の動きではあった。（後略）

　これらの描写に多層構造が現れている、現在と歴史、私ともうひとりの私、都市と自然、そして生と死、それらが重なりあい幾つもの層をなして現前する。そしてそれはまた、原の『集落の教え』のなかの一項「死者とともに生きよ」を思い起こさせる。

　　　バリ島の集落の住居には先祖を祀る一画があり、そこには小塔が立ち並んでいる。住居は分棟形式であるが、中央にあずまやがあり、まさに死に直面した人は、最後にそのあずまやに移され、そこから生きてきた世界＝住居を展望する。そして、小塔が群立する場所へ移っていく。
　　　バリ島の住居は、死と住居の関係を示す際立った事例であるが、中南米のインディオの集落の住居の床には死者が埋葬されていたりして、集落の多くは〈死者とともに生きる〉ことを私たちに教えている。

（傍点原著）

　小説と建築的空間との類似は、もはや構造のみにとどまらない。生と死の感触までもが、共有されている。まるで「集落の教え」を学んだかのように、リカルド・レイスは自らの死者とともに生き、ジョゼ・サラマーゴは彼らの死者とともに生きる。

10. 重ね合わせに生じた小さな亀裂

　だが、重ね合わせは、必ずしも美しい——あるいは悲しい——調和を生むばかりではない。時として、重ねあわされた層の間に隙間ができ、それが亀裂のようにして成長しながら、やがて決定的な崩壊の危機を生むこともある。

文学の計画——第2章　*113*

—It was not a street any more, but a world, a time and space of falling ash and nearly night.

The novel *Falling Man*[64], written by Don Delillo[65] begins like this. It is a story about the 9/11 terrorist attack.

The twin towers of the WTC were designed by Minoru Yamasaki[66], and they were 110 stories, and 1, 362 feet high. There was an infrastructure shaft in the center of every floor. The shaft and walls which made up the physical structure looked like a bird cage. The shapes were two simple cuboids. There was no column inside, and every floor had almost the same planning, so we can say that the space was homogeneous. It means that the space could accept any type of office, or nationality of the companies. It is called 'International Style,' which was made possible by the wave of modernism and economy from the end of the twentieth century. The style can fit any city over the world which is economically developed. The twin towers looked like copies of each other, so that they gave a kind of illusion that the towers were going to be endlessly reproduced all over the world.

A character in *Falling Man* says the following:

Weren't the towers built as fantasies of wealth and power that would one day become fantasies of destruction? You build a thing like that so you can see it come down. The provocation is obvious. What other reason would there be to go so high and then to double it, do it twice? You are saying, here it is, bring it down.

The design competition for a new building on the site where the WTC used to exist was won by Daniel Libeskind[67]. Now the proposal has been

114   Chapter 2———*The Planning behind Literature*

もはや街路ではなかった。世界だ。落ちてくる灰で夜のように暗く
　なった時空間の世界。

　ドン・デリーロ[66]の小説『墜ちてゆく男』[67]はそのように始まる。それは9.
11テロをめぐる物語だ。
　実際には9.11で破壊されたWTCツイン・タワーは、ミノル・ヤマサキ[68]
による設計で、110階建てで高さは400メートルを超えた。各階の平面中央
にエレベータ等のインフラ・シャフトがあり。このシャフトと、建物をく
るむ鳥かごのような外壁が、構造体になっている。形態は単純な直方体、
内部空間も柱がなく1階から110階まで面積もほぼ同じという、極めて明
快に均質な空間だ。それはつまり、どのようなタイプのオフィスでも、ど
この国の会社でも、容易に受け入れられるという性質でもある。インター
ナショナル・スタイルと呼ばれたこうした建築のありかたは、20世紀の
モダニズムと経済がもたらしたもので、世界中の経済的に発展した都市なら
どこにあっても違和感を生じさせない。互いが互いのコピーであるかのよ
うなツイン・タワーという形式は、これがそのまま世界の別の場所に増殖
していくような幻想すら抱かせる。

　『墜ちてゆく男』の登場人物はこんなことを言う。

　　富と権力の幻想としてのタワー。それは、いつの日にか破滅の幻想
　にもなるように建てられたんだ。ああいうものを建てるのは、それが
　崩れ落ちるのを見られるようになんだよ。挑発的な意味は明々白々だ。
　ほかに理由なんてあるかい、あんなに高くして、それをダブルにする
　なんて？　おなじことを二回するなんて？　これは幻想なんだから、
　二度やったっていいだろって言ってるんだ。さあ、できた、壊そう
　ぜって。

　WTC崩壊の跡地にはその後新しい高層ビルが計画され、設計コンペで
ダニエル・リベスキンド[69]が勝ち、そしてその建築案は実現した。グラウン

realized. It is an ordinary, but slightly fashionable office building with a monumental park on the ground level in memory of 9/11. The crack which terrorism showed us—a crack between layers of culture, religion, civilization, history and the world—has been driven out of the United States. Faith in the notion that 'wealth and power' can never be destroyed by cowardly terrorism might put it to rest.

Falling Man has an emotional story, but doesn't get into the crack. Keith, the protagonist, grabs someone else's attache case. He visits his wife, whom he has not seen for a while, and afterwards stops by to have an affair with a woman to whom the attache case belongs to. Downtown, he watches a performance where a man mimics a falling man from WTC. In this way, the novel shows us some cracks existing in our daily life, but not in history and the world.

In the final chapter of the novel, one of the terrorists in one of the planes set for WTC talks himself into forgetting this world. "Forget the world," he says. He sees something fall off the counter. At this moment, the narrative subject switches from the terrorist to Keith. Keith sees a bottle fall off the counter. He sees a white shirt, hands up, falling from the sky.

An American protagonist, and a terrorist from the Middle East, their consciousness change the narrative subject by having both of them experience the shaking of catastrophe.

Why didn't Don Delillo begin the novel with this final chapter? If he did, then the crack would show a cross-sectional surface of history and the world.

Of course, we can't say that describing a small crack is meaningless. A novel is not an editorial, or an essay. A novel might find significance in carefully representing the feeling of a small crack. Literature in Japan,

116   Chapter 2——*The Planning behind Literature*

ド・レベルに記憶を喚起しようとするモニュメンタル公園的な空間がある以外は、通常の、少ししゃれたオフィス・ビルだ。テロの風景が垣間見せた亀裂——文化、宗教、文明、歴史、世界そして人間の亀裂——は、アメリカ国外のどこかに追いやられた。「富と権力」はテロごときによって破壊されないという信念（あるいは幻想）のためもしれない。

　『墜ちてゆく男』も亀裂に入り込むような物語を持たない。主人公のキースはWTC崩壊の現場で他人のアタッシュケースを摑む。別居して久しい妻のもとに帰る一方で、アタッシュケースの持ち主の女性を訪ね、不倫関係を始める。街なかで、崩壊直前のWTCから飛び降りたビジネスマンの姿を模倣する男のパフォーマンスを見る。たしかにこの小説には、日常生活の、あるいはそこに生きるものたちの生の時間のいたるところに開いた亀裂の存在を伝える。だがそこから歴史と世界の亀裂にまで入り込もうとは、しない。

　この小説の最終章。WTCに衝突寸前の飛行機内で、テロリストのひとりは自分に言い聞かせている。世界を忘れろ。世界と呼ばれるもののことなど気にするな。飛行機はWTCに突っ込み、調理室のカンターから何かが落ちるのをテロリストは見る。この瞬間、描写の主体はテロリストからキースにスウィッチする。キースはWTCの調理室のカウンターからボトルが落ちるのを見る。空からシャツが降ってくるのを彼は見る、シャツは腕を懸命に振りながら落ちてきた——。

　アメリカ人の主人公と中東のテロリスト、両者の意識がカタストロフィの振動に促されるようにして、語りの座が入れ替わる。

　ドン・デリーロはなぜ、この最終章をむしろ序章として、小説を書き始めなかったのか。この最終章が始まりとなるならば、亀裂はきっと歴史と世界の断面を露わにしたに違いないのに。

　むろん、小さな亀裂を描くことに意味がないわけではない。小説は新聞の社説でも思想の論文でもない。むしろそうした小さな亀裂を丹念に描くところにこそ価値があると考えることもできる。特に日本文学、そのなか

especially novels after the turn of the millennium tend to do so. They have historical catastrophes like the "East Japan Great Earthquake and Tsunami," from 2013. The sight of a Tsunami coming up the coast, travelling over 300 miles is apocalyptic. Someone might foresee the end of the world by looking at the news of the hydrogen explosions in the Fukushima nuclear power plant. This catastrophe clearly showed us a dark crack opening in the future of Japanese society. Nevertheless, no one has expressed it as a crack in the structure of the world through brutal imagination.

'Brutal imagination' means, for example, the power shown in *The War of the End of the World*,[68] a novel by Mario Vargas Llosa.[69] Based on a true story, and set in Brazil in the nineteenth century, it begins with a prediction of the end of the world.

> —*It was necessary, therefore, to be prepared. The church must be restored, and the cemetery as well, the most important construction after the House of the Lord since it was the antechamber of heaven or hell, and the time that remains must be devoted to what was is most essential: the soul. Would men or women leave for the next world in skirts, dresses, felt hats, rope sandals, and all that luxurious attire of wool and silk that the Good Lord Jesus had never known?*

People said that the man was a saint. A robust community was built around him, "Around the time before the Empire had come to an end, and the Republic had just begun." Later, this religious community would begin the furious war against the Republic of Brazil.

The religious community denies culture from the West, like skirt and dresses, and insists that they have to change this world to the "antechamber of heaven or hell." On the contrary, the modern state is based on economy, tax and wealth, and power, law and military. An ugly killing

118   Chapter 2———*The Planning behind Literature*

でも2000年代以降の小説にその傾向は強い。2013年には日本にも「東日本大震災」という歴史的なカタストロフィがあった。東北沿岸500キロにわたって襲来した津波の風景は黙示録的とすら言えたし、福島第一原子力発電所の水素爆発には、この世の終わりを予感するものすら、いただろう。現実に、このカタストロフィは日本社会の未来にパックリと開いた闇の亀裂を鮮明に見せつけた。にもかかわらず——それを日常の亀裂として描いた小説は少なからずあっただろうが——、野蛮な想像力とともに世界の構造に入った亀裂を語るものはなかった。

　野蛮な想像力とは、たとえばマリオ・バルガル゠リョサの小説『世界終末戦争[70]』[71]で発揮されているような力のことだ。これは19世紀のブラジルで実際に起こった事件に基づいた小説だ。ある男がこの世界の終末を予言して、物語ははじまる。

　　　それゆえ、準備をしておかなければならない、と男は言うのだった。だから、主の家の次に大切なもの、教会と墓地を修繕しなければならない。というのは、教会と墓地こそ、天国と地獄につながる控えの間なのだから。残された時間は一番大切なものに捧げられなければならない、つまり、魂に。イエス様が一度たりとも身につけたことがなかったようなもの、スカートやドレスや、フェルト帽や編みあげ靴をつけたまま、あそこに送られたことがあっただろうか？

　男は聖人とみなされ、そのまわりに強固な共同体が生まれる、「ブラジル帝国が終わりを告げる前から、あるいはブラジル共和国が発足するころから」。この辺境の宗教的共同体はやがてブラジル共和国軍と熾烈な戦争を始める。
　「スカートやドレス」のような西洋文明がもたらした文化を否定し、この世界を「天国と地獄につながる控えの間」として整えるべきと主張する、宗教的共同体。対して、経済（富／税）と権力（法／軍備）に基礎を置く近代国家。そのふたつがやがて凄惨極まりない殺し合いを始める。様々な

文学の計画──第2章　　*119*

field would be created by the two communities. Various stories are told by various subjects' consciousness, and it does not follow chronological order. The successfully described the real and imaginary world through its use of overlapping stories.

Is it impossible to describe worlds like this after 9/11?

11. How to Forget the World

Architecture and literature is about the difficulties of face the world and its history. It is a crisis that I have already mentioned in the first chapter of this book. We will discuss it again in the fifth chapter. Here I would like to argue two points.

The age called "modern" is now close to its end as the nation state is vanishing.

Someone might say that the idea of a nation state will never vanish, but rather become more stable. But in reality wars after 9/11 has become a fight not between state and state, but 'state and terrorism. *The War of the End of the World* takes place during the conception of the modern state, and 'the war of the end of future' occurs when modern states follow this idea modern state to its conclusion. I do not condone terrorism in any way, shape or form. The state of Iraq faces a crisis of collapse. Not only in the Middle East, but also in Africa there is crisis. States that European countries determined the national border of are always unstable because of frequent ethnic disputes. In any region over the world, national borders are rendered ineffective in the war of economy and information. That is why nationalism seems to be on the rise. The nationalism of today is a kind of futile struggle to deny its fate, which is to disappear. Current examples of this are President Trump in the United States, and Brexit in the United Kingdom.

120   Chapter 2——*The Planning behind Literature*

主体の意識を通して、幾多の物語が時系列に従わずに語られる。その多層な物語によってそこにある世界（あるいは、そこにはない世界）を描き上げたのが、この小説だ。

　こんなふうに世界を描くことは、9.11以降においてはもはや、不可能なのだろうか？

11.　コマーシャルの言葉と世界

　建築や小説が、世界や歴史と対峙することの困難。これは、序章で論じた文学や建築の危機の問題でもある。そしてこのことは後に第5章で詳しく論じたい。ここではそれに先んじてふたつの論点を記しておきたい。

　「近代」という時代は、国家の「消滅」とともに終わりに近づいている。

　国家は消滅などしない、むしろナショナリズムはいたるところで勢いを増していると思うひともいるかもしれない。しかし9.11以降、戦争は「国家対国家」ではなく、ほぼ「テロリスト（と欧米が呼ぶ集団）対国家」という図式で行われてきた。『世界終末戦争』は近代国家が生まれる頃に行われ、これからの終末戦争は国家の寿命を見据えて戦われる。実際、ISIS（イスラミック・ステート）の台頭によりイラクという国家は崩壊の危機を迎えているし（2016年現在）、アフリカの国家（多くはヨーロッパ諸国がその国境を定めた）も部族間などの闘いが多く、国家として常に不安定だ。現代ではどの地域においても、経済や情報において国境という名のボーダーは実質上、無効化している。一見、ナショナリズムが台頭しているかに見えるのは、むしろそのゆえんだ。つまり、消えて行ってしまう運命に対し、いやだいやだと悪あがきをしているようなのが、現在のナショナリズムだといっていい。トランプ大統領のアメリカにせよ、EUで起こりつつある逆戻り現象にしても、そうだ。

文学の計画──第2章　　*121*

'Hiroshima' was a tragedy for the state of Japan and its people. People from other nations were also exposed to radiation. In 9/11, about 2,800 people were killed, 21% were born in other countries, and 1% had another nationality. Even so, the number of Caucasians victims seems high proportionate to the general racial distribution in New York City. It might be because the people working in the WTC were the so-called elites. The destruction of the WTC during 9/11 was a symbolic act, not only towards the United States, but also towards the global economy. It must have been the symbol of *Empire*,[70] as Antonio Negri[71] called it. "Empire" is not restricted to a national territory, but extended globally.

Architecture in modernism is about designing for the public or the state, like Kenzo Tange[72] did. Especially in a process of rapid modernization which Japan has previously undergone, architects were expected to do so. Of course, architects designed houses and apartments as a model of the modern space. Some architects, like Mies Van Del Rohe,[73] and Minoru Yamasaki, designed great office buildings. However, just a few architects in modernism designed commercial buildings, or retail shops. Hans Hollein[74] became famous at once through the candle shop he designed in Vienna, as Post Modernism was gaining traction, Signifying the end of modernism. It's pretty hard to imagine that master architects of modernism like Le Corbusier, Mies, and Tange, designed a retail shop.

Today, the situation has changed. A retail shop can be a representative work of the architect, like *PRADA*, designed by Herzog & de Meuron[75] in Tokyo. Now commercial activity can be the biggest supporter of culture.

Architects already know we have no words to prevent another "war that will end the world." The role of the architect picturing the future of state is ending, as a new empire rises. The domain of the "empire" is de-territorial, with no center. Architecture can only be a space showing branded products in this domain.

The 'Commercial' is becoming the main stage for today's architecture.

122   Chapter 2——— *The Planning behind Literature*

「ヒロシマ」は、日本という国家とその国民の「悲劇」だった（実際には他民族も被爆したが、シンボルとしては、そうだ）。それに対して、9.11の犠牲者約2800人の内、21％は他国で生まれたもので、１％が多国籍のものだった[72]。これでも、ニューヨーク市全体から比べると白人の被害者の割合が多いが、それはWTCで働くものはエリート層だったからということなのだろう。9.11で破壊されたのはむろんアメリカの象徴だが、それ以上に、世界経済の象徴でもあった。それは国家の象徴というよりも、ネグリの言う〈帝国〉[73]——脱領土的でグローバルな領域を飲み込んでいくもの——の象徴に違いない。

　モダニズムにおいては、建築家とは、たとえば丹下健三がそうであった[74]ように、国家や公共のための建築を設計するものであった。とくにかつての日本のように、国家の近代化が急速に進む過程においてはそうだった。もちろん建築家は、近代的空間の模範としての住宅や集合住宅の設計もした。ミース・ファン・デル・ローエやミノル・ヤマサキ[75]のようにオフィス・ビルの名作をものしたモダニズムの建築家たちもいた。だが、商業施設、とくに店舗の設計をする建築家というのは殆ど見当たらなかった。ハンス・ホライン[76]はウィーンの蠟燭店のデザインで一躍有名になったが、それはポスト・モダンと呼ばれる時代の到来、つまりはモダニズムの終焉を告げていた。ル・コルビュジェやミース、丹下といった近代の巨匠が店舗を設計するという情景は、今から考えても想像しにくい。

　しかし現在はそうではない。ヘルツォーク・アンド・ド・ムーロンの『PRADA』[77]のように、建築家の代表作になるものもある。それは今や商業こそが文化の最大の担い手になったからだ。

　新たなる「世界終末戦争」にむけて、建築家が建築を持って何かの意見をいうのは、もはや難しい。国家の未来像を描いてきた建築家の役割は、この新たな〈帝国〉の出現とともに終わった。〈帝国〉は中心を持たず、脱領域的な「場所」だ。その「場所」において建築は、グローバルなブランド商品を陳列する空間をつくるだけだ。

　現代建築の主舞台となりつつある商業建築。それを形作るのは、美しく、

文学の計画——第2章　*123*

Beautiful, bright, but ephemeral fragments of the future which will never make a full picture, are the words of the architectural language. Which means that architecture cannot talk about the world with its language.

We will find the same situation in the language of the novel.

The novel in the modern sense assumed the role of the 'novel of the nation.' For example, Alexander Pushkin[76] wrote novels and poems in a colloquial style, and he had such an impact that the language in his his works became normal Russian. Russian people still have an incentive to read Pushkin in elementary education even today. In Japan there was a movement to unify the written and the spoken language, which occurred in the Meiji era. (1886-1912) Shoyo Tsubouchi[77], Shimei Futabatei[78], and other novelists began to write in colloquial style so that the language in literature could be widely shared by the general nation, including those who didn't have enough education to command a literary language. It made it possible for the novel to be shared as a general experience by the nation. For instance, the query and distress of Natsume Soseki's[79] ego was discussed by a lot of Japanese writers in modernism. *No Longer Human*, written as a quasi-autobiography by Osamu Dazai[80] often move the minds of young people as if it is their own story.

The language of the novel enabled us to sympathize like this. But it changed its behavior in the last decades of the twentieth century. The economic and commercial powers are part of the reason of the change, and it was the same for architecture.

We had such buzzwords as "delicious life." At the time of the so-called Bubble Economy in Japan in the 1980s, there were advertisements seeking a copywriter at the SEIBU Department Store in Shigesato Itoi. Copywriter became one of those jobs that young people aspired to, after the "delicious life"—marketing prevailed. Some copywriters turned into novelists as well.

And some critics and thinkers[81] estimated highly the value of the language

利那的で、明るい未来の断片——決して全体像を結ばない断片の集合
——としての建築言語だ。そんな言語が「世界」を語れるはずもない。

　小説の言語についても、おなじことが言える。
　近代小説は、「国民小説」としての役割を担うことがあった。たとえば
アレクサンドル・プーシキンは、口語で小説や詩を書き、それは国語とし
てのロシア語の規範ともなった。実際、今でもロシア人は、初等教育のな
かで一度はプーシキンの「言語」に触れる。日本でも、坪内逍遥や二葉亭
四迷などによって「言文一致体」が提唱され、文学の言語は広く一般的な
（文語の知識を持たない）国民にも共有されることになった。そして小説の
なかの経験——エクリチュール上の出来事——は、国民全体の普遍的な経
験として共有され、あるいは批判されることも可能になった。たとえば夏
目漱石の「自我」についての苦悩＝「こころ」が、近代日本人のそれとし
て論じられる。あるいは太宰治が私生活に基づいて書いた小説『人間失
格』が、青春期の若者に「我がこと」のように迫ることもある。

　小説の言語はこのように「共感」を可能にした。だが、それは20世紀の
終わり近くに大きく性質を変えた。それを変えた力のひとつは、建築の場
合と同じく、経済あるいは商業の力だろう。

　「おいしい生活」。バブル景気が始まろうとする時代、そんな言葉があっ
た。糸井重里が西武百貨店の広告のために考えた言葉だ。この言葉がさま
ざまなメディアに出回った頃から一時期、「コピーライター」は花形の職
種となった。コピーライターから小説家に転身するものも多く出た。

　こうしたコピーライターの言語を、既成階級を無効化するもの、として

文学の計画——第2章　　*125*

of copywriting as words to destroy the existing classes of society. Yes, in developed society, poor or wealthy, they could have a "delicious life," but only if they engage in consumerism wisely. It means that an ideal and equal society was being realized by consumerism...

But of course, it was just a dream. They put too much faith in the magic of economy and commercial activity. Now the 'Bubble Economy' is just an historical term. In developed countries, economic growth has turned into deficit. A long time has passed since the society of Japan began to be referred to as a "polarized society." How is it possible for NEET's[82] to have a "Delicious Life?" They don't even have the means to protest the situation. Words have lost their power in the commercial world.

Novels in Japan from the 1970's to the 90's were influenced a lot by American literature, like my novel was. The United States is supported by a commercial capital, and a big economy. Regarding language, American English is the most spoken language in the world. It is not only because of the ease of learning the language, nor for reasons of region or nation, but because of distribution. It is important for the language to be easy to understand and to distribute.

Slaughterhous-5[83], a novel by Kurt Vonnegut[84] which was published in 1969. The story is based on a real event, the Bombing of Dresden, Germany, during World War II. Vonnegut experienced the bombing in his childhood. It was a cruel situation similar to what Tokyo and Osaka experienced toward the end. In 1969, when the book was published, the United States had been dragged into the Vietnam War since the Bombing of North Vietnam in 1965. Even if it's set in these severe conditions, the style of the novel is oddly light.

—*Listen:*

126   Chapter 2——— *The Planning behind Literature*

評価する批評家や思想家もいた。確かに、ある程度豊かになった社会では、富めるものも、そうでないものも、賢い消費をすれば「おいしい生活」が楽しめるかもしれない。平等で自由な社会は、消費こそが実現する――。

　だが結局のところ、それはあまりにも商業資本あるいは経済の魔力を信頼しすぎる態度だった。バブルは彼方に過ぎ去り、経済成長はマイナスに転じた。「格差社会」と呼ばれて久しい日本で、ニートやひきこもり、あるいはワーキング・プアと呼ばれるひとたちに、どうして「おいしい生活」が可能だろう？　しかし、彼らにはその不平をいうための言葉がない。一旦商業に引き寄せられた言葉には、もはやそれ以前の力は宿らない。

　1970年代から90年代の日本の小説は、アメリカ文学の影響を強く受けた（僕自身がそうだ）。アメリカが日本以上に商業資本、巨大経済に支えられているのは言うまでもない。また、アメリカ英語は、世界で最も流通している言葉だ。それは深く固有の場所に根ざすというよりも、流通のしやすさ、つまりわかりやすさにこそ準拠しようとする。

　カート・ヴォネガットが1969年に発表した『スローターハウス5』は、第2次世界大戦中、ドイツのドレスデンを襲ったアメリカの空襲を題材にしている。ヴォネガット自身が、子供の頃に現地でこれを体験した。太平洋戦争末期に東京や大阪などを襲った空襲同様、相当悲惨な状況だったとされる。また、発表時の69年といえば、66年の「北爆」以来のベトナム戦争の泥沼に、アメリカがどっぷりと浸かり込んでいた時期だ。そうした重い諸条件にもかかわらず、この小説の文体は、異様なまでに軽い。
　文体を話題にしているので左の英文ページでぜひ原文を読んでみてほしい。英語が不得手なひとでも、これが随分と平易な文章であることはわかるだろう。僕なりに日本語に訳すと、

　　聞いてくれ。

Billy Pilgrim has unstuck in time.

Billy has gone to sleep a senile widower and awakened on his wedding day. He has walked through a door in 1955 and come out another one in 1941. He has gone back through that door to find himself in 1963. He has seen his birth and death many times, he says, and pays random visits to all the events in between.

Not only the style, but also the structure of the story, as the protagonist is dragged into war because he unintentionally moves across time and space, is so light like an illustrated novel.

And the lightness was attractive.

In 1987, my first novel was published. I had to consider my style of writing when I began to write it. I intentionally chose to build a story with a light style.

Because didn't think I could express my reality without a light style.

The bubble was swelling and we had "delicious lives" for several years. Seven years had passed after John Lennon[85] was murdered. A heavy style, like the beginning of The Temple of the *Golden Pavilion*, by Yukio Mishima[86] never gave any reality to whatever I was trying to convey. American English that has ease of distribution can give more reality. That is why Japanese novelists were influenced by American literature.

It marked the end of the age of writing novels for the nation.

Also, a lot of American novelists today intentionally choose words that distribute easily.

—Get a grip on yourself, boy. You're fighting a war. What did you think this was? A trip to Fun World?

What war? Does that mean we're in Iraq?

ビリー・プリグリムは時間の流れから開放されたんだ。

　ビリーは年取った男やもめとして眠って、目覚めると自分の結婚式の朝になっている。1955年にドアをくぐると、1941年に出てきてしまう。そのドアから戻ろうとすると、今度は1963年に自分が来てしまったことに気づく。彼は自分の誕生も死も、もう何十回も見たと言ってる。その間のいろんな出来事に、それはもうデタラメに行ってきたんだと。

　文体も軽いが、時空を超えることで時々戦場に放り込まれるというストーリーも、ライトノベル的な軽い構造だ。

　そしてこの軽さこそが魅力だった。

　87年に、僕は最初の小説を発表した。それを書き始めるとき、僕は文体を考えなければならなかった。その時に、意図的に軽い文体で構築することを選んだ。

　理由はひとつだ。そうすることでしか、リアリティを感じることができなかったからだ。

　「おいしい生活」から数年が過ぎ、バブル経済がまさに膨らみ始めていた。ジョン・レノンが死んで7年がたっていた。何を書くにせよ、重厚な文体（たとえば三島由紀夫の『金閣寺』の書き出しのような）で書くことに、リアリティはなかった。流通しやすいことを前提としたアメリカ英語の表現のほうが、ずっとリアリティがあった。だからこそ日本の作家たちはアメリカの小説に影響を受けた。

　それは、「国民小説」の時代がとうに終わっていたということを意味する。

　アメリカ現代文学の書き手たちの多くも、流通が容易な言葉を、意図的に選びとっている。

　しっかりしてくれよ、戦争をやってるんだぞ。なんだと思ってたんだ、楽しい世界への旅行だとでも？

　何の戦争かって？　つまり俺たちはイラクにでもいるのか？

文学の計画——第2章　　*129*

Iraq? Who cares about Iraq?

America's fighting a war in Iraq. Everyone knows that.

Fuck Iraq. This is America, and America is fighting America.

This is a passage from *Man In The Dark*[87] by Paul Auster.[88] Auster wrote a story of another possible world after 9/11 with a light style.

12. Possibility of Lightness in Architecture and Novel

As novel has style, architecture does too.

Architecture has learned the light style from literature, and it has become the ideal. Most of all, architecture in Japan attracts attention because of its lightness.

The physical structure of architecture has become slender. This is a result brought forth by technology that can analyze complicated structures with the computer, and made it possible to think beyond columns and beams.

Traditionally, Japanese architecture was made of wood and paper, which is lighter than European masonry which used stone or brick. The Japanese architecture of today must be regarded as taking over the traditional characteristics.

It's not only limited to physical structures becoming more slender. Ideas in terms of space became lighter because of the novel as well.

Kazuyo Sejima[89] is one of the leading architects in Japan today. His *Museum of Louvre-Lens* (2012), *Rolex Learning Center* (2009), and the other works have a very light structure and space. Let's have a look at *Public Apartment in Kitakata* (2000) and analyze its lightness.

130 Chapter 2———*The Planning behind Literature*

イラク。誰がそんなところを気に掛けるかって。

　　確かにアメリカはイラクと戦ってる。誰でも知っている。

　　でもイラクなんてどうでもいいだろ。アメリカはアメリカと戦って
るんだよ。

　これは、ポール・オースターの小説『闇の中の男』からの引用（鈴木
訳）だ。9.11以降の、もうひとつの可能性の物語を、オースターはこうし
た文体で書いていた。

12. 〈軽さ〉の可能性──建築において、物語において

　小説に文体があるように、建築にも文体がある。

　そして小説の文体が軽くなったことに学んだかのように、現代建築もま
た軽さに価値を求める。特に、日本の現代建築はその点で世界からの注目
を集めてもいる。

　まず、建築の力学的な構造体が、細く薄くなった。これはテクノロジー
の進化がもたらしたもので、どのように複雑な構造でもコンピューターに
よる解析が可能になった結果、柱や梁といった単純な構造体で考える必要
がなくなった。

　もともと、伝統的な建築においても、木や紙でつくられる日本建築は、
石を積み上げるヨーロッパの建築に比べて軽い。日本の現代建築はその特
質を引き継いでいると考えられているのだろう。

　だが、もちろん、構造体が細く薄くなったことだけが、軽さを表現する
のではない。空間に対する考え方自体が、小説の感覚と同様、軽くなった
のだ。

　妹島和世は世界が注目する日本の建築家のひとりだ。『ランスのルーブ
ル美術館』(2012)、『ロレックス・ラーニング・センター』(2009) など、そ
の構造体や空間はとても軽い。その軽さをさらに詳しく見るために、『ハ
イタウン北方』(2000) に注目してみよう。岐阜県の県営集合住宅だ。

文学の計画──第2章　　*131*

Generally in Japan in the past, or even now, public apartments had a standardized planning for each house, built for mass-production. How was this made possible? They were made for only one type of family. The family of a married couple, and their one or two children. During the era of rapid economic growth, many young single people came to big cities in search for work. They would marry and have a couple of children. Now the types of family have come to vary throughout the population, and some mega cities are growing ever larger.

Seijima took advantage of this situation to design various plans and made the into connecting cubes. Each cube was given a function: living room, bedroom, and so on. The cubes connect to form an "L." Sometimes a cube was omitted from the structure to make up a terrace. Sejima made various plans reminiscent of "Tetris." People would choose one of the Tetris-blocks as their home.

The lightness of The Apartment in Kitakata by Sejima depends on the spatial structure like it was a game. Random combinations of spaces, and random numbers which fit together like puzzles. Here we can see a puzzle-like structure that we have already seen in the novels *Hopscotch* and *Portrait in Number*.

Sejima used thin walls for the physical structure, and glass to form the façade as a method to depict a light spatial structure.

If there were thick pillars in the apartment, the physical structure would contradict the spatial structure in the combinations of the cubes. This style is only made possible by by stacking cubes made up of thin walls. And supplementing that structure with transparent glass is most adequate.

Sejima's works have the sort of lightness like it is released from the heaviness that modernism received from historical European architecture. This is why Sejima's architecture is highly regarded. A lot of Japanese

かつての公営住宅は（今でもそうだが）、いわゆる「公団タイプ」の標準間取りがあり、それを増産する形で建設された。どうしてそんなことになったのか（あるいは可能だったのか）というと、入居する家族像がたったひとつだったからだ。つまり、若い夫婦とその子ども。高度経済成長期には、田舎から多くの若い単身者が労働力として都市部にやってきて、やがて結婚し、ふたり程度の子どもをつくった。だが、今では、大都市圏への人口集中という事態はむしろ極端になりつつありながら、家族の様態は大きく多様化した。

　妹島はそのことを盾にとって、様々な間取りを、幾つかの立方体をつなげることで実現しようとした。立方体は予め、居間や寝室などの機能が与えられていて、それを横並びに、時には「Ｌ」字型につなげる。ところどころ、ネガとしての立方体、つまり抜けとしてのテラスが挿入される。こうして様々に出来上がった「間取り」を、ゲーム『テトリス』のように組み立てる。入居者はこの『テトリス』のなかで自らの家族様式に適った『テトリスのピース』を選んでそこに住む。

　『ハイタウン北方』の『妹島棟』の「軽さ」は、何よりもまずこの空間の構造──ゲーム的な、乱数的な、あるいはアド・ホックな──に由来する。一意に空間が決まるのではなく、偶然に生じた複数の空間が、パズルのように組み合わさる感覚。パズル的という点ではこの構造は小説『石蹴り遊び』や『ポートレイト・イン・ナンバー』にも通底する。

　『ハイタウン北方（妹島棟）』では、この空間構造を「記述」するために必要な「文体」として、壁構造という力学的な建築構造と、ガラスのファサードが用いられた。

　太い柱が出てしまえば、それは既に立方体の組み合わせという空間構造と矛盾してしまう。立方体自体を薄い壁でつくりそれを積み重ねることでしか、この空間構造は記述し得ない。そしてこの空間構造をそのまま正しく見せるには、透明なガラスでそれを挟みこむのが最適だ。

　妹島和世が世界中から評価されるのは、モダニズムの建築が、ヨーロッパの伝統を引き継いだ「重さ」を持っているのに対し、そこから開放された「軽さ」が妹島の作品にはあるからだろう。そしてそうした「軽さ」は、

architects these days, even Americans, are designing with the lightness of Sejima's works.

On to my novel, *Terrain of Future* (*Mirai no Chikei*)[90], which was criticized by Ōe Kenzaburō:

> *Their [the protagonist "I" and his girlfriend's lives are described with the light style representative of the present. Their sex is described objectively and fleetingly. It reminds me of the depictions of Murakami Haruki. It also reminds me of the idea of lightness in the book Six Memos for the Next Millennium by Italo Calvino[91], who did a series of lectures in the United States based on his long writing experience in Italy.*

—Harvard University Press

> *In the book, Milan Kundera[92] says the following about the novel: "His novel shows us how everything in life that we choose and value for its lightness quickly reveals its own unbearable heaviness. Perhaps nothing escapes this fate but the liveliness and nimbleness of the mind —the very qualities with which the novel is written, qualities that belong to a universe other than the one we live in."*

—*Experience of Novel / Shosetsu no Keiken*[93] (translated by Suzuki)

The unnamed, first-person protagonist, or "I," has a job as a video editor. One day, he is asked to edit a movie for a cult which is gaining traction. His girlfriend Ruiko, who watches the video with him, says, "This guru used to be my classmate in junior high school." The guru teaches people to "Change the Terrain," as its main doctrine. Ruiko says that "Change the Terrain" is not the guru's original idea, but a story that their history teacher told them.

> —*The guru was not referred to as such when he was your classmate, was he? I asked Ruiko. "No way," she replied. "He did not look like an*

134   Chapter 2——— *The Planning behind Literature*

多く日本人建築家に、あるいはアメリカの若い建築家たちに受け継がれつつある。

　ところで僕自身は、僕が書いた小説『未来の地形[93]』を、大江健三郎に、次のように批評されたことがある。

　　……かれら（引用者注：『未来の地形』の主人公「僕」と主人公の恋人）の生活はいかにも当世風に軽く書かれる。（中略）かれらのセックスもまた、即物的な明瞭さで描かれる。これは村上春樹が切りひらいた世界だ。また、イタロ・カルヴィーノ[94]がイタリアでの永い作家生活の経験に立ってアメリカへの連続講義に行くためにまとめた、『次の千年紀のための６つのメモ』の軽さについての意見を思い出させる。
　　　　　　　　　　　　── Harvard University Press（大江訳）
　　そこにはクンデラ[95]の小説をめぐってこう書かれていた。《彼の小説は、われわれが人生においてその軽さによって選びとり、価値づけるものがすぐさまその本当の耐えがたい重さをあらわすことを示す。おそらくはただ知性の活発さと動きやすさとのみが、この運命をまぬがれる──これらの特質によって小説は書かれるのだ、われわれの生きている世界からはまったく異なった世界に属している特質によって。》
　　　　　　　　　　　　　　　　　　　　　　　　　──『小説の経験[96]』

　『未来の地形』の主人公「僕」は映像の編集を仕事にしている。あるとき、カルトの宗教団体から、ビデオの編集を依頼される。ビデオをともに見ていた恋人の「類子」は、この教祖は自分の昔の同級生に違いないと言う。「同級生の教祖様」は教義の中心に「地形を変える試み」というものを据えている。類子はそれを、教祖のオリジナルではなく、昔自分たちを教えた「歴史の先生」が語ったものだと話す。

　　教祖様は昔から教祖様と呼ばれていたわけではないんだろう？　と僕は訊いてみた。それはそうよ。別にオカルト的な趣味があったとい

文学の計画──第2章　　*135*

occultist or a religious freak. Not the prom king type, but a little more
somber. He was good at studying, I think."

Why would someone like that go and become the guru, and start-up a
movement to "Change the Terrain"? I say rhetorically. Who came up
with this?

"It's so simple," Ruiko replies. So simple, because it's all historical fact
which our teacher taught us. We learned it in history class. (omission)

"The guru's teaching reminds me a lot of beloved things," Ruiko sais.

"The guru's teaching reminds me of a lot of beloved things," Ruiko says.
Ruiko talks on about the teacher and the guru. They tried to change the
terrain twice, in 1917 and 1957. By coincidence, "I" and Ruiko learn that
the history teacher was killed in a traffic accident. It seems like a strange
sign, so we begin to explore Ruiko's Memory to find the hidden truth.
The history teacher might have been murdered by the guru....

It might remind you of the real cult, Aum Shinrikyo. Actually, the novel
was published in 1992, and the sarin terrorist-attack happened in 1995,
so the story is not based on that case. But already in 1989, the attorney,
Sakamoto, who set up a team supporting Aum's victims, was missing. It
turned out that Sakamoto had been kidnapped and killed by Aum after
the sarin terrorist-attack. However, the real cult must have given me a
kind of inspiration or divination.

In reality, many people were critically injured by Aum. Should I have
written the novel with a heavier style because of that? At any rate, I didn't
go with a heavy style.

うこともなかったし、熱心なクリスチャンとか仏教徒だったという噂も聞いたことはない。特に目立つ子ではなくて、若干陰気な感じがしたけれどそれも度が過ぎてというのでもないし。勉強は、どちらかといえばできたほうだったかしられ。

それがどうして、ああやって教祖様を名乗り、「地形を変える試み」なんていう運動を起こそうとしているのかね。僕は自分に言うようなつもりで言った。まったく不可解だな、そういう少年がいつどんなところで思いついたのか、見当もつかないよね。

すると類子は、あら、それは簡単なのよ、と答えた。あの「地形を変える試み」の話はね、写真に写っていた先生からの受け売り。(中略)

教祖様の話は、だから私には、とても懐かしい話だったのよ。

「地形を変える試み」は、「類子」が言うには、そして「同級生の教祖様」によれば、1917年と1957年の2回、実践された試みだという。そんな時、その「歴史の先生」が交通事故で死んだことを、「僕」たちはニュースで知る。なにか奇妙な符号を感じた「僕」と「類子」は、真相を探るために、「類子」の記憶を巡る旅を始める。ひょっとしたら、「歴史の先生」は「同級生の教祖様」に殺されたのじゃないか？──そんな物語だ。

かつてのオウム真理教による一連の事件を連想させるストーリーだが、小説が出版されたのは1992年、地下鉄サリン事件が1995年なので、実際には事件を下書きにしたようなことはない。ただし、「オウム真理教被害対策弁護団」を結成した坂本堤弁護士は、1989年に「失踪」していたから（これが教団による拉致と殺害事件だったと判明するのは、サリン事件の後だが）、何らかのインスピレーションを受けていた（あるいは予感めいたものを得ていた）ことは間違いない。

現実として、オウム真理教が引き起こした事件の被害は重大だった。執筆時にすべてがわかっていたのではないとはいえ、インスパイアされ、あるいは予感も得ていたのであれば、小説はもっと重いものになるべきだったのかもしれない。だが、そうはしなかった。

文学の計画──第2章　　*137*

I divided the story of 145 pages into 80 short segments. I classified the segments into 4 groups, A: memory, B: landscape, C: information, and D: history and noted the classification in the beginning of each segment. All segments are short, and the shortest is just one line.

This classification is related to the "stream of consciousness" and the subject of écriture. And the structure is made to be light.

You can see the lightness through reading the excerpt. Heavy topics are also shown by short conversations.

New religions including Aum appeared around the time of the bubble economy. People who didn't feel at ease in the booming economy might have been the type of people who got involved in such cults. It is well known that Aum believers who commit felony were very serious young men. The reason and the result, both were very severe, but still there was something comedic and cartoonish to be found.

It was there, in 9/11 as well. Quite a few people probably had the thought that this was similar to a scene from a film. We feel déjà vu in real tragedy that we see for the first time, and overlap it with a media-made fiction. We saw the "simulacra" of Jean Baudrillard,[94] a copy without an original.

Against these situations, heavy structure and style has no effective power. Like the words of Calvino which Ōe quoted, we can only "escape" from "unbearable heaviness" with "liveliness and nimbleness of the mind."

Can we say the same today? In the age when ISIS denies the framework of the modern nation state, and advocates the Caliph state; in the age where they bomb modern cities, is lightness still an effective power?

138   Chapter 2——*The Planning behind Literature*

まず、単行本上で145ページの長さを、80の短いセグメントに分けた。そしてセグメントをその内容から4種類《Ａ：記憶　Ｂ：風景　Ｃ：インフォメーション　Ｄ：歴史》に分類し、各セグメントの冒頭に記した。各セグメントは短く、もっとも長いものでも５〜６ページ、短いのは１行のものもある。

　この分類は、「意識の流れ」の分類でもあるし、「エクリチュール」の主体の分類でもあった。そしてそれは、「軽さ」を生み出すための構造でもあった。

　文体の持つ軽さは、先に引用した部分を見ればわかる。重要な問題も、短い会話文で示される。

　オウム真理教をふくめ、いくつものいわゆる新興宗教が、バブル経済の前後あるいはさなかに生まれた。好景気の風景に違和を感じたものが嵌っていったのかもしれない。重罪を犯したオウム真理教の信徒たちが、極めて真面目なそしてナイーブな青年たちであったことは既に知られている。結果も成り立ちも、とても深刻なものなのに、しかしどこかに漫画的な滑稽さも潜んだ。

　9.11にしてもそうだ。あれが起きた時、その光景を多くのものが「まるで映画で見たようなことが起こっている」と感じた。初めての光景に既視感を感じ、メディアがつくりだした虚構を思い返してしまう。ボードリヤールが、シミュラークル（オリジナルのないコピー）と呼んだものが確かにそこにあった。

　このような事態に面して、重たい構造や文体は、力を持たなかった。大江が引くカルヴィーノの言葉のとおり、《耐えがたい重さ》から《ただ知性の活発さと動きやすさ》を持って《まぬがれる》しかなかった。

　それはつまり、リアルからの「脱出」のことだ。

　しかしそれは今日においても同じだろうか？　ISISが近代国家の枠組みを否定し、カリフ国をつくると主張して近代都市の隙間に爆弾を仕掛けまくっている今も有効だろうか？

　ここで、第1章8.に書いた文章を振り返っておきたい。その項は「リアルからの『脱出』」と題されていた。そこに僕はこう書いた。

文学の計画——第２章　　*139*

What if we could escape from "reality" and travel to "fiction"? We know that the "dream" means nothing to us in the real world. The shared illusion has totally lost generality. As the evidence, insurance is now invalid as a "future."

Meanwhile, we can picture various "futures" as another possibility. It will be different from the dream of the nation state. It will be separated from the shared illusion of the majority. The people should nevertheless not be be categorized into trivial subsets of taste or hobby. But we should find "fiction" that is free from illusion or taste.

I believe that it is still effective. Lightness can reposition and reform time and happenings. It has a possibility to give another history and future to the world. It can make another time, another event, and new space. We can describe and design the world as a world with no other possibility. The only problem is that many architects and novelists are attracted only by the comfort and popularity of lightness.

We need to remember that reposition and reform are the devices that work best in literature and architecture.

13. Memories of Future

Everything is memory in literature.

Something that has not happened can also be a memory. What may or may not happen in the future—terrorism, for example—must be viewed in the light of the further future. Thus, we can write a "false history" by reforming and repositioning real events and time. It shows us another face of the world.

Using the method of writing "false history," we can take a retrospective glance from the future to the present, and write a novel as "history."

We have already come to know that we can plan and design a novel in

私たちは一旦、リアルから脱出し、フィクションに赴けばいい。リアルな社会において共有されるべき「夢」などは消えた。共同幻想は、今や普遍性を持ちえない。リアルな〈未来〉に備えての「保険」は無効だ。

　だが、リアルとは別の可能性としての〈未来〉は、いかようにも描きうる。それはかつて国家が見たような夢とは異なる。多くの人々に共有された幻想ではない。かといって、直ちに一部の人たちのためだけの趣味・趣向にカテゴリーズされない。むしろ、幻想や趣味から自由なフィクションが、あるのではないか?

「軽さ」はリアルからの「脱出」を可能にする。その意味で、それは有効だと僕は思っている。軽さは、時間や出来事の配置と変形を行うことで生まれる。それは世界に別の歴史と未来を与える可能性がある。別の時間、異なる出来事、違う場所を作り出すことができる。世界を、もうひとつの可能性を持つ世界として描くこと、そして設計することができる。

　だが問題は、そのような可能性をすっかり忘れて、ただ「軽さ」の心地よさや流行性に目を向ける作家や建築家が多いということだろう。

13. 〈未来〉という名の記憶

　小説においてはすべてが記憶である。

　実際にはおきなかったことも記憶として語られ、これから起こるかもしれない未来も（たとえばカルト教団による事件も）、その先の未来から見た記憶として語られるしかない。従って、リアルな時間や出来事を変形し配置しなおすことで、いわゆる偽史を書きあげることができる。それが世界の別の様相を浮かび上がらせる。

　偽史を書きあげる手法で、未来から現在を振り返り、その「歴史」を小説にすることも可能だ。

　私たちはすでにこの章で、小説は計画可能で、設計することもできるこ

文学の計画──第2章　*141*

this chapter. We learned about the relationship between existing and non-existing works, cites, persons and cases. We know that it's possible to share memories with fictional characters and renew our perception of the world with through them. We have a sense of lightness in our imagination. And we have learned that the lightness can help us escape from the heaviness of reality.

On the other hand, we have looked at the negative effect of the lightness as well. The lightness is something that no one invented, but for the changing structure of the world, which asked for it. And the fact that literature and architecture seized the lightness created a big possibility. The possibility to confront the real world.

In today's novels, any war or act of terrorism is described with lightness because it can never have an oppressive background. One might think Islamic fundamentalism is nothing but an oppressive power. But it's just a fiction with no real background. Young terrorists of today have enjoyed the culture of the West, the lightness of desire and information through their smart phones. They are young men of the present, not of the eighteenth century. They only want to escape from reality and throw themselves into the fictional story that is fundamentalism.

Until early modernism, religion was heavily oppressive. In the twentieth century, the nation state took its place. The gap between religious oppression and the individualism of modernity gave heaviness to expression. During two World Wars and the Vietnam War, novels permeated with heaviness were written. The kind of heaviness found in works by Jack Kerouac, a poet and novelist of the Beat Generation, supported by hippies. On the other side, the novel by Kurt Vonnegut could successfully escape from heaviness, with his story based on the bombing during World War II, Vonnegut relativized the oppression of the age with his science fiction device, *Time Machine*.

Salman Rushdie[95] wrote a novel called *The Satanic Verses* which became

とを知った。現実に存在する、あるいは存在した人物や事件、建築や都市とフィクションとの関係を学んだ。想像力によって、フィクショナルな人物と記憶を共有し、それによって世界への認識を更新できることもわかっている。そしてその想像力によって、「軽さ」を獲得し、その「軽さ」がリアルからの「脱出」を手助けする感覚も身につけた。

　だが同時に、その「軽さ」の危うさも詳細に見てきた。「軽さ」は誰かが発明したという類のものではなく、世界の構造の変化がひとびとに要請した態度だった。だが小説は、そして建築も、その「軽さ」を獲得したがゆえに大きな可能性を手放した。世界と対峙する可能性だ。

　戦争やテロリズムですら、小説では軽さとともに描かれるようになった。なぜなら現代のテロリズムには、抑圧的な「背景」が欠如しているからだ。まさか、と思う人がいるかもしれない。イスラム原理主義が「抑圧的な『背景』でなくて、なんだ？」と。だがそれは、「背景」のように見えるフィクションでしかない。今テロを実践している若者たちは現代文明をよく知り、スマートフォンを操り、快楽の「軽さ」を経験している。かれらは18世紀からやってきた者たちではない。ただ、「現実」から「脱出」して、フィクションとしての原理主義に身を投じているだけだ。
　かつて宗教や国家という抑圧があった。その抑圧と近代的個人の間のギャップが、重い表現を生んだ。20世紀のふたつの世界大戦、そしてベトナム戦争中にも、そうした重たさとともに小説は書かれた。ヒッピーに支持されたビートニックの作家ジャック・ケルアック[98]の小説にも、今読めば、ぬぐいがたい重たさがある。一方、すでにみたように、第二次世界大戦中の無差別爆撃を題材にとったカート・ヴォネガットの小説は、いち早く軽さを獲得している。時代が持つ抑圧を、タイム・トラベルというSF装置で相対化しているからだ。

　サルマン・ラシュディ[99]という小説家がいる。『悪魔の歌』という小説で

文学の計画──第2章　　143

protested. Some Muslim readers claimed it disrespected Islam. The Supreme Leader of Iran called for him to be assassinated. Rushdie certainly had heavy themes, but he could write it with lightness through a device called magical realism, in his novel *Midnight's Children*, depicting Islam in India.

The protagonist of *Midnight's Children* is a boy born on August 15, 1947, Independence Day in India. The story is about a history of the past looked back on from 1981 when the novel was written. Facts in the history were written with a focus on realism. On the other hand, the protagonist has supernatural powers like telepathy and use it to invite the *Midnight's Children* who were born on the same day, for the purpose of discovering a secret behind the official history of India. It's realistic, but obviously fictional. This is called "magical realism." Compared to SF, the descriptions are very realistic, and without scientific imagination. The difference is small so that we can say they are almost same. Generally, *Slaughterhouse-Five* is labeled as SF, but can be called "magical realism" because historical facts are described with realism. Whether it's SF or "magical realism," the device might be the best in terms of activating the imagination of the novel.

Let's go back to the real world.

How many people predict that the problem of terrorism will be resolved before the end of the twenty-first century? Honestly, we have to assume that terrorism will not come to an end, but become more severe because terrorism cannot change the world, and the unchanged world cannot stop producing terrorists. We can assert that no novel describe such a future with a heavy style because the issue has already been analyzed. Vonnegut and Rushdie wrote their novels with high fictionalization and lightness because the heaviness of reality made it too painful. You cannot

イスラムを「侮辱」したという理由で、一部のイスラム教信者から抗議を受け、さらにはイランの最高指導者がラシュディを暗殺する呼びかけを出した。ラシュディが重たいテーマを扱っているのは確かだが、彼の小説『真夜中の子供たち』(1981) は同じようにインドのイスラム問題を扱いながら、マジック・リアリズムという、フィクショナル性を高めた手法、つまりはSFに近い方法で、「軽さ」とともにその問題を描くことに成功している。

　『真夜中の子供たち』は、インド独立の瞬間すなわち1947年8月15日に生まれた少年を主人公にする。つまり、小説発表時の81年からすれば過去の歴史についての小説だ。歴史上の出来事はすべてリアルに描かれる。だが主人公はテレパシーの超能力を持っていて、その能力を使って、仲間の子供たちを集め、公式な歴史の背後に隠れている秘密を暴こうとする。リアルだが、あからさまなフィクションだ。こうした手法がマジック・リアリズムと呼ばれる。SFとの違いは、科学的な想像を持たないこと、描写は徹底的にリアルであること、が挙げられる。逆に言えば、両者の違いはそれしかない。カート・ヴォネガットの『スローター・ハウス5』は通常SFに分類されるが、歴史的事実はリアルに描いているのだから、マジック・リアリズムの例として挙げられてもおかしくはない。マジック・リアリズムにせよSFにせよ、小説の「想像力」を発揮するという点では、これらの手法に勝るものはないかもしれない。

　世界の現実にいったん戻ってみよう。

　21世紀の半ばまでに、テロリズムの問題が解決すると推測するものは、どれだけいるだろうか？　それはおそらくは激化し、さらなる重篤な悲劇を生むだろう。なぜなら、テロでは世界は変わらないし、変わらない世界ならこれまで通りテロリストは必ず生まれる。

　推して、これもこれまで分析してきた結果から断言できるのだが、そうした未来を重い文体で表現できる小説は、決して現れない。カート・ヴォネガットやサルマン・ラシュディが、重い現実を、身を切るような痛さとともに感じながら、そのフィクション性をあえて高め、「軽さ」とともに

文学の計画——第2章　*145*

see the oppressor because it is not a man, but a system. Even the oppressed are part of the system. We might be able to imagine and write a story that the system destroyed the system itself, but we would fail to express what people actually felt. That is why they chose to write with the lightness.

Meanwhile, present day Japanese novels seem to be totally isolated from the history of the world. For example, we have the Akutagawa Prize for young Japanese novelists which has served to discover and highlight new talents for decades—but its role has come to an end. Recent winners still believe that 'reality' means 'world,' and consists of poor jobs like part-timers at a convenient store, or workers in an auto factory. They describe 'reality' like realists applying the trend that is 'lightness.' As a result, the young generation or middle-aged singles who must live in this 'reality' have stopped reading novels altogether because they are only tracing 'reality' with literary prose. Japanese novelists no longer have the brutality needed in the background of the 'reality'. That is true reality.

We need look for the heaviness of the future. To quote Kundera, it can be found only through "the liveliness and nimbleness of the mind." That is why we need "lightness."

My novel, *The Perfect World*[96], was published in 2014. Greg Manos[97], an American screenplay writer, gave me the original idea and a plan to build together the story for a film. It is my first work in science fiction.

In 2084, there is a huge work of architecture shaped like a cylinder on the top of Mt. Everest. The work has an empty cone-shaped center which is 3,600 feet tall. A man named Ari'X is seated at the bottom of the void, surrounded by twelve judges. The sun shines through the hole at the top of the cone, barely reaching the circle where the thirteen people are [fig. 14] (p. 186).

それを表現したのは、そうすることでしか表現ができなかったからだ。抑圧者の姿は見えない、なぜならそれは個人というよりもシステムなのだから。抑圧される側の個人ですらその同じシステムに参加しているのだ。システムが自壊していく様子を想像力で構築し描くこともできたかもしれないが、それでは個人がその生と死のなかで感じていることは表現できない。だから彼らはそうした「軽さ」とともに表現することを選んだ。

　他方で、いまや世界史から完全に疎外されたかのような、日本の現代小説がある。日本には「芥川賞」という新人作家のための賞があり、歴史的に実力のある作家を発見してきたが、今はすでにはっきりとその役割を終えた。なぜなら今日の「芥川賞作家」たちは、コンビニエンス・ストアのアルバイト店員とか、期間工とか、そういう貧しい職業に「現実」が、つまりは世界が表れていると、今も信じている。現実主義者＝リアリストのようにその「現実」を描きながら、流行の「軽さ」をも身にまとう。結果、そうした「現実」を実際に生きているはずの若者や中年の独身者は、決して小説など読みはしなくなった。なぜなら今や日本の小説は、文学用語で「現実」をなぞっているにすぎないからだ。そして日本の作家たちは「現実」の背景に踏み込むような野蛮さを持たない。それこそが本当の現実だ。

　私たちは、未来の重さこそを探さなければならない。先に引いたミラン・クンデラの言葉を使えば、「ただ知性の活発さと動きやすさとのみ」によって、それは探し出される。「軽さ」は、ただそのためだけに存在価値がある。

　2014年に僕は小説『パーフェクト・ワールド』を出した。アメリカの映画脚本家グレッグ・マノスから原案をもらい、映画の制作のための物語をして作り上げた。僕にとっては、初めての「SF小説」になる。

　2084年、エベレストの山頂に建つ、巨大な建築。円筒状のその建築の内部には高さ3600フィートの巨大な吹抜け空間があり、円錐状のその空間の底面にアリエクスという名の老人が座っている。彼の周りを、12人の審判員が囲む。円錐の頂点から差し込む光が、かろうじてその場所にまで届いている [fig. 14]（p. 186参照）。

The huge cylinder is called "Everest Colony." Ari'X takes advantage of the confusion and fear from when big meteors nearly hit the earth to set his plan in motion. We need to settle on Mars to guarantee the survival of humanity. The idea Ari'X advocated was approved by the United Nations, and then the construction of an experimental dwelling facility began on Mt. Everest. But in 2050, around the work's completion, no one has noticed that it's not only an experimental facility, but also a "Perfect World." All the wealth, resource and talent has been sucked into the "Perfect World." As such, the existing world has begun to decay. The man presented and executed his plan, and as a consequence, the existing world lost everything. Ari'X is found to be still alive after hiding himself for long time in the colony, and awaits his judgment.

The original purpose of the plan was for mankind to immigrate to Mars, but it always in the preparation stage, and was never executed. Ari'X admits that the true purpose never was to immigrate to Mars, but to build a perfect world on earth, concealing his true intentions. He says that he only took advantage of the illusion of the purpose.

Judges ask him if he could not imagine what would happen as a consequence of his actions. He answers, "Why wouldn't I?" He tells them that he had foreseen everything. He knew he would be judged someday. He has survived for the sake of judgment, even going so far as to fake his own death.

The judges object. "No way, how is it possible to foresee what would happen 50 years later?" Ari'X replies as if it were nothing.

"If you sow an appleseed," Ari'X says, "You can calculate how the sprout will grow, and how the branches will spread out when it becomes a full-fledged tree. It will grow fruit, and someone will eat it. If you analyze the seed before sowing it, and find out that the seed will produce fruit that taste bitter, you can foresee that the tree will be cut down by

148   Chapter 2——*The Planning behind Literature*

巨大な建築はエベレスト・コロニーと呼ばれる。2028年の巨大隕石のニアミスが引き越した恐怖と混乱に乗じてアリエクスという男が計画を主導した。人類の存続を保証するために、火星にもうひとつの世界をつくる。アリエクスの主張を国連が承認し、そのための実験居住施設の建設がこのエベレストに始まった。だが2050年、この巨大建築が竣工するころには、世界中のだれもが気がついていた。それはもはや実験施設などではなく、すでに「完璧な世界」なのだと。地球上の富と資源と才能はすべてこの「完璧な世界」のなかに吸い込まれた。その代わりにこれまでの世界は破たんし、衰退の道をたどっていく。この計画を発案し実行させ、結果これまでの世界を破壊した男、アリエクスは死を偽ってコロニー内で生きているのが発見され、審問にかけられる。

　計画のそもそもの目的だった火星への移行計画はなかなか実行されない。審問でアリエクスは、火星移住は幻の目的で、その目的を喧伝することで地球上に「完璧な世界」をつくったのだと認めた。隕石も火星も、そのために利用したに過ぎない、と。

　それがどういう結果を招くのかを、考えなかったのかとアリエクスは問われる。アリエクスの答えはシンプルだった。まさか。もちろんすべてを予見していた。こうして私が審判をされる日が訪れることも。そのために、私は死を偽ってまで、生きながらえてきたのだ、と。

　50年もの先の未来を、どうやって予見するなんて、不可能に決まっている。そういう審問員に向けて、アリエクスはこともなげにこう答える。

　　「……リンゴの種を植えたとしよう」アリエクスは言った。「そこからやがて芽が出て、枝葉を張り、樹木にまで成長することは計測できる。やがて実がなり、それを誰かが食べることも計測できる。植えた種を予め分析しておき、それが甘い実をもたらさぬことがわかっていれば、それを食べたものが不満を持ち、次の日には木を切り倒すか、

文学の計画──第2章　149

those who hate it. Then another smart guy will invent a better seed that can make better fruit. Just by analyzing and sowing the seed of an apple, you can foresee what will happen years later. I sowed the seed of this world. Is it really all that mysterious that, at that time, I could foresee what's happening today?"

Future and history's only difference is that of reading the story from the beginning or the final chapter. We see an "appleseed," and when we sow it, we look back the memories from the future having a lot of fruits. We should look at it.

Future is always fiction, just like memories.

To design architecture is to design the flow of time into the future. Architects imagine things that will happen in the space. They imagine space as filling a role.

To design novel is to design memories found in the future. Novelists can describe the present as the past remembered in 2084. They can describe the nineteenth century as the past remembered in the present.

In architecture and literature it's important that we can imagine or remember something unattached from the present. That is the possibility of the novel, and the power of architecture. These days however, the novel is a pompous mirror called "literature" which reflects reality only through the lens of the eyes. Or, at best, it could be a self-satisfactory ploy to attach itself in a cowardly way to history by a kind of parody called "conscious imitation." It's only fit to be reproduced for historical value.

Some illustrated novels are written in the setting of "transcending space and time," but they only represent enclosed relationships of love and sex. Such an enclosed relationship is ultimately lacking in possibility.

There are various methods of transcending past and future, memory and

150   Chapter 2———*The Planning behind Literature*

あるいは自らもっと甘い実をつける品種を発明しようとするだろうことが予測できる。種を分析し植えるだけで、そこまで先のことが予測できるのだ。私は種を植えた。この世界の種を。その時点で、今日のこの日が予見できたとして、それほどの不思議があるかね？」

　未来と歴史とは、同じひとつの物語を、最初から読むか、最終章から読むかという違いでしかない。リンゴの種を植えるとき、実はリンゴがたわわになった未来の時点から記憶を振り返る眼で、私たちはその種を見ている。というよりも、見るべきなのだ。
　未来とは常にフィクションである。同じように、記憶もまた、常にフィクションなのだ。
　建築を設計することは、未来に流れ出す時間を設計することである。この建築を作れば、その空間内でこんなことが起こるだろうと想像する。50年後に、この建築の空間が果たすだろう役割を、想像する。
　小説を設計することは、未来に発掘されるだろう記憶を設計することである。小説では、2084年の時点から現代を過去として叙述することもできるし、現代から19世紀の過去を振り返ることもできる。
　重要なことは、小説も建築も、現実の時間を離れて予測し、記憶することができる、ということだ。それこそが小説の可能性だったし、建築の力でもあったはずだ。ところが、小説はいま目に見える現実を「文学」という名の気取った鏡で映すだけのものになってしまった。あるいはせいぜい、「本歌取り」のようなパロディで、姑息に歴史に取り入った自己満足に落ち入っている。それはただ歴史や記憶を縮小再生産する方向にしか向いていない。

　あるいは一部のライトノベルのように、「時空を超える」ような設定がなされながら、結局のところ恋愛＝性愛の閉じた関係しか表現されえない。そうした閉じた関係には、何の可能性もない。
　小説的構想力の重要性は、過去と未来、記憶と予測との関係を超えられ

文学の計画──第2章　　*151*

prediction, in the imaginative power of the novel. Architecture must learn from this unrestricted way of depicting something.

14. About Emotion

First of all, why does that which we call emotion exist only on the earth in the limitless universe? No emotion or no receiver for it would be around a star far from here even if it exploded and vanished after existing for billions years. Why does this exist only in our world on Earth?

Ari'X asks this.

If no emotion or no receiver for it existed on the earth, we would never write or read any novel. Progression of science and technology is also caused by emotion called desire. Anytime, we need also a space for our emotion. Emotion is made from experiences and memories for it. We cannot tell why but that someone who transforms happenings into experiences and tells the memories exist only on the earth.

In Search of Lost Time[98] by Marcel Proust[99] gives us various descriptions about how experienced spaces transformed by working of memories. For example, the protagonist who tells his memories recalls his hometown like this.

And so it was that, for a long time afterwards, when I lay awake at night and revived old memories of Combray, I saw no more of it than this sort of luminous panel, sharply defined against a vague and shadowy background, like the panels which a Bengal fire or some electric sign will illuminate and dissect from the front of a building the other parts of which remain plunged in darkness: broad enough at its base, the little parlour, the dinning-room, the alluring shadows of the path along which would

Chapter 2———*The Planning behind Literature*

る多様な記述方法があることだ。そして、建築はその無制限な記述からこそ学ばなければいけない。

14. 感情について

　――そもそも、宇宙のなかで、なぜこの地球にだけ感情などというものがあるのだろう？　どこかで数億年を生きた星が爆発し消滅したとしても、そのまわりには感情は一切なく、その受容器も存在しない。それがなぜ地球上の世界にだけ存在する？

　小説『パーフェクト・ワールド』のなかで、主人公のひとりアリエクスはこう問う。
　感情がなければ、ひとは小説を読みも書きもしなかっただろう。科学や技術の発展ですら、欲望という名の感情こそが引き起こしたものだ。空間にも、ひとは感情のための場所を求めてきた。そして感情を形作るのが、経験とその記憶だ。地球上にのみ、出来事を経験に変換し、さらにはその記憶を語る主体が存在する。

　マルセル・プルースト[101]の『失われた時を求めて』[102]には、経験された空間が、記憶の働きによって変形する様子がよく描写される。そしてその記憶を語る主人公は、故郷の町コンブレーをこんなふうに思い出す。

　　（前略）コンブレーを思うとき、私の頭には、ちょうど燃えあがるベンガル花火か電気の光りに照らされて、夜の闇に沈んだ建物のほんの一角だけがほかと区別されて浮かび上がるように、混沌とした闇の真ん中から切り取られた一種の光っている壁の一部が浮かぶばかりだった。その底辺はかなり広く、そこには小さな客間、食堂、自分ではそれと知らずに私の悲しみの作者となったスワン氏のやってくる薄暗い道の最初の部分、玄関があってその玄関から私は階段の最初の段

文学の計画――第2章　　*153*

come M. Swann, the unconscious author of my sufferings, the hall through which I would journey to the first step of that staircase , so hard to climb, which constituted, all by itself, the tapering 'elevation' of an irregular pyramid; and , at the summit, my bedroom, with the little passage through whose glazed door Mamma would enter; in a wood, seen always at the same evening hour, isolated from all its possible surroundings, detached and solitary against its shadowy back ground, the bare minimum of scenery necessary (like the setting one sees printed at the head of an old play, for its performance in the provinces) to the drama of undressing, as though all Combray had consisted of but two floors joined by a slender staircase, and as though there had been no time there but seven o'clock at night.

(Translated by C.K. Scott Moncrieff and Terence Kilmartin)

In the novel, space is distorted by memories and by the text.

On the contrary, spaces in architecture are not distorted in the process of designing and building. Any work of architecture cannot be physically realized if no one correctly understands and expresses the spaces imagined in such complex shapes.

Yet, an architect can picture memories in advance, which would remain in the architecture. It is this imagination that Proust gave his protagonist *In Search Of Lost Time*, sometimes regarded as Proust's autobiography, though it's not exactly that. Proust's real hometown is not "Combray." Michihiko Suzuki, translator of the novel into Japanese, called this novel "a fictional autobiography" in his book *Reading Proust.*[100]

No one has experienced a work of architecture when it is designed. On the other hand, spaces in novel seem to be experienced by the author as a fact, but actually it is only lived by a protagonist in fiction. So just like a novelist, an architect must be able to write memories like fictions in

の方へと歩いて行ったわけだが、心をえぐられながら上がった階段は、それだけで、このいびつなピラミッド型のひどく狭い胴体を形成していた。頂上には私の寝室があって、ママの入ってくるガラスのはまったドアのある狭い廊下がついている。一口に言えば、常に同じ時刻に、周囲にあったと思われるいっさいのものから引き離されて、それだけが闇から浮き出ている舞台装置、私の着替えの悲劇にとって（昔の戯曲の冒頭に、地方公演用に指定されているあの装置のような）必要最小限度の舞台装置である。あたかもコンブレーとは狭い階段で結ばれた二つの階でしかなく、またコンブレーには夜の七時しか存在しなかったかのようだ。

　これは小説だから、空間はテクストと記憶によって二重に歪んでいる。
　建築の空間は、その設計過程、実現過程においては、歪まない。たとえそれがどんなに複雑な形態として発想されたとしても、それを正しく理解し表現しないかぎり、建築は物質として立ち現れることはないからだ。

　だが同時に建築家は、やがてその建築に刻まれるだろう記憶を、先回りして想起することもできる。それは想像力によってであり、プルーストが主人公の「私」に託したのと同じだ。
　『失われた時を求めて』は自伝的要素が強いと言われているが、もちろん自伝そのものではない。プルーストの故郷の町はコンブレーではない。鈴木道彦は『プルーストを読む[103]』の中で、これを「虚構の自伝」と呼んでいる。
　建築家が建築を設計する時、その建築は未だ経験されていない。一方、小説のなかに描かれる空間は作家によって「事実」として経験されたかに見えるが、実際には主人公によって「虚構」として「生きられた」ものでしかない。だとすれば、建築家もまた、これから立ち上がる空間に、「虚

文学の計画──第2章　　155

spaces that will be realized only later.

A built architecture is not a fiction. Architects cannot foresee what will happen there in the future. However, what will happen in the work of architecture has been planned when it is designed. Architects plan where they would have a dinner, read a book and sleep. Architects can design "the little passage through whose glazed door Mama will enter." Architects can design "a bedroom seen always at the same evening hour, isolated from all its possible surroundings, detached and solitary against its shadowy back ground, the bare minimum of scenery necessary (like the setting one sees printed at the beginning of an old play script, for its performance in the provinces) to the drama of undressing." Still, architects cannot predict exactly what kind of experiences would appear and memories will remain there in the future. But if an architect can design a space with intensity, the architect can foresee that impressive experiences will emerge and would change into unforgettable memories. Architects can design a "sort of luminous panel, sharply defined against a vague and shadowy background" and imagine that the scenery would remain as a memory with what would happen there later in a head of the resident, then the memory might evoke "the panels which a Bengal fire or some electric sign."

Memories are important for architecture not only in house but also in a school, for example. Young people stay in the space called school only for several years. Experience in school should be well planned, and moreover, memories recalled throughout one's life after graduation are important. School exists not for living in the school but living outside of the school.

I designed *Kyoto Seika University Main Building*.[101] The university is where instructors and staff stay for the long-term, but students visit regularly for only a half-decade or so. They must leave there after some several years. I came up the idea to first design a tall void inside a shape of tower. It

156　　Chapter 2——— *The Planning behind Literature*

構」としての記憶を書き込むことができるはずだ。

　むろん、実際の建築はフィクションではないし、そこで何が起こるかを見通すことなどできるはずはない。だが建築家が建築を設計^{plan}する時、そこでどのような行為が起こるかも当然計画^{plan}されている。どこで食事をし、どこで本を読み、どこで眠るのかを計画する。子どもの「寝室」をつくり、その母親が「入ってくるガラスのはまったドアのある狭い廊下」を設計することができる。「同じ時刻に、周囲にあったと思われるいっさいのものから引き離されて、それだけが闇から浮き出ている舞台装置」、子どもの「着替えの悲劇にとって（中略）必要最小限度の舞台装置」のような空間を設計することができる。そこでどんな経験が得られるか、どのような記憶が形成されるかは、わからない。だが強度のある空間を設計すれば、特別な経験が生まれ、それが後々まで残る記憶へと変化していくことは予測できる。建築家は「夜の闇に沈んだ建物のほんの一角だけがほかから特別されて浮かび上がるように、混沌とした闇の真ん中から切り取られた一種の光っている壁」を設計することができる。その風景が、今はまだ起こっていない経験とともに刻まれ、後々までその住人の頭に、「燃えあがるベンガル花火か電気の光り」を想起させるかもしれない。

　記憶は「家」にだけではなく、たとえば「学校」のような建築にも重要なことだ。若者たちは、決められた数年間だけを学校という空間で過ごす。その年限のなかでの経験も重要だが、それと同じくらい、あるいはもっと重要なのは、その学校の記憶がその後の生のなかでどう甦るかだ。学校は学校で生きるためにあるのではない、学校の外で生きるためのものだから。

　僕はかつて『京都精華大学本館』¹⁰⁴を設計した。大学という場所は、教職員にとっては長い年月を過ごすところだが、多くの学生にとっては４年かそこらの限られた時期を過ごすだけの場所だ。二十歳前後の若い時間を過ごした後、必ずそこを去ることになる場所。

文学の計画──第２章　*157*

runs from the ground level to the highest story. Sunlight through a window at the top of void would barely reach the bottom… As you see, this is same as a void in a huge architecture that I described in the novel, *The Perfect World*. In the University, the structure is much smaller than *the Perfect World*. This void has no function. The bottom is the space only for confirming a light from a top of the void. Or the bottom might be used for "judgment" someday, just as in *The Perfect World* [fig. 15] (p. 186).

Someone objected to the idea for the void inside a tower shape when I was designing it. Because there is no function to the void, as they point out correctly enough. I told them it is a space needed to find a small bit of sky, but they still didn't like it. I earnestly insisted, "Students will climb up the stairs in the building to travel for some sky." They looked at me as though I were insane. But I was telling the truth. A university is a place for students to find a tiny bit of sky and figure out how to get there. Nothing but dreams can be given. That's it. However, I can easily foresee students will remember their school days —along with the void and the staircases. I designed the void and staircases as a novelist would describe memories of the future. A student who looks up at the small patch of sky from the bottom of the void can climb up the "blue stairway" or "red stairway." The stairways are colored blue and red because the colors help them to remind of school days. They can share their memories only if they talk about blue or red stairs with their schoolmates.

Light from the sky would be coming closer. The blue staircase is filled with blue light, while the red staircase is filled with red light [fig. 16-17] (pp. 186-7).

After finishing climbing up the stairway, they would find a small court on the top floor modeled on the traditional Japanese garden called "KARESANSUI." What looks like gravel is actually pieces of glass that can store up the sunlight and discharge it as illumination after dusk. A mass centered in the court is designed to resemble a rock. It is actually the top of the tower that they looked up toward from the bottom. They will see

この建築を設計する際、最初に考えたのはひとつの塔状の吹抜けだ。それは地上レベルから最上階までを貫通する。その頂点の窓から差し込む光がかろうじてその底にまで達している——そう、これは小説『パーフェクト・ワールド』で描いた巨大建築の中の吹抜けと同じだ。それよりもずっと小さいが。この空間には何の機能もない。小さい空からの光を確認するためだけの空間だ。ひょっとして、ここも小説同様、審判がやがて行われる場所なのかもしれない [fig. 15]（p. 186参照）。

　設計をしている最中、この塔状の登場の吹抜けをつくることに反対したひとも少なからずいた。何も機能を持たない空間だからだ。「小さな空を発見するための場所だ」と言っても、賛成してくれるものは増えなかった。「その後に空まで行こうとして、別の場所にある階段を登るのだ」。皆、僕が冗談でも言っているとでも思ったようだった。だが僕は本気で考えていた。大学とは、小さな空を見つけて、そこに行こうと決意をするための場所だ。ほかにどんなご利益もない。ただそれだけの場所で、やがてはきっと皆そんなふうに、学生時代を思い返すのに違いない、と。

　僕はここで、未来の記憶を記述する小説家のように、その吹抜けと階段とを設計していた。塔の底から小さな空を見上げたものは、「青階段」「赤階段」を登っていく。階段をこうした色にしたのは、これも記憶のためだ。やがて卒業生が、どこかで別の卒業生と出会った時、彼らは「あの青い階段」とひとこと言うだけで、場所の記憶を共有できる。

　階段を登って行くと、空からの光が近づいてくる。「青階段」では青い光が、赤階段では赤い光が壁の際に満ちる [fig. 16-17]（pp. 186〜187参照）。
　階段を登り切ると、小さな庭がある。日本の伝統的な庭園形式「枯山水」を模した庭だ。砂利に見えるのは、蓄光ガラスで、昼に蓄えた光を夕暮れ時にかすかに灯す。庭の中央の塊は、岩に模している。それは実は、入口で見上げたあの塔の頂部分だ。覗きこめば、さっきまでいた場所、空を見上げていた塔の底が、見えるだろう。《塔の底 − 階段 − 小さな庭》は、

文学の計画——第2章　*159*

where they were and look at small patch of sky through glass at the top of void. "Bottom~stairway~court" is a circuit of a short memory for where you were.

The sky is not here at the top of the void when they arrive. It can be seen over the mountains to the west. The framed landscape is brought to the court as "shakkei," meaning "borrowed scape."

The court has no function. There are not even chairs here for students to talk with their friends. Students can only see the western mountains and the sky. The landscape of sunset over the mountain will put into his or her memory. The figure of the student forgetting time passing to look at sunset might be reminiscent of Basho under a willow.

Another memory is planned into the architecture. It is created by a huge triangle of glass facing a square. After dusk, it becomes a huge luminescent triangle. There is a bus stop in the square, so students finishing the school day come here under the illumination of the triangle. They wait for the bus with easiness of the days as university student, anxious only of the future or nervousness as a mortal, in every evening for a half decade [fig. 18] (p. 187).

I planned so that the huge triangle would revive in their memories in the future as a "sort of luminous panel, sharply defined against a vague and shadowy background."

In both architecture and novels, memories belong not only to the past. Memories of the future can be planned.

15. **From Words to Pictures**

But now literature is in a crisis.

As discussed in the Chapter One, the novel has been required as a cultural base for a community sharing empathy, an imaginary community like a "nation." Karatani Kojin argued that the intellectual class and the

160   Chapter 2——*The Planning behind Literature*

短い記憶の回路なのだ。

　空を探してこの庭にやってきても、塔の頂の近くにはそれはない。それは西の山の彼方にある。その風景を、借景の手法で切り取り、この庭のなかに引き込んだ。

　この庭にも、機能はない。カフェのテラスやパティオとは違う。椅子もないここでは、学生は友とも語りあわないかもしれない。ただここで、西の山と空を見つめることはできる。山の向うに夕日が落ちていく風景を、記憶にとどめるだろう。風景を見つめて時を忘れる学生の姿は、ひょっとしたら柳の下の芭蕉の姿に似ているかもしれない。

　もうひとつ、この建築には、計画された記憶がある。それは、外部の広場に面した、巨大な三角形のガラス壁だ。ここは夕暮れを過ぎると、全体が三角形に光る。広場はスクールバスのロータリーを兼ねており、学校での一日を終えた学生たちは、この三角形の照明の光の下に、集まってくる。学生時代特有の気楽さや、将来への漠然とした不安、あるいは本人によってしか治療しえぬ苦しさを抱えて、彼らはここで、バスを待つ。毎夕、4年の間ずっと [fig. 18]（p. 187参照）。

　この大きな三角形のガラスが、「混沌とした闇の真ん中から切り取られた一種の光っている壁」として、学生たちの《未来の記憶》としてよみがえることを、僕は計画した。

　建築においても小説においても、記憶は過去にのみ属するのではない。こうして《未来の記憶》の計画が可能なはずだ。

15.　言葉から映像へ

　しかし文学はいま危機にある。

　第1章で見たように、近代文学は「『共感』の共同体、つまり想像の共同体としてのネーションの基盤」として、求められた。柄谷行人は、「小

文学の計画——第2章　*161*

working class, along with any number of other classes, can be united and given identity through empathy, and then a nation would appear involving all of these classes.

What would an imaginary community actually consist of? The answer is memories and the future [fig. 18].

Imaginary communities requires history as a collective memory. The "story" termed "History" must be written by the imaginary community. Japan for example, one such imaginary community, sometimes tells the story of "TEN-NO Emperor" or at other times of the "Samurai" as one historical reason for differing accounts of national origins. For another example, in *The Year of Death of Ricardo Reis*, Reis and Fernando Pessoa trace the history and memory of Portugal and themselves. That is, "I" as an imaginary community begins to tell its memory with "numbered portrait."

One of the reasons for this crisis that modern literature faces is that these memories now can be shared not only in small communities but in large ones as well. Not only with social classifications dividing to community horizontally but also with tastes dividing it vertically; thus, the imagination that should have unified the community is now fragmented. "Taste" may sound petty. Tastes have no particular reason, so we cannot control them at all.

Any imagination is shared, be it by internet-nerds or journalists active in real war zones. We can say they have a different philosophy or life. But we cannot say why they are different or why the difference has come up. It isn't rooted in a difference of social class. Education or the surroundings may have been one of the roots, but not necessarily so. We can only say they have chosen their own way which we call taste.

On the other hand, what is the difference between a politician and someone who just presents their opinions on the internet? Trump, President of United States, uses Twitter as his most powerful weapon. His words are the same in statements, his interviews like tweets. "I would

説が知識人と大衆、あるいは、様々な社会的階層を『共感』によって同一的たらしめ、ネーションを形成」してきたのだと言う。

　ではその「共感」あるいは「想像の共同体」を構成するのは具体的には何か？　それは記憶と、未来だ[fig. 18]。

　「想像の共同体」は、共有されるべき記憶としての歴史を求める。「想像の共同体」こそが歴史 (history) という物語 (story) を書くのだとも言える。日本という「想像の共同体」が時に「天皇」、別の時には「武士道」という物語を「国民」の歴史の基礎として語り出すように（言うまでもないが、天皇と武士とではもともと全く別の文化なのにもかかわらず）。『リカルド・レイスの死の年』のレイスとフェルナンド・ペソアがポルトガルと彼らの歴史と記憶を辿るように。あるいは「僕」という名の「想像の共同体」が番号付きの記憶を語り出すように。

　近代文学が危機を迎えているのは、ひとつにはこうした記憶が大きな「共同体」性を保証しなくなったからだ。共同体を水平に分割する「階層」のみならず、垂直に無数に分割する「趣味」によって、共同体をまとめ上げるはずの「想像」力は細分化された。「趣味」といえば軽く聞こえるかもしれないが、それは無根拠ゆえに、どのようにもコントロールし得ない。

　ネット・オタクと、海外の戦地を飛び回るジャーナリストとの間には、共同の想像力は成立しない。それを生き方の違いとか、思想の差だと評することはできるだろう。だがその違いがどうして生じたか、どこから出て来たかを探しても、きっと確固とした理由は見当たらない。それは階層の違いに根差さない。教育や周辺環境は影響したかもしれないが、していない例もあるだろう。結局のところ、どちらも、好きな道を選んだとしか言いようがない。それは「趣味」の違いと言うしか他にない。

　一方、SNSで自分の「意見」を垂れ流すものと、政治家とは何が違うだろうか？　トランプ米大統領の武器はもっぱらツイッターであり、その言語は演説であれインタビューであれ、あまり変わらない。「メキシコとの

build a great wall, and nobody builds walls better than me, believe me, and I build them very inexpensively." (BBC News Web 6 February 2017) "If the ban were announced with a one week notice, the "bad" would rush into our country during that week. A lot of bad "dudes" out there!" (Twitter by @realDonaldTrump, 1 January 2017). These statements just like Twitter have garnered such a substantial number of votes that Trump managed to become the President of States, an office in which he must perform the center act on the world stage. It means the protagonist of the world can be selected by people who share a little taste.

I do not wish to argue that we should accept the situation today, even if many people think the difference or a little sharing of taste has the value. There is no chance of conversation or contradiction in the difference or the sharing because only you can say you like it or don't like it. Lifestyles marked by the "taste" for social withdrawal, or the life of the seasonal worker, for example, are united through being classified according to richness and poorness. Questions of national borders can never be solved without long and complicated discussions. Inevitably, the discussions are shared via Twitter-like language. The differences appear only emotionally. Can we emotionally share tastes, or not? For a simple answer to the question, Twitter must be the best media for the expression or comprehension of the taste.

Memories cannot play a main role in a fragmented community. Even with history, they can only tell it according to their tastes. You can an example of this merely by searching through statements by geeky right-wing nationalists on the internet.

The novel, which yet retains the potential to be a strong form of expression by digging out common memories and rendering our times through the narrative of a common history, is now facing a crisis.

The future is as necessary for an imaginary community as memory. It is common knowledge that we have believed in a future predicated on an

国境に壁を建てろ！」「モスリムの入国を禁じろ！」（正確な文言は英文参照）。このあまりにもツイッター的な言語が、多くの支持を集めてトランプは世界で中心的な役割を果たす国家の大統領になった。つまりは、「趣味」を薄く共有する者たちによって、世界の主人公ですら決まるのだ。

「趣味」の違いや薄い共有が有効になったからといって、現状のすべてを肯定していいとは思わない。根拠を欠くこの差異や共有には、対話どころか矛盾の契機すらない。本当は、ひきこもりやフリーターといった「趣味」による生活形態は貧富という「階層」の問題とも結びつくはずだし、「国境」をめぐる問題は長く複雑な議論を経てしか解決されえない。だが今それらはすべて、ツイッター的な感情表現によってのみ共有され、あるいは差異が表面化する。趣味が同じか違うか。この問いに答えるだけならば、確かにツイッター的言語で表明できるし、そのほうがわかりやすい。

「趣味」によって細分化された共同体にとって、記憶は大きな力を持たない。そこでは歴史すら、趣味的に語られるのだから（たとえばいわゆるネトウヨがそうである）。

共通の記憶を掘り起こし、あるいは今日という時間を同時代の記憶として定着させることで強力な表現たりえた小説は、こうして危機を迎えた。

記憶同様、未来も、「想像の共同体」には必要不可欠なものだ。序章に

文学の計画──第2章　*165*

endless trajectory of growth, for which in modernism we saw the prologue. Now, such a future has become just a myth of the past.

However, this situation might tell us something about the possibility of foretelling our future beyond the end of that myth called "growth."

The Future can have various meanings according to "tastes," just as with History. However, we who live today must have one common presentiment about the future.

We are sensing that the natural environment of earth will be irrevocably destroyed if we can't find any effective change. This presentiment has scientific grounds.

The dark foreboding sounds like a low dissonance throughout the base of the global community beyond the modern frame of the nation-state.

The only potential for the novel must be found in the place where this dissonance sounds.

Still, the novel faces another crisis.

It is one brought about by the limitations of language.

We first learn a national language. Most people first acquire a native language, then go on to study another foreign language.

As we have already discussed, the novel forms a base of national language. For the Japanese language, a movement to unify the written and spoken language occurred in novel at the beginning of the modern age. Standard Japanese was accumulated and codified, and it unified the society of Japan through a common language. At the time, regional language was reduced to dialect.

The formulaic association, "common language = national language," was designed as a memory to be shared with all people of the nation. Japanese can feel the memory of Japan with language, "I spring it is the dawn that is most beautifl" (translated by Ivan Morris) in Sei Shōnagon's classic, *The Pillow Book*, for example, and citizens memorize what they

166   Chapter 2——*The Planning behind Literature*

も記した通り、近代社会は、「成長」という未来を信じていた。今ではそれはただの神話となった。

しかしこのことは、「成長」神話終了後の、共通の予感を可能にしているかもしれない。未来も歴史同様、「趣味」によって捉えかたは異なるだろう。

にもかかわらず、今を生きるものたちが、否が応にも共通に持たざるをえない予感がある。

その予感とは、この地球の自然環境が、このままなら必ず壊れるというものだ。この予感には、科学的な根拠がある。

国 = nation state という近代的な枠組みを超えて、この暗い予感は、低い不協和音のようにこの「世界」という名の共同体の底に響いている。

小説にまだ可能性が残されているとすれば、この不協和音が響く場所の他にない。

それでも小説には、もうひとつの危機がある。

それは言葉の持つ限界だ。

言葉は、まず national language すなわち国語として学ばれる。まれに native language = 母語を持たずに育つものもいるが、大多数は先に何かのネイティヴとなり、その後に他国語も理解するようになる。

すでに論じたことだが、小説は national language の基本を担う。日本の明治期の言文一致運動もその役割を果たした。規範としての日本語ができあがり、それは日本の共通語として日本社会を統合した。「お国言葉」はその時ただの「方言」となった。

共通語 = 国語（national language）がつくりだしたのは、その国民に共有されるべき記憶だ。「春はあけぼの」という『枕草子』の言葉によって、日本人はこの国の記憶を体感する。あるいは、学んだものを体感として記憶する。

文学の計画──第2章　*167*

learned in literature as their experience.

In the beginning of the modern age, language and memory became strongly correlated. Memory was identified with language. History couldn't exist any more without language. That is why the novel became the most important medium for expression.

How about today? Language will remain an important medium of course. Nevertheless, what language can function for a nation that has become small and is predicted to go on shrinking? (Report by Cabinet Office, Government of Japan, 2012)

We can understand the situation only if we think about a new common-or "general" we should say-language, which is English. It doesn't matter if anyone can speak English or not. It matters because anyone who speaks any language can get some feeling from the common language, for example, from an English word "kiss." It means that we need no unique language like literature in our mother tongue to build up sympathy in the nation any more.

Comparing the present to the age of Natsume Soseki and Mori Ogai over a century ago, the significance of Japanese language for the nation is diminishing. Japanese people can feel what the word "kiss" expresses without any translation. They can know the experience, the psychological effect and the historical meaning.

English is not the only common language of today. Motion pictures like film or TV have given what "kiss" would bring for Japanese or any non-English speaker. After the twentieth century, which was a century of motion pictures, movie and TV have functioned as the common language for the world.

Motion pictures have become the primary form of expression since the dawn of the modern age, just like language, or more than language. Witness how well the novel has expressed war memories and how well pictures have conveyed our reality. The realities of Hiroshima and

近代の初期において、言葉と記憶とは極めて強力に結びついた。記憶は言葉そのものとなり、歴史は言葉抜きには存在しなくなった。だからこそ、小説は表現の最重要メディアになることができた。

　しかし今は違う。もちろん、言葉は現在も未来も重要な役割を担うことは間違いない。にもかかわらず、languageがnationに果たす役割は既に小さくなり、これからも縮小を続ける。

　それを理解するには、英語という「共通語」の存在を考えるだけで足りる。だれもが英語を話せるかどうかは問題ではない。ただ、どのような言葉を話す者たちも、世界の共通語の感覚を得ることができてしまう。たとえばkissという英単語から。

　漱石や鷗外の時代から比べれば、日本人にとって日本語の重要性は明らかに縮小している。21世紀の日本人は、kissという語の感覚を、日本語を経由せずに得ることができる。その言葉が持つ体感も、心的な重要性も、歴史的な意味合いですらも。

　「共通語」はまた、英語という言語を通してのみもたらされたものでは、もちろんない。日本人はkissという感覚を、映画やテレビがもたらす映像から得た。20世紀という映像の世紀以降、共通語の役割を担ったのは映画やテレビだったといえるのかもしれない。

　映像は、言葉とともに、近代以降の表現の主役になった。あるいはそれ以上に。戦争の記憶をよく表現するのは小説だが、映像抜きにそのリアリティを伝えるのは困難だ。たとえばヒロシマやナガサキのリアリティは、

文学の計画——第2章　*169*

Nagasaki, or the impacts of 9/11 and 3/11, cannot remain without images. Images are also another possibility for the novel. This possibility is a presentiment of a future released from national language.

We will discuss the possibility in the next chapter.

＊ notes

1   Novelist. Argentina. Born in 1914.

2   The 30th *GUNZO* literature award in 1986. The book was published by *GENDAI-KIKAKUSHITU* in 1988.

3   Novelist. United States. Known for hardboiled detective fiction. 1888-1959.

4   Novelist. United Kingdom. Known for intellectual detective fiction. 1890-1976.

5   Published in 1982 in Japan.

6   Novelist. Born in 1949. Debut in 1979 with the 22nd *GUNZO* Literature Award.

7   Published in 2013. A protagonist "Tazaki" has a travel to see his old friends for knowing his own secret.

8   Shinchosha Publishing, 1985.

9   Kodansha Publishing, 2009-2010.

10   Anthropologist. France. 1908-2009.

11   Linguist. France. 1857-1913.

12   Architect and design theorist. Austria. Born in 1936.

13   Published in 1964. Later it was published as a book with another essay "Notes on the Synthesis of Form." Another representative book is *Pattern Language*, 1977.

14   Kodansha Publishing, 1983.

170   Chapter 2——— *The Planning behind Literature*

そして9.11や3.11の衝撃は、残された映像とともにしか存続し得ない。

　映像は、小説のもうひとつの可能性でもある。「国語」から開放された未来の予感としての可能性だ。

　次の章で、その可能性について詳細に見てみよう。

※注

1　小説家。アルゼンチン。1914年生まれ。

2　土岐恒二訳、集英社、1984年（原題 *Rayuela* ／英語題 *Hopscotch*）。ここでは英語版に基づき筆者が和訳した。

3　1986年第30回群像新人文学賞。1987年現代企画室から単行本として出版。

4　探偵小説作家。アメリカ。1888〜1959

5　推理作家。イギリス。1890〜1976

6　小説家。1949年生まれ。1979年第22回群像新人賞を受賞してデビュー。

7　講談社、1982年（『ユリイカ』1982年7月号）

8　文藝春秋社、2013年。主人公「多崎つくる」は自己の謎を探るため過去の友人に会いに行く。

9　新潮社、1985年

10　講談社、2009〜2010年

11　文化人類学者。フランス。1908〜2009

12　言語学者。フランス。1857〜1913

13　鹿島出版会、2013年

14　講談社、1983年

15　ジル・ドゥルーズ、フェリックス・ガタリ（宇野邦一ほか訳）『千のプラトー――資本主義と分裂症』河出書房新社、1994年

16　Formalization.「形式」は「内容」の反意語。例えば「1」は「リンゴが1個」のような「内容」を意味できるが、「形式」としては数学の定義（例えば自然数の最初の数）以外の意味を持たない。

15 "Form" is antonym of "content." For example, "one" can designate the content as "one apple" but as a form it has only mathematical definition, like the first number of natural numbers.

16 Magazine *Eureka*, March, 1983.

17 Poet. Born in 1931.

18 Architect. Born in 1956. Co-leading SANAA with Ryu'ei Nishizwa.

19 Novelist, France, born in 1936.

20 Original title is *La Vie mode d'employ*, 1978.

21 Novelist, born in 1956. The original was published in 2010. English title is *The Map and the Territory*.

22 Architect, poet, art theorist. Opposite to mass-product movement and re-estimate works by hands. Advocating "Arts and Craft's movement" that aspire unifying art, craft and life.

23 Novelist. United States. Born in 1930.

24 Written by Laurence Sterne. 1713-1768.

25 Methodology to describe real and unreal things in real space.

26 No translation in English is as yet available. Referring to *Silent Cry or M/T and the Narrative about the Marvels of the Forest*.

27 Hiroshi Hara precisely analyzed Ōe's novel when he designed magazine *Elementaly School in Uchiko-cho in KENCHIKU-BUNKA*, 1992-11.

28 Kodansha Publishing, 1993.

29 Methodology of naturally describing objects without intentional view points.

30 Methodology of accurately describing objects. The theme is also real matter.

31 Architect. United States. 1867-1959.

32 The shortest style of poem in the world. It consists of 17 syllables as 5-7-5.

33 Translated by Donald Keene. The original book title is *Narrow Road to Oku*.

34 Waka poet. 1118-1190.

17 「文学と建築」(『ユリイカ』1983年3月号「特集：幻想の建築 〈空間〉と文学」)

18 詩人。1931年生まれ。

19 建築家。1956年生まれ。西沢立衛と協働。

20 小説家。フランス。1936年生まれ。

21 酒詰治男訳、水声社、1992年（*La Vie Mode d'Emploi*, 1978.）

22 野崎歓訳、筑摩書房、2013年（*La Carte et Le Territoire*, 2010.）

23 19世紀の建築家、詩人、芸術思想家。大量生産に反発し手仕事を再評価、アート・工芸と生活の一体化を目指すアーツ・アンド・クラフト運動を提唱した。

24 志村正雄訳、筑摩書房、1994年（*Sabbatical : a romance*, 1982.）
著者ジョン・バースはポスト・モダン文学を代表するアメリカの小説家。

25 ローレンス・スターン（朱牟田夏雄訳）岩波文庫、1969年（Laurence Sterne, *The Life and Opinions of Tristram Shandy, Gentleman*, 1759.）

26 小説家。1935年生まれ。

27 非現実的なものと現実的なものを同一のリアルな空間のなかで描く手法。ガルシア・マルケス『百年の孤独』（Gabriel García Márquez, *Cien años de soledad*, 1967）がその代表例。

28 新潮社、1979年

29 原広司はその四国の谷に『内子町立大瀬小学校』を設計する際、大江の小説の詳細な構造分析を行っている（『建築文化』1992年11月号）。

30 講談社文芸文庫、1993年

31 世界最短の詩形。17音節からなる。

32 歌人。1118～1190

33 実際には、この柳がその柳であったのかどうか、確かではない。しかしそれはあまり問題ではない。芭蕉にとっては、西行の歌こそ重要なのだから。

34 様々な歌人による和歌の撰集。10世紀初頭に編纂。

35 パブロ・ピカソ（1881～1973）による絵画。立体派の代表的作品。

36 ポップ・アートを代表する芸術家。1928～1987

37 ロックを象徴するミュージシャン。1943～

35 It consists of 31 syllables as 5-7-5-7-7.

36 A painting by Pablo Picasso, 1881-1973. A representative work in Cubism.

37 Representative Artist of Pop Art. 1928-1987.

38 Musician symbolizing Rock music. 1943-

39 Movie Actress known as a sex symbol. Born Norma Jean. 1926-1962.

40 Artist. 1951-

41 Artist. 1962-

42 Architect. United States. 1925-. *Complexity and Contradiction in Architecture* (1966), *Learning From Las Vegas* (1977).

43 Architect. Germany. 1944-. *Delirious New York* (1978).

44 As same as the Atomic Bomb Memorial, they existed and were partially destroyed in 1945 and are still existing.

45 Hiroshima City Government is uploading 86 buildings as a list of atomic-bombed memorial on the official website.

46 Established in 1915. The name at the Atomic Bomb Dome was *The Building for Promoting Industry.*

47 Claude-Nicolas Ledoux, 1736-1806. Architect. Drawing *Eye Enclosing the Theatre at Besançon.*

48 Jean-Jacques Lequeu, 1757-1826. Architect. Drawing *Temple dedicated to the Equality.*

49 Architectural group formed in 1960s in Lindon. Main members were Peter Cook, or Herron and some. Drawings *Plug in City, Walking City, Instant City.*

50 Philosopher, Germany. 1724-1804. *Critique of Pure Reason* (1781), *Critique of Judgement* (1790).

51 Philosopher, France. 1905-1980. *L'Imaginaire* (1940), *Being and Nothingness* (1943).

52 "Schema" is the word Kant uses in his epistemology. A sense impression becomes cognition with accompanied by schema.

53 Published in magazine *AXIS*, 1998. 7-8.

38 映画女優。セックス・シンボルとして知られる。本名ノーマ・ジーン。1926
〜1962

39 芸術家。1951〜

40 芸術家。1962〜

41 建築家。アメリカ。1925〜

42 建築家。オランダ。1944〜

43 R. ヴェンチューリ（伊藤公文訳）『建築の多様性と対立性』鹿島出版会、198
2年（*Complexity and Contradiction in Architecture*, 1966.）

R. ヴェンチューリ他（石井和紘・伊藤公文訳）『ラスベガス』鹿島出版会、1
978年（*Learning From Las Vegas*, 1977.）

レム・コールハース（鈴木圭介訳）『錯乱のニューヨーク』筑摩書房、1995年
（*Delirious New York*, 1978.）

44 米川良夫訳、河出書房新社、2003年（*Le città invisibili*, 1972.）

45 「原爆ドーム」同様、広島に原爆が投下された時に存在し、部分的に破壊さ
れながら、その後も存在し続けた建物。

46 広島市はWEB上の「被爆建物リスト」に86箇所を載せている（2015年時）

47 1915年竣工。原爆投下時の建物名称は『広島県産業奨励館』。

48 建築家。1736〜1806。ドローイング『*Oeil reflétant l'intérieur du Théâtre de
Besançon*』など。

49 建築家。1757〜1826。ドローイング『*Temple consacré à l'Egalité*』など。

50 ロンドンで1960年代に結成された建築グループ。主なメンバーはピーター・
クック、ロン・ヘロンなど。ドローイング『*Plug In City*』『*Walking City*』
『*Instant City*』など。

51 哲学者、ドイツ。1724〜1804。『純粋理性批判』『判断力批判』など

52 ドイツ語「Einbildungskraft」は英語で「imagination」と訳される。つまり
サルトルの言う「想像力」と同じ語だということに注意したい。

53 哲学者、小説家。フランス。1905〜1980

54 「図式」は、カントがその認識論のなかで使ったキーワードである。感覚は
図式に落とし込まれることで認識となる。

55 『AXIS』1998年7〜8号掲載。

文学の計画──第2章　*175*

54 *Hon-no-mado*, Shougaku-kan Publishing, 2009. The title of a series of essays coauthored with Kei Nakazawa, the novelist, is "I Came Up with the Idea to Build a House in the Countryside."

55 A protagonist of a novel *Crime and Punishment*.

56 Russian Novel, 1866, written by Dostoyevsky.

57 Novelist, Russia. 1821-1881. *The Idiot* (1869), *Demons* (1872), *The Brothers of Karamazov* (1880).

58 Essay, 1967. In English book, *Image-Music-Text*, 1977.

59 Critic, Philosopher. France. 1915-1980.

60 'écriture' in French. An opposite idea to 'parole' that means 'speaking.'

61 Novelist. Portugal. 1922-2010. 1988 Nobel prize winner. *Blindness* (1995) and *The Doble* (2003) were made into movies.

62 Witten in Portugal, 1984. English translation, 1991, Harcourt Inc.

63 Published in Japanese, 1998.

64 2007.

65 Novelist. United States. Born in 1936.

66 Architect. United States. 1912-1986.

67 Architect. United States. Born in 1946.

68 *La Guerra Del Fin Del Mundo*, 1981. English translation, Faber & Faber Co.

69 Novelist. Peru. Born in 1936.

70 Michael Hardt and Antonio Negri, *Empire,* Harvard University Press, 2000.

71 Philosopher. Italy. Born in 1933.

72 Tange designed "Imperial East Asia Memorial" in during World War II, and project for Hiroshima, Tokyo Olympics 1964, Expo 1970 in Osaka, Tokyo City Hall.

73 Architect. Germany, United States. 1886-1969.

74 Architect. Austria. 1934-2014.

75 Architects unit by Jaqcues Herzog and Pierre de Meuron. Swiss. Both are born in 1950.

56 小学館『本の窓』2009年4月号及び5月号、小説家の中沢けい氏との共同連載「田舎に家をたてようと思った」より。「Kちゃん」他の人物の年齢等も2009年当時。

57 小説『罪と罰』の主人公

58 ロシアの小説。1866年

59 小説家、ロシア。1821〜1881。著書に、『白痴』『悪霊』『カラマーゾフの兄弟』など

60 フランスの思想家。1915〜1980

61 1967年に書かれたエッセイ。日本では花輪光訳『物語の構造分析』(みすず書房、1979年) 所収。

62 écriture　フランス語で「書かれた言葉」の意味。話者が明らかな「話し言葉 (parole)」の対比的概念。

63 小説家、ポルトガル。1922〜2010。1988年ノーベル文学賞受賞。『白の闇』『複製された男』は映画化もされた。

64 岡村多希子訳、彩流社、2002年 (ポルトガル語の原著 *O ano da morte de Ricardo Reis*, 1984.)

65 彰国社、1998年

66 小説家。アメリカ。1936年生まれ

67 上岡伸雄訳、新潮社、2009年 (*Falling man : a novel, Scribner*, 2007.)

68 建築家。アメリカ。1912〜1986

69 建築家。アメリカ。1946年生まれ。

70 小説家。ペルー。1936年生まれ。

71 旦敬介訳、新潮社、2010年 (*La Guerra del Fin del Mundo*, 1981.)

72 http://www.cdc.gov/mmwr/preview/mmwrhtml/mm51SPa6.htm による。

73 アントニオ・ネグリはイタリアの思想家。マイケル・ハートとの共著『〈帝国〉グローバル化の世界秩序とマルチチュードの可能性』(水嶋一憲他訳、以文社、2003年) にその概念は詳しい。

74 戦中の大東亜建設記念計画をはじめ、戦後のヒロシマ、東京オリンピック、70年万博等に関わる建築の他、東京都庁舎 (旧新とも) などを手がけた。

75 建築家。ドイツ、アメリカ。1886〜1969

76 Novelist, Poet. Russia. 1799-1837.

77 Novelist, Critic. Japan. 1859-1935.

78 Novelist. Japan. 1864-1909.

79 Novelist. Japan. 1867-1916.

80 Novelist. Japan. 1909-1948.

81 Taka'aki Yoshimoto, for example.

82 Not Educated, Employed or Trained.

83 Kurt Vonnegut Jr., *Slaughterhouse-Five, or The Children' Crusade: A Duty-Dance with Death*, 1969.

84 Novelist. United States. 1922-2007.

85 Musician. UK. 1940-1980. Ex The Beatles. Also known as an anti-war activist. Shot by a self-called fan.

86 Novelist. Japan. 1925-1970. Remembered for his ritual suicide by HARAKIRI after a failed coup d'état attempt.

87 Published in 2008.

88 Novelist. United States. Born in 1947.

89 Architect. Japan. Born in 1956.

90 Kodansha Publishing, 1992.

91 Novelist. Italy. 1923-1985.

92 Novelist. France. Born in Czech in 1929.

93 Asahi Shimbun Publishing. Published in 1998. This quotation is from a chapter titled "From Architecture of Today."

94 Philosopher. France. 1929-2007.

95 Novelist. UK. Born in India in 1947. He used to be a copywriter in Pakistan.

96 RONSO Publishing, 2014.

97 "Cutaway" (2000), and the others.

98 Original French title is *À la recherche du temps perdu*, 1913-1927. Translated by C.K. Scott Moncrieff and Terence Kilmartin ; revised by D.J. Enright, 1992-.

76 建築家。オーストリア。1934〜2014

77 ジャック・ヘルツォークとピエール・ド・ムーロンの2人の建築家によるユニット。スイス。両者とも1950年生まれ。

78 小説家、詩人。ロシア。18799〜1837

79 小説家、批評家。1859〜1935

80 小説家。1864〜1909

81 小説家。1867〜1916

82 小説家。1909〜1948

83 1982年。ウディ・アレンをキャラクターに起用したコマーシャル・フィルムもつくられた。

84 吉本隆明（1924〜2011）など。

85 Not Educated, Employed or Trained.

86 小説家。アメリカ。1922〜2007

87 カート・ヴォネガット・ジュニア（伊藤典夫訳）早川書房、1973年（*Slaughterhouse-5 or the Children's Crusade: a Duty with Death*, 1969.）

88 ミュージシャン。イギリス。1940〜1980。元ビートルズ。反戦運動でも知られる。ファンを名乗る男に射殺される。

89 小説家。1924〜1970。自衛隊にクーデターを呼び掛けたが失敗し、切腹によって自殺。

90 小説家。アメリカ。1947年生まれ

91 柴田元幸訳、新潮社、2014年（*Man In The Dark*, 2008.）

92 建築家。1956年生まれ。

93 1992年講談社刊

94 小説家、イタリア。1923〜1985

95 ミラン・クンデラ。小説家。フランス。1929年チェコ生まれ。

96 同著「現代建築から」の章から。朝日文庫、朝日新聞出版、1998年

97 哲学者。フランス。1929〜2007。『象徴交換と死』（*L'Échange Symbolique et la Mort*, 1976)、『湾岸戦争は起こらなかった』（*La Guerre du Golfe n'a pas eu Lieu*, 1991）など。

98 詩人、小説家。アメリカ。1922〜1969

99 Novelist. France. 1871-1922.

100 Shueisha Publishing, 2002.

101 Magazine *SHINKENCHIKU Japan Architect*, April, 2009.

99 小説家。イギリス。1947年インド生まれ。パキスタンでコピーライターをしていた時期もある。

100 論創社、2014年

101 小説家。フランス。1871〜1922

102 鈴木道彦訳、第1篇 〜 第7篇、集英社、1996〜2001年（*À la recherche du temps perdu*, 1913-1927）

103 集英社新書、2002年

104 『新建築』2009年4月号

current   "Portrait In Number"

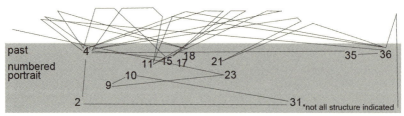

past
numbered
portrait

[fig. 1]

Paris   "Hopscotch"

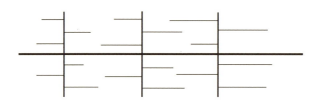

Buenos Aires   *not all structure indicated
[fig. 2]

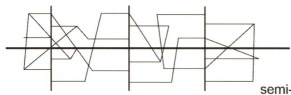

tree structure

[fig. 3]

semi-ratice structure
*not only as streets but also semiotic

[fig. 4]

182   Chapter 2——— *The Planning behind Literature*

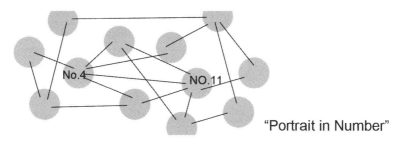

[fig. 5]

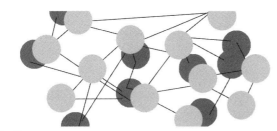

[fig. 6]

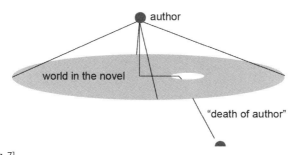

[fig. 7]

文学の計画——第2章

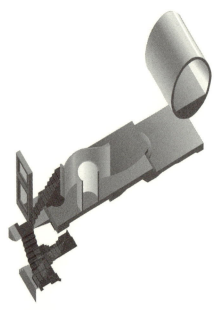

[fig. 8]

[fig. 9]

[fig. 10]

184   Chapter 2———— *The Planning behind Literature*

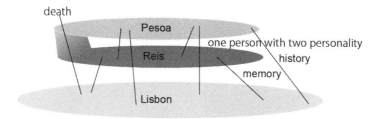

[fig. 11]

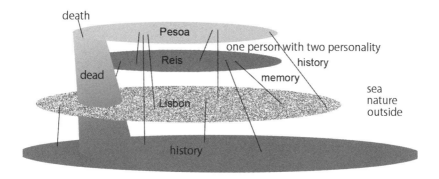

[fig. 12]

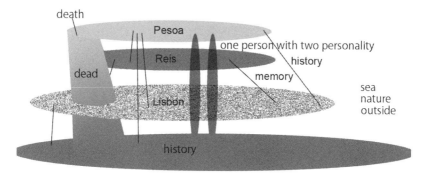

[fig. 13]

文学の計画――第２章　*185*

[fig. 14]

[fig. 15]

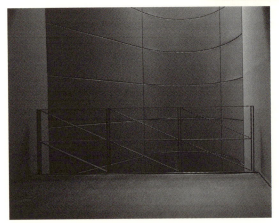

[fig. 16]

186   Chapter 2——— *The Planning behind Literature*

[fig. 17]

[fig. 18]

文学の計画——第2章　　*187*

Chapter Three

Film

1. Moscow —*Four Timelines*

The Embassy of Japan in Moscow holds an event called *J-FEST* every year in able to introduce contemporary Japanese culture such as manga and animation, which fascinates young people. I have participated in the event several times myself. In 2011, I made a short film with a team from Kyoto Seika University, and presented it in Moscow.

It did not have a story. *J-FEST* is more like a festival than an exhibition, and as such it is pretty difficult to make a quiet environment for the audience to watch the film. It was also a kind of gathering for Russian girls and boys who cosplay. The setting makes it difficult to comprehend and appreciate architectural drawings and works of literature, so I made a point of bringing a short film instead. Four screens for four films were projected horizontally at the same time. One score, and no lines. The films ended every five minutes, and were played repeatedly.

Four screens for four spaces, Russia, Moscow, Japan and Kyoto. One world projected on the four screens. Four timelines for four places, and a world after 11 March 2011 (a date now commonly referred to as "3/11" in

第3章

映　画

1.　モスクワ──4つのタイムライン

　モスクワの、日本大使館が主宰するJ–FESTというイベントがある。日本の現代文化を、マンガやアニメなどモスクワの若いひとたちにも人気の「コンテンツ」を中心に紹介する。これに何度か参加した。2011年には、京都精華大学のチームで制作したショート・ムービーを持って行った。

　劇映画ではない。J–FESTはフェスティバルであって、展覧会でもないので、静かな環境で長い時間をかけて見てもらうという形式は似合わない。日本のアニメに憧れてコスプレをしているロシアの美少女たちが歩きまわっているようなイベントだ。建築案でも小説でもなく、映像をつくっていったのも、同じ理由による。

　4つの画面を横並びに同時に映す。音楽はひとつ、セリフはない。長さは5分間、それを繰り返す。ロシア／モスクワ／日本／京都という4つの空間あるいは世界という名の共通の空間。それぞれの時間あるいは『3.1

189

Japan).

Four screens were dedicated to these places, however, each screen was not fixed on any place or time. Images of the afflicted areas of 3/11 were projected on one screen, and then moved to another screen, and occasionally shown on all screens. In the next moment, darkness filled all the screens.

I wrote a screenplay using the spreadsheet software Excel. The program was never intended for screenplays, but it is useful in composing for four screens that need to be synchronized, and work together [fig. 19] (p. 228).

One box has five seconds, and there are 60 boxes in total, making up five minutes for the film.

The boxes are classified into five image categories: 1) turning to blackness; 2) the scene in Moscow; 3) the scene of 3/11 disaster projected on a wall; 4) messages in Japanese, Russian and English; 5) "a protagonist" in a landscape of reality projected in Moscow and Kyoto [fig. 20] (p. 228).

These five categories appear in each timeline in numerical sequences. The numerical sequences have common multiples so some frames of pictures would be synchronized with the other pictures in the common multiples. Three out of four timelines would have three synchronized frames turning black when the film is halfway. All four frames would synchronize to project one large picture of the 3/11 disaster at the end of the spreadsheet. All frames turn to darkness, and the film ends [fig. 21-25] (p. 229).

Various accounts of time and space which appear in the film are sometimes synchronized to change to a different scene. This structure is similar to what we have found in several novels in the previous chapter.

This film visualizes the structure with four screens. It can also be visualized as a drama film utilizing only one screen.

The films by Alejandro Iñárritu[1] show us this possibility.

190   Chapter 3———*Film*

1』以降の今という時間。

　それらを映し出すために、4つの画面を用意したわけだが、ひとつの画面にひとつの場所や時間を固定して割り振ったのではない。たとえば3.11の被災地の映像が、ある画面から別の画面へと移動しながら映しだされ、時にそれは4つの画像すべてを覆い尽くす。あるいは別の瞬間、ある画面がただ闇を映し、次にすべてをその闇に飲み込む。

　この映像の脚本を、僕はEXCELを使って書いた。EXCELは誰もが知る「表計算用ソフトウエア」だ。脚本用ではない。だが4つの画面を5秒毎に入れ替え、時にシンクロするような《script＝脚本》を構成するには適していた。[fig. 19]（p. 228参照）が、その《script＝脚本》だ。

　左から右へ、5秒毎に1コマ、それが60個まで5分間分ある。上下に4段、それぞれの段がひとつの画面を意味する。

　ひとつのコマは5つの性格にわけて分類されていて、それは■■□■□に色分けされている。「P」すなわち「主人公」がその画面のなかに配される場合もある [fig. 20]（p. 228参照）。

　■■□■□は、それぞれの段《それぞれの画面》に、ある数列規則とともに現れる。数列は公倍数を持つので、その公倍数ごとに他の画面とシンクロする。左側から時間が立ち、ちょうど中間ほどで、3つの画面が「■」すなわち「暗転」でシンクロする。右端、すなわち5分間のムービーの最後の近くで、4つすべての画面が「□」すなわち3.11震災後の風景をひとつの大きな画面として写しだし、次の瞬間にはすべてが暗転して終了する（■）[fig. 21-25]（p. 229参照）。

　この映像作品に現れるのは、それぞれの時間、別々の空間であり、そしてそれが時にシンクロして違う風景に変化する様子である。その構造は、先の章に示した様々な小説の構造に近い。

　その構造をここでは4つの画面を使って映像化したが、同じような構造をひとつの画面で、劇映画としてつくり上げることもできるだろう。

　アレハンドロ・イニャリトゥ監督による映画作品群は、そのことをよく示している。

2. The Magic of Film
—"Cutting" and "Editing (Montage)"

The film *Amores Perros* by Iñárritu consists of three storylines. They develop simultaneously and alternate on screen.

A robber commits the sin of coveting his brother's wife. Something happens to Valeria, a beautiful and sensual model. It tells the story of an elderly man who collects garbage, and his love for his dog. These three stories progress fragmentally and alternate.

In the beginning of the film, a car collision happens and suggests a connection between the stories, but nobody knows for sure. Later, the collision appears again in the film so that we get to know the three stories that intermingle with each other in the traffic accident.

This kind of a "designed structure" can be found in the literature of today as we have seen in many examples. However, it would work better in a film that combines visual expression with audio.

In designing architecture, the visual sense is the most prevalent. We can perceive the relationship between spaces, the results of movement and functional efficiency through visual imagination. Actually, we first recognize space visually. Sound, smell, and touch follow suit. We shouldn't regard various senses as less important, but nevertheless, we say that architectural space is visually recognized at first. That is why architecture is recorded or expressed through visual media as drawings or perspectives.

Spaces emerge one after another when we actually experience a work of architecture. Amid the "one after another" sequentiality of the development of the spatial story, some scenes have little relation to the story. The scenes jump into the story like a landscape viewed through a window, or some objects seen through a door to another room.

In a work of architecture called *Amores Perros*, three rows create spaces

192   Chapter 3——*Film*

2. 映画の魔術——「カット」と「編集（モンタージュ）」

イニャリトゥ監督の映画『アモーレス・ペロス[2]』には、３つのストーリーがあり、それらが同時進行的に次々に現れる。

強盗犯罪者で、兄の妻を愛するという「罪」も犯す青年の物語。美しく官能的なモデル、バレリアをめぐる出来事。犬に自身の最上の愛を注ぎながら、ごみ収集の仕事をする初老の男についてのストーリー。これら３つの物語が、断片的に交互に現れる。

冒頭に交通事故のシーンがあり、それが映画全体の物語を統率するように暗示されるが、詳細はわからない。やがて再度同じ事故のシーンが現れ、そこで観客は３つのストーリーがこの事故によって深く交錯することを知る。

このような「仕組まれた構造」はすでに多くの例に見てきた通り、現代文学においては常套手段とすら言ってもよい。だが映画というビジュアルな、そして聴覚を伴う表現においてそれが現れる時、新鮮な衝撃が生じる。

建築を設計する時、第一義的に考察する感覚は、ビジュアルだ。空間と空間との関係、ひとの動き（動線）に伴う効果、そして機能的な効率性すらも、視覚的な想像力で感知できる。そして実際、空間がそこにあるとき、まずは視覚的にそれを認知する。もちろん、音や匂い、あるいは触覚がすぐにそこに参加してくるだろう。それら様々な感覚を、決して過小評価することはできない。だがそれでも、建築空間は、「最初」としては、ビジュアルに表現され認知されるものだと言ってそう間違いではないだろう。その証左として、建築は図面／パースペクティブといったビジュアル表現で記録／表現されるという事実がある。

建築を実際に体験するとき、空間は「次から次へ」と順次現れる。その「次から次へ」の空間的な物語展開の間に、時々その物語とは関係がないように見える風景が挿入される。風景は窓の外のものとして、あるいは別の部屋のそれとして、入り込んでくる。

『*Amores Perros*』という名の建築には、３つの空間系列が平行して配置

parallel to each other. These parallel rows are isolated so it seems not to have any cross point, but it may share an unexpected accidental space.

An experience of film has no difference from a memory of architectural space. People watch what is happening in the scenery and share the experience. In films, time can be shortened and extended, and there is no limit on the space which can be instantly visited through editing and camera work. In real architecture, that is something we cannot do.

It might take years for something to happen. The transfer in real space takes a longer time than in films.

Experiences that are limited in real architecture can easily appear in a film because a film has processes called "cutting" and "editing."

If you shoot everything in one cut, the film has to be limited spatially and temporally. If B happened five hours after A in a one-cut, a camera must continue to shoot for five hours, and B would be projected five hours after A. "Cutting" and "editing" can make it shorter, or play with rearranging the order altogether, such as having B appear on screen before A.

Iñárritu has established his ideal narrative for film by taking maximum advantage of these methods, as can be shown in *Amores Perros*, *Babel*, *21 Gram* among other films. The narrative represents multiple timelines and happenings in various spaces.

Does this only work for film?

Could the processes of "cutting" and "editing" be useful for architecture as well?

We should study his films more closely to consider these possibilities.

されている。別の系列に属し交わることもないと思われていたものが、突然アクシデンタルな空間を共有する。それが、この映画の空間／時間的な構造だ。

　映画の経験と建築空間の記憶とは酷似している。風景のなかで出来事は起こり、ひとはそれを目撃し、半ばその出来事を共有する。とはいえ映画では建築と異なり、限られた時間（上映時間）のなかにそれ以上に長い時間が流れ、幾つもの場所に瞬時に行くことができる（カメラが切り替わる）。建築での経験は、そうはいかない。何かが起こるには長い時間がかかるかも知れず、場所の移動には制約がある。

　建築では制約がかかる経験が、映画では容易に生じ得るのは、「カット」と「編集」という過程があるあるからだ。

　ムービー・カメラをオンにしたまますべてを撮り続け、そしてそれをそのまま映し出すのであれば、映画は建築と同じように現実の時間と空間の制約を受けるしかない。ＢがＡの５時間後に起きたなら、カメラは５時間撮影を続け、上映時にもＡから５時間を経なければＢは映し出されることはない。しかしカットと編集さえあれば、Ａの直後にＢを見たり、あるいはＢを見た後にＡを経験することすら可能になる。

　『Amores Perros』のみならず、『Babel』や『21gram』など多くの映画でイニャリトゥ監督は、この映画の特質を活かしきって独自の話法を確立した。それによって、複数の時間の流れ、別々の場所での出来事が観客の目の前に差し出される。

　だがこれは本当に映画に限った話法なのだろうか？

　建築においても、この優れた話法、そしてそれを可能にする「カット」と「編集」という手法は、有効なのではないだろうか？

　そのことを考えるためにも、もう少しイニャリトゥ監督の映画を見てみよう。

映　画——第3章

3. Time in Reality / Space in Illusion

Birdman (The Unexpected Virtue of Ignorance) won the Academy Award for Best Picture in 2015. It doesn't represent various times and spaces like *Amores Perros*. The setting is limited to in and around a theater on Broadway in New York where there is a general-probe. Iñárritu shows us a story limited in time and space, captured through a mobile perspective and for a length of time much longer than actual projection time, like one long take with no cuts. It looks like a one-cut film.

Many directors have used this method called "long take" using no or few cuts. Actually, *Birdman* is not a one-cut at all. It has a lot of hidden cuts in superb timings, and is edited with precision.

It cuts when a camera goes through the dark space of the entrance while it follows the protagonist. Time passes quickly after a camera looks up at the night sky following a character until dawn breaks. The camera following tracing the protagonists face when he passes another character then begins to follow that character. This camera work creates a viewpoint that moves freely like a bird, and compresses the timespan of several days into the time it projects.

We watch what happens in and around a theater during the course of several days, in several hours. This is similar to relation between experience and memory in architecture.

We surely experience spaces in and out of the theater around 44th Street and Broadway when we watch *Birdman*. We see a world on and behind a stage and inhale the air of a bar in New York. There is a camera in

3. リアルな時間／幻想の空間

『バードマンあるいは（無知がもたらす予期せぬ奇跡）』は2015年にアカデミー作品賞を受賞した映画だ。『Amores Perros』のように様々な場所の様々な時間が現れたりはしない。場所はニューヨークのブロードウェイにある劇場と、そのごく近所のみ。時間もある演劇のゲネプロあたりから公演初日直後のときまでに限られる。

その限定された場所と時間における物語、とはいえ動きまわる視点および上映時間よりはずっと長い時間によって捉えられる物語を、イニャリトゥはカットなしの長回し撮影のように見せる。つまり、最初から最後まで、ひとつのカメラが休みなくずっと撮影を続けそれがそのまま映画になっているかのように見せるのだ。

カットを入れない長回しという手法を取り入れる監督は珍しくない。しかし、最初から最後までひと続きの長回しというのはあまりない。そして、実のところは『Birdman』もまったく、「ひと続きの長回し」などではない。絶妙な瞬間に隠れたカットが多数入り、それらが注意深く編集されている。

たとえば、カメラが主人公を追ってバーに入るとき、暗い入口空間を通るところで画面は暗転し、実際にはカットが入る。登場人物の目線を追ってカメラが夜空を見上げ、直ぐに空が明るくなることで時間が素早く過ぎる。あるいは主人公を追っていたカメラは、他の登場人物とすれ違う瞬間から、回れ右してその登場人物の方を追いかけ始める。こうすることで、視点は鳥の眼のように自由に動き回ることができ、数日間の時間を上映時間のなかに畳み込むことが可能になる。

建物の内外の場所で数日の間に起こる出来事を、数時間で見る。これは建築の経験と記憶の関係に似ている。

この映画を見るときたしかに、私たちはブロードウェイ44丁目辺りにある劇場内外の場所を経験している。ステージの世界の表裏を見、ニューヨークのバーの空気を吸っている。私たちの眼の代わりにカメラがうろつ

映画——第3章　*197*

place of our eyes. The experience is edited in the same way our memory is made in the process. Think about the process of our perception of reality. We recall days not as the entire timespan, but as an edited and shortened film including imagination.

The protagonist remembers his days on Broadway. He remembers a character named *Birdman* who acted in a Hollywood film. *Birdman* suddenly appears behind the protagonist and gives him advice. This *Birdman* is just a figment of the protagonist's imagination, just like "Boggy" who advises the protagonist in the film *Play It Again, Sam* directed by Woody Allen.[2] It is someone who exists in the protagonist, so it must be part of the protagonist. The actual protagonist has a dialogue with the imaginary protagonist, himself.

One shot and the compression of time resembles the experience and memory you get from architecture. However, can we talk about imaginary experiences and memory in architecture? Can architects design imaginary spaces?

We should ask what an "imaginary space" is.

4. A City in Your Brain

Charlie Kaufman[3] who directed the film *Synecdoche, New York*, is also known for writing the screenplays to *Being John Malkovich* and Eternal Sunshine. He is proficient at mixing illusion with reality.

The protagonist in *Synecdoche, New York* is a theater director by the name of Caden Cotard, played by Philip Seymour Hoffman. Cade, a middle aged guy whose wife and child left him, whose recent performance was met with severe criticism, is now frightened by the approach of his old age. Armed with a grant, he is determined to create the play of his lifetime about New York, a city which he lives in and loves. He wants to represent the entirety of New York, so he begins to build the city not as

198   Chapter 3——— *Film*

きまわり、私たちがその風景を記憶する過程とおなじように編集がなされる。現実における私たちの知覚の過程を考えてみればよい。私たちは数日という時間を見たままにまるごと記憶するのではなく、他者の視点も想像的に取り込んだ上で、編集された短編映画のように思い出すのだ。

この映画に描かれた数日間の時間にも、記憶という別の時間は流れこむ。ここではそれは、主人公がハリウッドでかつて演じたヒーローのバードマンだ。バードマンは不意に主人公の背後に現れ、語りかけ、忠告する。ウディ・アレンの映画『ボギー！　俺も男だ』で主人公にアドバイスする「ボギー」同様、バードマンも主人公の幻想だ。主人公の過去の存在なのだから、主人公自身だとも言える。リアルな主人公と、幻想の主人公が対話する。

カットなしのように見えるワン・ショット、そのなかに畳み込まれた時間と空間。それは確かに建築の経験と記憶に似ている。だが、幻想はどうだろうか？　建築家は幻想の空間を設計し得るか？

そもそも、幻想の空間とはどのようなものだろうか？

4．脳内都市

『脳内ニューヨーク』(2008) を監督したチャーリー・カウフマン[3]は、『マルコヴィッチの穴』や『エターナル・サンシャイン』の脚本家としても知られる。つまり、幻想と現実とが入り交じる物語を書くのに長けた作家だ。

『脳内ニューヨーク』は演劇家を主人公とする物語だ。主人公の名はケイデン・コタードといい、フィリップ・シーモア・ホフマンがこれを演じる。中年男のケイデンは妻と子に去られ、演劇作品を酷評され、自らの老いに怯えている。彼はある助成金を得たのを契機に、一世一代の演劇を創りだそうと決意する。それは彼が暮し愛したニューヨークの物語だ。ニューヨークをまるごと表現したいと考え始めた彼は、舞台の上の小さな背景としてではなく、廃屋と思しき巨大な建物のなかに、もはやセットと

映　画───第3章　*199*

a small background, but as a ridiculously huge mock-up in an abandoned warehouse.

It is a huge miniature of New York. Caden is unable to realize his idea for the coming 17 years, and finds himself an old man. Even after a mock-up has been created, it has become unclear if the miniature is a real stage setting, or just an illusion in his brain. We are watching something projected in his brain, which gives us a distorted perception of New York.

Was a huge miniature of New York really built in the warehouse? It might be empty, and Cade might have wasted 17 years of his life for nothing.

In the process of losing reality and clearness, we can extract the following truth:

It is possible for illusion to be built in reality.

New York exists in real as a city space where many people live, stay, and memorize their own "New York." The longer you experience the city space, the more unique the memory is shaped, and another image of "New York" emerges in the mind. Not only Caden in New York, but everyone depicts their city in their mind.

"Another New York" is an "image" by Henri Bergson[4] used in his theory of philosophy. It's not an existing object, and not subjective consciousness, but something in between. It can also be built as an actual city in an abandoned warehouse.

"Abandoned warehouse" refers to the space losing its function. "Another city" means that the city is revived from memory. If it can be called "illusion," its space can surely be designed.

Synecdoche, New York is titled "Inside the Brain New York" in Japanese.

200   Chapter 3——*Film*

は呼びがたい大きさのニューヨークをつくり始める。

　ガラス屋根の下の、巨大なミニチュアとしてのニューヨーク。この建設と、一向に演劇としてまとまらない彼の構想のせいで、17年という長い月日が過ぎ、気がつけばケイデンは老人の域に差し掛かっている。巨大なセットとしてのニューヨークは建設されたが、それが本当の舞台装置なのか、それともケイデンの頭のなかにある幻想のニューヨークなのか、次第に区別が付き難くなっていく。現実のニューヨークが、ケイデンの歪んだ知覚で彼の脳内に再生されている、それを観客は見ているだけなのだろうか。

　そもそもガラス屋根の下に、本当にニューヨークは構築されたのかどうか？　そこは今も本当はがらんどうで、ケイデンはただ無為に17年を過ごしただけなのかもしれない。

　現実性があいまいになっていくこの状況の中で、こう言うことは可能だ。

　幻想はこのようにして、リアルに構築される可能性がある、と。

　ニューヨークは現実に存在する都市空間だ。多くのひとがそこに暮らし、あるいは滞在し、それぞれのニューヨークを記憶する。この都市空間での経験が深くなれば、記憶は独自のかたちをとり始め、やがて脳内にもうひとつのニューヨークが像を結ぶ。ニューヨークのケイデンのみならず、誰もがそうして、自分が暮らす町や村の形象を脳内に構築しているはずだ。

　「もうひとつのニューヨーク」は、アンリ・ベルクソンがその哲学の理論のなかで言ったような意味での、イマージュである。客観的に実在しているそのものではなく、かといって主観のうちにのみあるのではなく、その両者の間に存在するもの。そしてそれは、廃屋のなかのもうひとつの都市として、リアルに構築もされうる。

　「廃屋」とは、機能を捨象した空間のことだ。「もうひとつの都市」とは、記憶の風景から再生された都市のことだ。そのようなものが幻想であるのなら、幻想の空間を設計することは十分に可能なのではないだろうか？

　『脳内ニューヨーク』の原題にあるSynecdocheとは統辞法における「提

I think the Japanese title is better than the original, though New York works variously as a synecdoche for another New York, because this is a film whose illusion is built by working in images, not in words. We can find the possibility in another type of images besides literal character, syntax for example.

5. The Camera which Captures Inter-Subjectivity in Space

Where is the camera shooting from? It is often situated as a third party viewer that sees what happens, but in some cases it functions as the eyes of the character.

Caden, a protagonist in *Synecdoche, New York*, becomes gradually more insane. Is the camera shooting a real scene, or is it Caden who is experiencing an illusion? The director, Kaufman, intentionally made it seem vague.

In *Being John Malkovich* (1999), the perspective of the camera has a vital meaning because anyone can see the world from the perspective of John Malkovich by putting his or her head through a hole in the wall.

John Malkovich is a real actor, and plays himself in the film. Many people want to put their head into the hole to be Malkovich, a Hollywood celebrity. He is well connected, so any guy who wants to meet his favorite actress can do so by putting their head into the hole. One guy and his female boss come up with an idea to earn money by using the hole.

It is a ridiculous concept that someone can put their consciousness into another person's head. However, could it happen in reality? The technology to realize this, including glasses and cameras which connect to internet have been explored. We have been able to watch the world through the glasses which someone else watches. We are not "being

202 Chapter 3———*Film*

喩」を意味する。確かに、この映画のなかの様々なニューヨークが、別の
ニューヨークを提喩しているとは言える。それでも、邦題のほうが原題よ
りも優れているように思う。なぜならこれは映画であり、映像の力によっ
て幻想が構築されているものだ。言語ではない。映像の、言語的な性格
（たとえば統辞法）から逃れたところにこそ、その力を見出すことができる。

5. カメラ、空間の主観性として

　カメラはどこから見ているか？　映画の場合、それは最大に重要だ。そ
れは第三者的に状況を眺める位置にある場合も多いが、登場人物の眼とし
て、何かを見ることもある。
　『脳内ニューヨーク』では、主人公ケイデンは次第に狂気に蝕まれてい
く。カメラがリアルな風景を見ているのか、それともケイデンの目として
幻想を写しているのか。カウフマン監督はその両者を意図的に混在させる。

　カウフマンが脚本を書いた『マルコヴィッチの穴』（1999）では、視点は
もっと重要な役割を果たす。なにしろ、ある壁の穴に頭を突っ込むと、誰
でも「ジョン・マルコヴィッチ」として世界を見ることになる、というの
だから。
　ジョン・マルコヴィッチは実在の俳優の名前で、この映画中にも本人役
で現れる。多くの人がその壁のなかに頭を突っ込んで、ハリウッド・ス
ターのマルコヴィッチになりたがる。マルコヴィッチは誰もが知る有名俳
優で、だから壁の穴に頭を突っ込めば憧れの女優とだって会える。その壁
がある部屋で働く男とその女上司が、この穴を使って金儲けを企む。

　他人の頭のなかに自分の意識を突っ込むとは、いかにも映画らしい荒唐
無稽な話だ。だが本当にあり得ないだろうか？　ネットワークに接続され
たメガネやカメラを使えば、これに近いことができるテクノロジーは既に
開発されている。つまり他の誰かの目に映った世界を、自分がかけたメガ
ネで見ることはできる。このテクノロジーで「マルコヴィッチになる」こ

John Malkovich," but seeing the iconic actress or actor in front of us. So what can be done in real architectural space without Information Technology?

Before answering this question, let us look at another example of point of view in film.

Wings of Desire (Der Himmel über Berlin, 1987), directed by Wim Wenders,[5] is set in Berlin after World War II. Angels soar above the city.

Men cannot cross the Berlin Wall, but angels can. The camera is set from the angel's perspective as it flies in the sky beyond the Wall.

The angels can see the suffering of the people living in Berlin. There have even been accounts of angels trying to stop people from committing suicide. But no one, with the exception of small children, ever notices the existence of the angels. In the film, the angles have a one-way perspective on the human characters. The audience shares the point of view of the angels, not the people.

Quentin Tarantino's[6] stories feel like comic books. His narratives have outstanding technique. Let us have a look at three different points of view appearing in middle of *Jackie Brown* (1997). Jackie, the protagonist, passes bunches of money to a gangster in a fitting room at a department store. Tarantino first shot it from the perspective of Jackie's, then from the gangster, and finally from a guy who is romantically involved with Jackie. An event in one timeline was shot from three different places, and then connected. The audience witnesses the event through the eyes of three characters.

We should look at the film, *Interstellar* (2014), directed by Christopher Nolan.[7]

It is a SF film about the near future which is filled with intensity. Most of all, the scenes in which the protagonist strays into four-dimensional space in the universe far from the earth are very impressive. It is

とはできなくとも、あこがれの女優や俳優を目の前に見ることはできるだろう。では電脳テクノロジーを使わない建築空間ではどうだろうか？

　この問への答えを考える前に、もう少し映画内の視点の例を見てみよう。

　ヴィム・ヴェンダース監督の『ベルリン・天使の詩』(1987) は、まだ壁によって東西に分割されていた頃のベルリンが舞台だ。この街の上空に、天使がいる。

　ひとはこのベルリンの壁の向こう側に行くことはできない。だが天使はむろん自由だ。その視点は壁の遙か上空を、思うがままに行き来する。

　天使は、ベルリンで苦悩とともに生きるひとびとの姿を見る。自死を決意するひとの隣に降りてくることもある。だが天使の存在に気がつくものは——子ども以外には——いない。天使から人間への、一方的な視線だけがそこにはある。そしてこの映画を見るものは、人間の視線ではなく、天使の視線こそを共有する。

　クエンティン・タランティーノは、通俗的な映画監督だ。お話はいつでもバカバカしい。だが、その語り方は極めて上質に技巧的だ。たとえば『ジャッキー・ブラウン』(1997)。この映画のなかほどに、主人公ジャッキーが、デパートの婦人服売り場の試着室で巨額の金をギャングに渡すシーンがある。このシーンを、タランティーノは、最初にジャッキーの視点から、次にギャングの視点から、最後にジャッキーに思いを寄せる男の視点から、描いてみせる。つまりはひとつの時間を、3つの別々の場所から見て、それらを繋げる。観客は3人の視点からことの成り行きを見ることになる。

　クリストファー・ノーラン監督の『インターステラー』(2014) の例も見ておこう。

　この、驚くべき映像の力に満ちた近未来SF映画のなかで、ひときわ強い印象を与えるのは、主人公が宇宙の果てで、4次元の空間にまよい込むシーンだ。4次元の空間を人間が視覚的に描くことは不可能だ。我々は3

impossible to visually draw four-dimensional space. We can do it only with our imagination or in mathematic theory, because we live in a three-dimensional world. Nolan visualized and pictured it using a "tesseract" which is the mathematic model of four-dimensions in *Interstellar*. The visualization fits the four-dimensional space that is captured in our imagination. We can relate to another time by entering geometry that time adds another dimension to. The protagonist looks at his daughter and himself in the past. Imaginary space is visualized as a model in the images.

We cannot have images like this in reality. Still, we can design the same images in a structure which resembles the pictures in imagination.

A perspective cannot be physically free from the body. It can see something from where the body is at the moment. Is a man's sight just a pulsation of nerves? It is an electrical signal from the eyes to the brain, and also an act of cognition that is called "noesis"[8] by Husserl.[9] Not only in the present, but also in memory can we foresee the flow into consciousness. The landscape of another place would be overlaid here.

We saw an example of consciousness flowing into another consciousness in *Being John Malkovich*. In reality we feel like we share a consciousness with someone when we enter their room for example. We feel embarrassed or confused because it feels like looking at someone from the inside, when we usually look at them from the outside. And we might see the landscape through a window of the room by borrowing the perspective of the host.

Not only "angels in Berlin," but we also have a view from the sky where we live because we have known the landscape from the top of a tall building, and have looked down the street from a crossing bridge. Thus we can imagine what a view from the sky looks like in our vicinity. The perspective of angels can be designed as a bridge or a passage over a

206   Chapter 3——*Film*

次元の空間で生きている。4次元は数学理論的に、あるいは想像的に思い描くしかない。『インターステラー』では数学的な4次元モデルである正八胞体「テッセラクト」を用いてそれを視覚化し、映し出している。そしてそれは、感覚が想像的に捉える4次元によく合致する。時間がもう一つの次元として加わった幾何学に入り込むことで、別の時間とかかわることができる。主人公はここで過去の自分や娘の姿を見る。ここに、想像的な空間が模式的に視覚化されている。

　現実には、これらの視点はつくりえない。だが、構造的に同一な、そして想像的に近似する視点を設計することは十分に可能だ。
　視点は物理的には、その持ち主の身体から自由になることはない。そのとき、その場所の身体からしか、物事を見ることができない。だが、人間の視点は、単にそのような神経的な感覚に過ぎないのか？　視点とは、目から脳へ神経的な信号であると同時に、意識としての作用——フッサール[8]によってノエシス[9]と呼ばれたもの——である。意識には、現在という時間だけではなく、記憶や予感が流れこむ。「ここ」という場所のなかに、別の場所の風景が重なりあいもする。
　『マルコヴィッチの穴』では、他人の視点に入り込む意識が描かれた。これも非現実的な設定だが、それでも普通ひとは、たとえば自分の親や友人、あるいは恋人の部屋に入ったとき、その部屋の主の意識をかすかに共有する感覚を持つのではないか？　いつもは外から見ているそのひとを、なかから見るような気がして気恥ずかしさと戸惑いを覚えたりしないか？
　その部屋の窓からの風景を、部屋の主の視点を思いながら見るのではないだろうか？
　ベルリンの天使ならずとも、私たちは空から自分たちが住む街を見る視点を持っている。というのも、高層ビルの最上階から見下ろす都市の風景を私たちは知っているし、自動車道路を歩道橋で渡りながら見下ろすこともある。そしてそうした経験を元に、今自分がいる空間を、上から見るつもりで想像することができる。天使の視点を、吹抜け空間の上を飛ぶ橋や

void.

We cannot see what is happening at the same time from various angles like in *Jackie Brown*. On the other hand, it is not so difficult to see space from different angles by taking one's time.

We cannot design four-dimensional architectural space. We cannot move on a timeline as we wish. Besides, it is always possible to see where we were from where we could be next as we can visit a school we have graduated. Relationships between space and time essentially work like this: No one lives only in the present. Everyone keeps looking at the past through places.

"Other minds" is a term in philosophy. It's an antonym to "ego." It is not just "other" but something found as "ego" in others.

For example, when someone says "my tooth hurts," I can understand what it means, but never feel the pain. However, I have experienced a toothache so I can subjectively feel the pain and cringe when that person twitches in pain.

When we see the opposite side of a river from our side, we can see our side from the opposite side in our imagination. We can see it just as visual with our intuition not as a result of calculation for a perspective image of ourselves from the opposite side.

Husserl explained it with the idea of "inter-subjectivity." Inter-subjectivity emerges in the multiple subjectivities. When I look up at the night sky with my significant other, my subjectivity, the other's subjectivity, and the inter-subjectivity between me and the other see stars. "We" see a shooting star and "we" miss time before dawn. What "inter" means is different from "common" or "shared." For example, inter-subjectivity can emerge between I and a cat. I can imagine the cat's subjectivity to some extent. I can also imagine that the cat can imagine my subjectivity. By looking at the cat's face, I can think that "we" are hungry. Thus I can get a view of "other

廊下で仮想することもできる。

　『ジャッキー・ブラウン』のように、特定の事件を同時に違う角度から見ることはできない。ただし、特定の空間を若干の時間差を伴って違う角度から見ることは、それほど難しくない。

　4次元の建築空間を設計することはできない。時間軸を自由に移動することも不可能だ。だがたとえば自分が卒業した学校を訪ねることができるように、「かつていた場所」を「次にいる場所」から見ることは常に可能である。と言うよりも、時間と空間とは、私たちにとって本質的にそのようなものである。現在にしか生きていないひとはいない。誰もが過去を、場所として見続ける。

　他我という哲学用語がある。自我に対応する言葉だ。他者ではない。他者のうちに見出される我のことだ。たとえば「痛い」という感覚は、本来その身体の持ち主にしかわかりえない。他者が「私の歯が痛い」というとき、私はそれを理解するが、その痛みを神経的に感じ取ることは絶対にできないはずだ。しかし私には、自分の歯が痛かった経験があるので、他者が歯痛に顔を歪めるとき、その「痛い」を半ば主観的に感じることもでき、場合によってはその想像力によって私の顔を歪める。

　川の此方から彼岸を眺めるとき、私たちは彼岸から此方を想像的に眺めることもできる。ここにいる自分が、あちらからはどう見えているのか、それを計算して理解するというのではなく、直感的に、視覚的に、感じることがきっと可能だ。

　フッサールはこれを、間主観性という概念とともに説明した。私に主観があるように、他者にも主観がある。それら複数の主観の間に生まれるものが、間主観性だ。恋人と夜空を見上げるとき、星を見るのは私の主観であり、恋人の主観であり、私と恋人の間に生じる主観だ。私たちは流れ星を見つめ、私たちは夜が明けるのを惜しむ。「間」というのは、共通の、とか、共有する、というのとは少し違う。たとえば間主観性は、私と猫の間にも生まれ得る。私は猫の主観をある程度想像し得る。猫が私の主観を想像しているだろうと、想像することもできる。私は猫の顔を見ながら、私たちは腹が減ったな、と思うことが可能だろう。だから私は、猫から見

映　画──第3章　*209*

minds" in imagination as I can picture what the cat thinks of me.

Architectural space can have the same scenery as film only if we think about it in terms of "inter-subjectivity." Film is architectural space, shot by "inter-subjectivity."

6. "Future" is Another Name for "Memory"

Interstellar is a science fiction film set in the near future. People begins to believe that the end of the world is inevitable as a result of climate anomalies becoming increasingly more extreme. No one can survive on earth. The protagonist has to travel through space to find another hospitable planet.

The future pictured in most films has been bleak since *Metropolis* (1927). It might simply be because a film depicting crisis will be more interesting than showing a happy world. They often intend to criticize the situation of the present which can trigger a dystopia. We also feel like a bleak future is more nestled in reality than a happy world.

As I have mentioned, the global environment is facing critical issues. Earth's population is still increasing beyond the capacity that nature allows. Some issues could be solved by improving science and technology. On the other hand, unknown and severe issues are brought to light every day.

La Jetée (1962, directed by Chris Marker[10]) also shows us a dismal future.

First, the film shows several images that a man recollects as a memory when he was a kid. The kid saw a guy was killed in an airport.

Later, World War III plunged the world into ruin. No life but death prevailed on the ground because too much residual radiation remains. A handful of people have survived underground in Paris. Scientists have been experimenting with time travel in order to acquire resources from

210   Chapter 3——*Film*

た私の像を得るようにして、他我の視点を想像的に得ることができる。

　他我の作用を考えれば、建築の空間にも映画と同様のシーンが浮かび上がる。この言い方は逆かもしれない。本当はこういうべきだろう。

　映画とは、建築の空間を、他我によって撮影したものなのだ。

6. 「未来」とは「記憶」の別の名

　先に例に出した『インターステラー』は近未来を舞台とした物語だった。異常気象が激しくなり、ひとは終末を予感する。地球上では、ひとはもはや生きていけなくなる。居住可能な地球以外の惑星を探しに、主人公は宇宙への旅に出る。

　SF映画に描かれる未来は、概ね暗い。『メトロポリス』(1927) の時から、そうだ。明るい未来を見せるよりも、危機的な状況を描いたほうが、映画として面白くなる。そういう単純な理由はある。あるいはディストピアとしての未来を描くことで、実際にディストピアをつくり出しかねない現在の世界を批判することもできる。だがもうひとつの理由がある。それは、明るい未来よりも暗い未来に、私たちがリアリティを感じるということだ。

　これまでにも述べたが、地球の環境が危機的な状況にあることは間違いない。世界の人口は環境が許容するだろう限度をはるかに超えて増え続けている。様々な科学技術の発展は、医療分野をはじめ多くの問題を解決してはいるだろう。それでも、取り返しのつかぬほどに新たなそして深刻な問題が日々生み出されているに違いない。

　『ラ・ジュテ』(クリス・マルケル監督、1962年) も、暗い未来を描く映画だ。

　最初に、ある男が少年の時に見た風景の記憶が映し出される。少年は空港にいて、ひとが殺されるのを目撃する。

　やがて第3次世界大戦が世界を廃墟に変える。地上は放射線が多く残り、死の場所となった。パリの地下では、少数の人類が生き延びている。そこで科学者たちはタイム・トラベルの実験装置をつくった。過去や未来からエネルギーや薬を持ち帰ることで、生き延びようと考えたのだ。少年時代

the future or past. A man who can never forget an ambiguous memory about an airport succeeds to travel to the past. He arrives at the airport before the outbreak of the war. His memory becomes clear. He witnessed a murder in the airport when he was a little boy. He discovers that the victim was himself. The little boy, himself, watches as he is killed in the future. He thinks the little boy is looking at him, he is watching himself dying...

This story inspired *Twelve Monkeys* (1995), a Hollywood action film. *La Jetée* consists of black and white still picture every few seconds. The story proceeds with no lines but for narration.

In 1962, when *La Jetée* was produced, film in color was mainstream. Nevertheless, Marker decided to go with this format.

We can clearly see what the method has brought. Images that were shown in the beginning appear again in the ending so that future, becomes memories in the film.

Photography was originally a media for memory. It memorizes what I see now and will remember it in the future. Black and white pictures can evoke a sense of distant memories because colors have been lost.

That is why this film evokes such a strange feeling. Has all of this already happened? Even the future beyond World War III has passed, so does this film try to remind us of the future as a memory?

This film creates the effect through a specific method; however, we can generally say that "future means memory."

Not only photography, but also film seemed to be a media just for recording and replaying. Soon, Georges *Méliès*[11] produced a SF film titled *Le Voyage dans la Lune (A Trip to the Moon)* (1902). *Méliès* introduced the concept that magical imagery, as a human face appears on the moon and

の、空港での曖昧な記憶に執着している男が、この時間旅行に成功する。彼は大戦前の空港に行く。そこで彼ははっきりと思い出す。少年時代に、彼は空港でひとりの男が殺されるのを見た。あの殺された男とは自分のことだった。未来から来た自分がこの空港で殺されるところを、少年時代の自分は見たのだ。少年が自分を見ている。自分自身が、自分の死を見ている……。

　この物語は、後にハリウッドでつくられた『12モンキーズ』(1995) の基になった。『12モンキーズ』はアクションもあるエンターテインメント映画だ。それに対して『ラ・ジュテ』は白黒で、しかも写真（静止画）だけで構成されている。映し出される白黒静止画は、数秒ごとに入れ替わっていく。セリフはなく、ナレーションが物語を進めていく。
　製作年の1962年は、もちろんカラー映画が主流である。それにもかかわらず、クリス・マルケル監督はこのような手法をとった。
　この手法が何をもたらしたかは明らかだ。最初に映し出された写真は、最後にもう一度映写される。それによって、未来は記憶になる。

　写真とは、そもそも記憶のためのメディアである。今見ているものを記憶として残し、未来に思い返す。白黒写真は色が失われているぶん、遠い記憶に似た感覚を思い起こさせる。
　だからこの映画を見ていると、不思議な気持ちになる。これはすべて、すでに起こったことなのかもしれない。「第3次世界大戦」以降の未来も、すべて既に過ぎ去った時間で、この映画はそれを思い出させようとでもしているのだろうか？
　この映画は特別な手法を使ってこの効果を生み出しているが、ひょっとしたら、未来というのは確かに記憶のことなのかもしれない。
　写真だけではなく動画もまた、リュミエール兄弟がその仕組を考えた頃、記録とその再生のためだけに役に立つと思われた。だがさっそくジュルジュ・メリエスが『月世界旅行』(1902) というSF映画をつくった。メリエスは、編集という映画特有の作業によって、魔法のような映像——月に

a rocket gets stuck in it, can be produced by "editing," which is the "magic" of film. Media for memory began to tell a story of the future through a method called "cinemagic."

The future told as a story behaves as memory when it is fixated on film. This is a property that film originally has.

It is not only about describing the fictional future of SF. For example, "death" is a future that will come for everyone. Thus a film picturing "death" is telling a story of future in the meaning.

Biutiful (2010) is a film directed by Iñárritu and set in Barcelona. At the beginning, a middle-aged man is with a younger man in a forest. The young man says that they will walk through the forest to another place. The middle aged man is anxious because he has not been there before. The beginning ends like this. The story doesn't connect to the next scene.

The story keeps the middle aged man as the protagonist and moves on. He is an immigrant from Mexico and makes a living by introducing other immigrants and illegal residents to employers. He has a connection with the underworld. On the other hand, he shows his good personality by providing care for poor immigrants. Then he is diagnosed with cancer. He worries about his small children. He can have conversations with dead people and sometimes uses the ability for the benefit of others.

It is a film filled with images of death. The protagonist gives sympathy and gas heaters as gifts to illegal immigrants from China who are working and living in a cold factory. One night, the cheap gas heaters cause incomplete combustion so that all the poor Chinese people are killed by carbon monoxide poisoning. Their employer loads the bodies onto a boat and throws them into the sea. The next morning, TV news reports that a lot of Asian bodies have drifted ashore.

The protagonist's illness keeps getting worse. He gazes absent-mindedly at the bedroom window which is swinging because of the wind, causing

214   Chapter 3——*Film*

ひとのような表情が現れたり、そこにロケットが突き刺さったりするような——をつくり出すことが可能だと考えた。「シネマジック」と呼ばれたその手法で、記憶のためのメディアは未来を物語ることを始めた。

　物語られた未来は、フィルムに定着した途端、記憶としての性質を帯びる。これは映画が本来的に持つ働きだ。

　SFのようなフィクショナルな未来だけではない。たとえば「死」は、誰にとっても間違いなく訪れる未来である。死を描く映画は、その意味で未来を物語っている。

　『*Biutiful*』（2010）はアレハンドロ・イニャリトゥがスペイン・バルセロナを舞台にして撮った映画だ。最初のシーンで、中年の男が、彼よりも若い男とともに森にいる。若い男が、これから森を歩いて別の場所に行くのだという。中年の男はそこには行ったことがないと、不安をのぞかせる。このシーンはそれで終わり、話は次にはつながらない。

　中年の男を主人公とするストーリーが始まる。男はメキシコからの移民で、他の移民や不法滞在者に職などを世話することで生計を立てている。闇組織ともつながりがあるが、彼自身は不遇の移民を思いやる善人であることが知れる。彼は自分がガンに侵されていることを知る。まだ幼い子どもふたりの行く末を案じる。彼は死者と会話をすることができ、時々その能力を他人のために役立てている。

　徹底して死について描いた映画だ。たとえば主人公は、中国からの不法移民たちが、寒い工場で働き生活もそこでしていることに同情し、ストーブを買ってプレゼントする。しかしある晩、その安物のストーブは不完全燃焼を起こし、中国人たちは一酸化炭素中毒で全員死んでしまう。彼らの雇い主は彼らの死体を船に積み、沖合で捨てる。次の朝、テレビは、砂浜にアジア人の死体が大量に打ち上げられていることを報じる。

　主人公の体も、日を追うごとに弱っていく。寝室の窓の雨戸が風に揺れ、閉じては闇をつくり、開いては白い光を導き入れるのを、主人公はぼんや

the room to alternate between darkness and sunlight.

Every shot included in this scene is beautiful. Even the grotesque scene of many bodies cast ashore has a strange beauty to it. The title, *Biutiful* comes from a scene where the protagonist gives the wrong answer when his little daughter asks him about the spelling for "beautiful." It's not correct, not generally understandable but a beautiful moment between the protagonist and his kids. The wrong spelling might have such a meaning.

The scene of the forest we have seen in the beginning appears again in the end of the film and we finally understand what the scene expresses. The young man is the protagonist's father who died young. The protagonist is much older than his father was when he died. The young man is leading the protagonist to where dead people should go. Now we can see why the protagonist was anxious. The protagonist enters the forest. He has died.

We can interpret the timeline of the film in two ways because part of the ending scene has been shown in the beginning as if it posed a riddle. In the first interpretation, the protagonist foresees his own death and decides to spend the last of his days with his children. In the second interpretation, the protagonist has already died. This is a film of a memory of future called death.

7. Imagine the Invisible Space

Film represents "the future" in time and space. Camera works, cutting and editing possesses a magic which can express the future. As I have mentioned, we can apply the magic to real spaces in architecture. What about the image of the future? Can the future really be represented in a real space? How can architecture relate to the future?

りと見ている。

　この光と闇が交互に訪れるシーンを始め、様々なカットが、本当に美しい。海辺に大量の遺体が打ち上げられたという残酷な場面ですら、なぜか不思議な美しさを伴っている。タイトルの『Biutiful』は、主人公が、娘に「美しい」の英語のスペルを聞かれて、間違えて教えてしまう場面から来ている。正しくもなければ一般にも通じない、しかし彼とその子どもたちにとっては確かに美しいもの。そんな意味がこのスペルミスを伴ったタイトルにはこめられているのかもしれない。

　冒頭の森のシーンは映画の最後にもう一度現れる。このとき、私達はそのシーンが何を表していたのかをようやく了解する。若い男は主人公の父親で、若くして死んだ。主人公は父が死んだ歳をとうに超え、そして今死んでゆく。若い男は、死者が向かうべき場所に、主人公を導こうとしているのだ。主人公が不安を見せたのも理解できる。そして、主人公は森のなかを歩いて行く。彼は、死んだのだ。

　最後のこのシーンの一部が、冒頭になぞかけのように示されていたことで、私達はこの映画の時間を二通りに捉えることができる。ひとつは、主人公は自らの死という未来を予感しながらも、子どもとともに最後の時間を生きた。そういう時間だ。もうひとつは、主人公は既に死を迎えていた。これは死という未来の記憶を物語った映画なのだ、と。

7. 見えない空間を夢想せよ

　映画の空間と時間には、このように未来が表れている。それはカメラ、そしてカットと編集という手法があるからこそ表現しえた未来だ。そしてこれもすでに述べたとおり、これら映画の手法自体は、現実の空間にも当てはめて考えることができる。では未来の姿についてはどうだろうか？　現実の空間はどのように未来の姿を描き得るか？　たとえば建築は、未来とどういう関係にあるか？

映　画——第3章　*217*

Architecture in modernism tried to picture the near future more than any other arts before it.

Le Corbusier envisioned *Radiant City*, and Mies van der Rohe drew the designs of today as their future. Antonio Sant'Elia[12] joined Futurism to announce his manifesto. Russian avant-garde[13] architects saw themselves as leaders of a new epoch. Their envisioned future has been partially realized through the city planning of Brasilia,[14] among other cities.

In modernism, architecture is science fiction and reality. Kenzo Tange and Kiyonori Kikutake[15] presented ideas of a city on Tokyo Bay. Kisho Kurokawa[16] actually designed a work of architecture titled *Chugin Capsule Tower*, which is modular like a robot. Peter Cook[17] and Archigram[18] drew images of Walking City.

The imagination of SF worked best in the important expressions of architecture in the twentieth century. The future was the motivating factor. Imagining the future was the job of the architect. The imaginations were mostly optimistic and filled with a sense of euphoria. Meanwhile, Arata Isozaki, Hans Hollein[19] and various architects depicted apocalyptic images of architecture in the future.

Images of future must be ambivalent. It is something that we cannot see now, but will in the future, unless we are dead. Any architecture, art, or literature wanted to represent the uncertain ambivalent future.

In Japan, we have a historical architecture called *Byodoin Hoo-Doh*.[20] It is engraved on the ten-yen coin, so that everybody knows it if they live in Japan.

Byodoin Hoo-Doh is designed for death. In Buddhism, They say heaven must be in the far west which would welcome the spirits of the dead. *Byodoin Hoo-Doh* is a gate to heaven.

There is a pond on the east side of the gate so that visitors can see the architecture from the lakeside in the east. The sky behind the gate turns

218   Chapter 3——*Film*

モダニズムの建築は他のどんなジャンルよりも雄弁に近未来を語った。

ル・コルビュジェは『輝く都市』の像を描き、ミース・ファン・デル・ローエは『ガラスの摩天楼』で現在の都市の姿を予言した。サンテリア[12]は未来派の宣言に加わり、ロシア前衛主義者[13]たちは時代の牽引者を自負した。ブラジリア[14]などの計画都市で、彼らの未来の一部が実現もした。

モダニズムにおいては、建築とはリアリティのあるサイエンス・フィクションだった。丹下健三や菊竹清訓[15]は東京湾上の海上都市を空想した。黒川紀章[16]はロボットの一部が入れ替わるような建築を実際につくった（『中銀カプセルタワー』）。ピーター・クック[17]とアーキグラム[18]が、都市が自ら歩き始める様子まで描いた。

こうした『SF』は、20世紀の建築の最重要の表現であったと言ってもよい。未来こそが原動力だった。建築家は未来のことだけ考えていればよかった。概ねは、楽観的で、幸福感に満ちた予感が示された。一方で、磯崎新の廃墟の未来図や、ハンス・ホライン[19]による終末論的建築イメージも提示された。

未来図は常にアンビバレントだ。今は見ることができないが、やがては目前にやって来るだろう世界。あるいは不可避の死。建築は、あるいは小説や様々なアートもすべて、そのアンビバレントな未来像のうちに揺れていた。

平等院鳳凰堂[20]という伝統建築がある。10円コインにもその姿は刻印されているのだから、日本で生活をしたことがあるものならば知らぬものはいない。

この建築は、死のためにある。ひとが死んだ後、その魂は西方浄土に迎え入れられる。その西方浄土の、門としてこの建築は設計された。

鳳凰堂の東側には池があり、来訪者はその東畔から西方にその建築を見る。夕暮れ時なら、鳳凰堂の背後にオレンジ色に太陽が傾く。

映画──第3章　*219*

orange at sunset.

It is so beautiful that even the impious might consider it to be heaven.

The times that religion showed value for life has come to an end. Some might say that it hasn't. This century kicked off with a whistle of terrorism by religious fundamentalists. President Trump brought a revival of conservatism based on Christianity. However, the values have changed. It is hard for the people of today to believe anything without evidence, or surrender oneself to faith. To believe is to gamble, even in the case of fundamentalists, or especially in their case. It is very difficult to physically share actions of believing or surrendering with others, but when it comes to gambling they can be shared. Faith in gambling even appears in the relationship between the fictional character and the fan. It is something which can be called conscious illusion, a dream we watch knowing it is a dream.

Architecture has been a representation of shared illusion. Shrines, temples, or even housing have. Modernism has crushed these illusions one by one, and it has built newer illusions like "future" and "growth." However, spaces designed just for function have little capacity for illusion. The last social illusions like "nation states" or "communism" cannot sustain in the world of "global economics."

Don't we need illusion anymore?

We know the negative side of illusion with spatial experiences. A solemn space in an old church in Europe would move us and physically make us notice how the religion strongly suppressed people for a long time. We also know that the ultra-nationalism in Japan had strong influence over the illusion in which the heavenly emperor functioned.

Nevertheless, we cannot give up our craving for illusions.

Few people believe that "love" is just a different term for animalistic sex. They seek illusions in tackling life. No one is so strong that they can

それはたしかに美しい。信心など持ち合わせないものでも、こんなふう
に死後の世界があってくれればと願いたくなるような、美しい風景だ。

　宗教がひとの生のなかで第一義的価値を持つ時代は過去になった。「そ
うではない」というひともいるだろう。21世紀は宗教原理主義者のテロに
よって幕を開けた。トランプ大統領の誕生で、アメリカにもまたキリスト
教的保守主義が復活しつつある。とはいえ、やはり過去とは決定的に異な
る。現代人には、証拠のない何かを「信じる」ことや、あるいはその何か
に自らの一切を「委ねる」ことは、なかなかできることではない。原理主
義者にとってすら……あるいは彼らにとってこそ、「信じる」ことは一種
の「賭け」である。「信じる」「委ねる」という行為を、身体的に他者と共
有することはさらに難しいが、「賭け」ならば可能だ。「賭け」としての
「信仰」は、今の社会なら、アニメのキャラクターとそのファンたちとい
う関係にすら現れる。それはいわば自覚的な幻想、つまり夢であることを
知りながら見ている夢のようなものだ。

　建築とは本来、共有された幻想の、再現だった。神殿であれ、寺院であ
れ、あるいは住宅ですらも。近代はリアリティの名のもとに古い幻想をひ
とつひとつ打ち砕いたが、代わりに未来や成長という新たな幻想を構築す
ることも忘れなかった。それでも機能を第一義的に考える空間は、幻想の
保有力が著しく低い。国家や共産主義という最後の社会幻想も、グローバ
ル経済という名の空間のなかでは存続することはできなかった。

　もはや私たちは幻想を必要としないだろうか？

　幻想には負の側面があることを、私たちは空間の経験とともに知ってい
る。ヨーロッパの教会に足を踏み入れるとき、その荘厳な空間に感動する
と同時に、宗教が精神的な抑圧として強く長く働いてきたことを身を持っ
て感じる。あるいは私たちは、「天皇」が幻想として機能した時代、超国
家主義が力を持っていたことを知っている。

　だがそれでも、ひとは何かの幻想を求めずにはいられない。

　恋愛を、性欲という動物的機能とまったく同一だと考えるひとは少ない。
幻想が今ここになくても、ひとは幻想を求めて生きる。やがて死ぬこの一

映　画──第3章　*221*

accept just one life and the end without turning to any illusions.

That is why *Byodoin Hoo-Doh* still elicits some kind of attraction in people's minds…or in my mind, at any rate.

Architecture as well must seek illusions to live, as many films depict. "Future" and "death" are the common themes for film and architecture.

As I have written in Chapter Two, I wrote my novel titled *Perfect World* as a story on which a film will be based. It is a story about illusions called "future" and "death." I wrote it in an attempt to find a path which connects film and architecture.

So, what was the path?

8. Architecture as "Another World"

One type of stories in SF films can be categorized as dealing with "Another worlds." They contain stories about worlds which present us with realities different from our own—alternative futures we cannot see, where something has slipped in the surface of our time, where there is a different law and order. That is "Another world" film.

I pictured two worlds in *Perfect World*. One is a real world where we live. Billions of people live in poverty, falsity and violence. Another one is "a new world." It exists in a huge architecture on the top of Mt. Everest where about 12,000 people reside. It is a perfect world that has a closed system of equilibrium. Only beautiful and gifted people can be accepted to live there. I focused on one of the stories that sought and found a secret to why and how this world wanted to, and succeeded in building another world.

The events in the perfect world are going to be a main story in the film we are planning. Entertainment film in Hollywood would need to move the setting to "another world," though a story in the real world would be interesting to a lot of social critics. The critics would never disappear

回性の生を生きるのに、幻想なしで耐えられるほどひとは強くはない。

今なお平等院鳳凰堂がひとの——あるいはこの僕の心を捉えるのは、そうした理由からだ。

建築もまた、何かの幻想を追い求めるべきだ。多くの映画がそれを見せているように。死や未来が、共通のテーマになる。

第2章ですでにふれたように、僕は自身の小説『パーフェクト・ワールド』を映画プロジェクトの原作として書いた。これは未来と死いう名の幻想を描いたものだ。それは映画と建築とをつなぐ回路を求めて書いたものでもあった。

はたして、その回路とはどのようなものだっただろうか？

8. 建築とは「もうひとつの世界」

SF映画には、「アナザー・ワールドもの」とでも呼ぶべきジャンルがある。今目の前にある現実、あるいはその延長線上に見えている未来ではなく、そこから何かがずれ、こことは違う秩序や法則に支配されている世界。それが「アナザー・ワールド」と呼ぶべき種類のものだ。

『パーフェクト・ワールド』でふたつの世界を描いた。ひとつは「新しい世界」。エベレスト山頂にそびえたつ巨大な建築のなかで1万2000余人が暮らす。閉ざされた系を持ち、美しく才能あふれる者たちが暮らす「完璧な世界」。もうひとつはその「外部」、すなわちいま私たちが暮らしているこの地球上の世界。数十億の人間が暮らす。貧困と虚偽と暴力に満ちている。小説では、この世界が、なぜ「もうひとつの世界」を欲し、つくりあげるにいたったか、その秘密を探り当てることを物語のひとつの軸にした。

映画では、すでに完成した後の「完璧な世界」内部の話が主となる。社会的批評を多く含みうる「外部」の物語も面白いと思うのだが、ハリウッドでのエンターテインメント映画としては、たしかに「アナザー・ワールド」の枠内で描くのが正解だろう。そしてそうしたとしても、今ここにあ

映画──第3章　*223*

even if only the events in "another world" make the story. We should say that "another world" can be designed only by critics of the real world of the present.

As we saw in the previous section, we can say the same thing for modern architects' projects toward future and historical works like *Byodoin Hoo-Doh*. They could never be designed without imagining what we never see in the real world.

I imagined what we had never seen in the real world when I wrote *Perfect World*. For example, a system of a perfect equability that denies the idea of growth. We can call it a kind of *faith*, an unwavering belief in the idea as a supreme value which modern society has never abandoned, even though it has brought us wars, disparities and environmental disruption. The architecture of *Perfect World* is also designed as a critic of the idea. It has a space of emptiness inside of itself. It opens only to the inside but never to the outside so that it cannot expand or grow. An illusion of extraterrestrial inhabitation. The architecture in the film will be designed for the story, and the film will be set within.

The story includes a critique if how we die in this world. In a growing society, they would do their best to prolong their lifetime, while neglecting the dead or dying. Meanwhile, in *Perfect World*, they give up the prolonging of their lifetime for the purpose of keeping the equability. With that goal in mind, they designed the time just before dying as a supreme experience realized in a space called the "loop room."

I would never claim that these systems and designs in *Perfect World* are better than our real world, or that it is something to aspire to. *Perfect World* is just another world in SF film, and the novel is written with emphasis on the story. It is not a theory made to change the real world. Nevertheless, the film must be able to picture the problems of reality.

Perfect World, the film, has not been completed as of yet. I need to work

224   Chapter 3——*Film*

る世界への批評性が消えるわけではない。というよりも、どのような「アナザー・ワールド」の構想も、今ここの世界への批評の上にしか、成立しえない。

　前節にあげた近代建築の未来志向のプロジェクトについても、あるいは歴史的建築物の平等院鳳凰堂についても、同じことが言える。この世界に決定的に欠けているもの。それを見つめることからしか、これらの建築プロジェクトは始まらなかったはずだ。

　『パーフェクト・ワールド』も、今この世界では欠けているものを構想する。例えば、完全平衡系の世界。それは、成長という概念を否定する。近代以降に社会に憑りついた「成長至上主義」は、戦争や格差あるいは環境破壊をもたらした末になお、ある種の「信仰」の対象ですらある。『パーフェクト・ワールド』はその成長への批評としての建築だ。内部に虚の空間を持ち、そこにのみ開かれて、外部には閉ざされて成長しない。唯一の外部は、地球外居住という幻想のみだ。この建築はそのようにデザインされ、映画ではその空間で起こる出来事を描くだろう。

　また、これは今この世界における「死」のありかたへの批評でもある。成長系社会では、寿命を延ばすことには熱心だが、死に近い者や死そのものについては疎んじられる。『パーフェクト・ワールド』では平衡を守るために、寿命はあらかじめ定められ、それを延長することには無関心だ。しかし死の直前の時間を最良にするための設計がなされ、それは「ループ・ルーム」と呼ばれる空間で実現されている。

　もちろん、こうした設定が、実際に優れているとか、この世界もそうなるべきだとか、そういうことを言いたいのではない。『パーフェクト・ワールド』はSF映画のなかでの「アナザー・ワールド」であって、小説もそのための物語に過ぎない。これは現実を変えようとする論理ではない。だが現実の問題をあぶりだす映像にはなりうる。

　この本を書いている現在、いまだ映画『パーフェクト・ワールド』は実

映画――第3章　225

out the particulars of the spaces in an "other world" to be able to realize the film. This is my next project as an architect.

Everything leads to architecture.

* notes

1   Film director. Mexico. Born in 1963.

2   Film Director. United States. Born in 1935.

3   United States. Born in 1958.

4   Philosopher. France. 1859-1941.

5   Film Director. Germany. Born in 1945.

6   Film Director. United States. Born in 1963.

7   Film Director. UK, United States. Born in 1970.

8   It is explained in phenomenology that consciousness consists of "noesis" being oriented and acting to something and "noema" captured by "noesis."

9   Philosopher. Germany. 1859-1938.

10 Film Director. France. 1921-2012.

11 Film director, producer. France. 1861-1938.

12 Architect. Italy. 1888-1916.

13 Art movement in Russia. 1910's~1930's.

14 A capital of Brazil designed by Oscar Niemeyer, 1907-2012.

15 Architect. Japan. 1928-2011.

16 Architect. Japan. 1934-2007.

17 Architect. UK. Born in 1936.

18 Avant Garde architecture group in 1960'. Peter Cook, Ron Herron, Michael Webb and the others joined.

19 Architect. Austria. 1934-2014.

20 In Kyoto, Japan. Built in 1053.

現していない。その実現のために、この「アナザー・ワールド」の空間を、より細かくデザインする必要があるだろう。それがこれからの、建築家としての僕の仕事だ。

　すべてが、建築につながっていく。

❖注

1　映画監督。メキシコ。1963年生まれ

2　2000年。原題『*Amores Perros*』

3　アメリカ。1958年生まれ。

4　哲学者。フランス。1859〜1941

5　映画監督。ドイツ。1945年生まれ。

6　映画監督。アメリカ。1963年生まれ。

7　映画監督。イギリス、アメリカ。1970年生まれ。

8　哲学者。ドイツ。1859〜1938年。

9　現象学では、認識は、対象を志向し作用するノエシスと、それによって捉えられたノエマによって成立すると説明する。

10　映画監督。フランス。1921〜2012

11　映画監督、製作者。フランス。1861〜1938

12　建築家。イタリア。1888〜1916

13　ロシアの芸術運動。1910年代〜30年代。

14　ブラジルの首都。オスカー・ニーマイヤー（1907〜2012）が設計。

15　建築家。日本。1928〜2011

16　建築家。日本。1934〜2007

17　建築家。イギリス。1936年生まれ。

18　前衛的建築集団。1960年代に活躍。ピーター・クックのほか、ロン・ヘロンやマイケル・ウエブなどが加わった。

19　建築家。オーストリア。1934〜2014

20　京都。1053年建立。

[fig. 19]

■ は暗転を示す
■ はモスクワの風景
□ は3.11震災後の風景を壁などに映写した映像をさらに撮影
■ は文字メッセージの黒字に白の文字。日本語、英語、ロシア語
P は風景(あるいはプロジェクトされた風景)に「主人公」を配する

[fig. 20]

[fig. 21]

[fig. 22]

[fig. 23]

[fig. 24]

[fig. 25]

映 画──第3章 *229*

Chapter Four

Architecture

1. "Another Time" in "Another World"

Time is not a single stream. Another time flows in "another world." We know that time consists of several streams. Without interfering with each other they sometimes meet, cross, make a vortex, stagnate, and break back into separate streams.

Designing architecture means to imagine "another world." Since that is the case, we also need to imagine "another time" for designing architecture.

In novels or films, the living and the dead can talk to each other. Different times can easily cross over. What about architecture? What if we want to overlap history and memory with the real space architecture of the present?

I have designed a spatial model of the idea.

I entered an architectural design competition with this design for the *Museum of the World War II* in Gdansk, Poland, in 2010.

Poland has been forced to walk on a tightrope since World War II. Today, fewer people remember it, however, so that it has become mere

第4章

建　築

1.「もうひとつの世界」の「もうひとつの時間」

　時間はひとつの流れではない。「もうひとつの世界」には「もうひとつの時間」が流れる。時間にはいくつもの流れがあり、それは互いに干渉することなく、あるいは何度も交わり、渦をつくり、淀み、そしてまた別々の流れに戻りもする。

　建築を設計することが、「もうひとつの世界」を構想することなのであれば、それは「もうひとつの時間」をも構想することにもなる。

　小説や映画のなかでは、生者と死者が語らう。別の時間が容易に交錯する。それでは建築においてはどうだろう？　たとえば歴史や記憶といった時間を、建築というリアルな空間のなかで、どのように現在と重ねあわせることができるだろうか？

　これについて、僕は次のような空間モデルを考えたことがある。

　ポーランドのグダンスクという都市で、「第2次世界大戦記念館」の設計コンペ（2010年）が行われた時、僕も出品した。

　戦後も厳しい道を歩んだポーランド。とはいえ、第2次大戦は、それを記憶するものも少なくなり、生々しさが消えた歴史へと変わっている。起

history lacking the sense of physical immediacy. Nobody can erase what has happened. People killed, and people were killed. No matter how many times we look back, the answer remains the same.

History is something which should be called "closed time." War begins, war ends. During the war, we see a lot of bloodshed, and hear echoes of crying. It never changes no matter how many times we visit the "closed time." With the end of the war, the time of the war morphs into a closed loop. War ends, war begins.

In my proposal for the competition, I put the looping "closed time" into a torus that is shaped like a doughnut. Inside the loop, the war repeats forever [fig. 26] (p. 300).

People who are alive today must enter the doughnut from outside to be able to watch the war. They need to be confined to the "closed time" at least once to be able to return to the present [fig. 27] (p. 300).

The time called the present is also confined to daily life. We physically have no "time" for anything but repeating daily life. So I came up the idea to make another torus. The visitors first enter the thin doughnut. Staying in the present, the thin doughnut goes inside of the big doughnut. Visitors find themselves slipping into the war time. They experience the time loop, and then get in the thin doughnut to come back to daily life [fig. 28] (p. 301).

These two doughnuts have the same topological hole. Two closed times run around a doughnut hole which means emptiness. The emptiness appears only when the time loop is there in the same way that doughnut holes can exist only if doughnuts exist.

For another architectural project, I designed "time" as the following.

It's a house for Kei Nakazawa,[1] a novelist and friend.

It is shaped like a crystal dug from soil. It has an inclined roof [fig. 29] (p. 301), like the kind found on traditional Japanese houses, but still different. The *Novelist's House* has a big roof built to follow a slightly twisted three-

きた出来事は取り消せない。何度振り返っても、殺すものがいて殺される
ものがいる。

　歴史とは言わば「閉じた時間」だ。戦争は始まり、そして終わる。その
間におびただしい量の血が流れ、叫び声がこだまする。何度その「閉じた
時間」を訪ねても、それは変わらない。終戦とともに、戦争の時間は閉じ
た円環へと変化する。戦争は終わり、そして始まる。

　コンペ案では、この円環に閉じた時間を、トーラスすなわちドーナツ状
の空間に入れ込んだ。戦争は、そこで永遠に繰り返される [fig. 26]（p. 300
参照）。
　今を生きる者たちがこの戦争を見るためには、外部からドーナッツに入
り込まなければならない、円環の時間にいったん閉じ込められなければ、
そこから現在へと戻ってくることはできない [fig. 27]（p. 300参照）。
　現在という時間もまた、日常の中に閉ざされた時間である。私たちは、
物理的には、日常を繰り返すしか他に時間を持たない。それで、僕はもう
ひとつのトーラスを考えた。訪問者はまずこの細いドーナッツのなかに入
る。それは現在という時間のまま、大きなドーナッツのなかに入っていく。
訪問者はいつの間にか自分が戦争の時間の中に紛れ込んでいることに気が
つくだろう。円環の時間を経験したのち、訪問者は再び細いドーナッツの
なかに入ることができ、そして日常の時間に戻っていく [fig. 28]（p. 301参照）。
　ふたつのドーナッツは、ドーナッツの穴をトポロジカルに共有する。ふ
たつの閉じた時間は穴という名の虚無の周りをまわる。ドーナッツがなけ
れば穴もまた存在しないように、虚無は円環の時間があって初めて姿を現
す。
　あるいは別の建築で、僕は次のような時間をデザインした。
　それは小説家で友人の中沢けいさんのための家だ。
　それは、土の中から掘り出された結晶のような形をしている [fig. 29]（p.
301参照）。日本の伝統的な住居と同じく傾斜屋根を持つが、同じようには
見えない。『小説家の家』の大屋根はわずかに歪んだ三次曲面になってい

建　築──第4章　　*233*

dimensional curve.

The shape is covered by copper plate. The glittering brown appearance accentuates the look like a crystal buried for a long time. We also know that the color and the glitter will change. The copper will develop verdigris, and the glitter will fade. The crystal which exudes presence will assimilate to the forest of the background as if it is going back to nature [fig. 30] (p. 302).

Novelist's House opens onto a landscape of nothing but rice fields in front of it. Ponds emerge in spring, where winter there was only soil. Rice plants are planted, and they turn green in summer. Finally, a golden landscape informs us that autumn is here, before it turns back into soil. This house will watch the repetition of time. A novelist will write a novel, watching the repetition [fig. 31] (p. 302).

Various times flow into a novel. A novelist transfers time. The landscape of rice fields helps the transfer, and sometimes gently connects it to the present.

In these ways, architecture can represent "another time."

2. "Cutting" and "Editing" in Architecture

I designed *Kyoto Seika University Main Building*. It was inspired by the architecture of "another world" depicted in my novel, *Perfect World*, where I designed a black tower located at the entrance of the building. However, it doesn't have a system closed to the outside, because it is an office building within a school campus. An office needs ordinary time. Therefore, "another time" flows in the other space, rather than the time of the functional space we call the office. It flows in spaces for circulation, like staircases, corridors, halls, outside paths and squares.

With the motion of the body and the abilities of consciousness, our eyes can move in the same way a film camera does. By moving and looking

234   Chapter 4———*Architecture*

る。

　この形態が銅板に包まれている。茶色にギラリと光る様子が、土の中に
長く眠っていた結晶の感覚を強調する。だが、この色と光が、やがて変化
していくこともわかっている。銅板はやがて緑青を吹き、光はずっと落ち
着いていく。存在感を誇示した結晶は、やがて背景の森に帰るように、同
化していく [fig. 30]（p. 302参照）。

　『小説家の家』は、水田の風景にのみ開かれている。冬にはただの土
だったそこに、春には水が張られ、苗が植えられる。夏にそれは緑一色に
染まり、秋は黄金色になる。そして冬にただの土の風景に戻る。繰り返さ
れる時間を、この建築は見つめる。小説家もまた、その繰り返しを見つめ
ながら小説を書くだろう [fig. 31]（p. 302参照）。

　小説には様々な時間が流れ込む。小説家もそれを書いているときは、そ
の様々な時間を移動してくだろう。水田の風景がその移動を助け、またあ
る時はそれを今という時間に緩やかにつなぎとめる。
　「もうひとつの時間」を建築でつくり出すのは、このように可能である。

2．建築空間の「カット」と「編集」

　第2章でも紹介したとおり、『京都精華大学本館』は僕が設計した建築
だ。そしてそのエントランスから立ち上がる黒い塔は、小説『パーフェク
ト・ワールド』に現れる「もうひとつの世界」の建築から、ヒントをも
らっている。とはいえ大学内のオフィス棟という機能を持つこの建築が、
外部に対して閉ざされた系になっているわけではない。オフィスには日常
の時間が流れなければならない。したがって、「もうひとつの時間」はこ
こではオフィスという機能空間以外の場所で流れる。それは階段や通路、
そして建物周辺の道や広場という交通空間において、ということになる。
　ひとの目は、身体の運動と意識の能力の助けを借りて、映画のカメラと
同じように動く。動きながら、そして様々な方向を向きながら、対象をと

建　築──第4章　　*235*

at various angles, they capture the objects. In spaces for circulation, the eyes shoot the objects with precision. It means that we can design architecture by imagining scenes which some eyes capture in spaces for circulation, as the pictures of a film camera would shoot.

In a film project, lots of storyboards are drawn. A director and his co-workers draw the storyboards that cameras would shoot, and plan the process of editing. This was also the case in designing the *Kyoto Seika University Main Building*.

These architectural drawings work as storyboards for film work. They represent a story as a series of scenes like a film. The story in the architecture looks like this: [fig. 32] (p. 303)

I look at a building. A huge triangle of glass radiates light. Many people are in a square illuminated by the light. I enter the black tower through the entrance. The tower contains a void open toward the sky, and I am in the bottom of the void. I look up. I find a sky, and there I see.

The idea occurs to me to go there.
I climb up the stairs. The spaces are stained blue and red.

I find a small court just after having climbed up the stairs. I find the head of the tower I saw from the entrance, but I cannot capture the sky I guessed would be there.
I see mountains westward. I find it over the mountains. Under a sky colored orange in the sunset.

I designed the circulation inside and outside the structure in order to develop these scenes.

The development of these scenes realized this: [fig. 33] (p. 303)

らえる。交通空間においてなら、ひとの目はまさしく移動とともに対象を見ていくだろう。そうであれば、交通空間でひとが見るだろう風景を、映画のカメラがとるだろう構図のように発想し、そこから建築を設計することもできるはずだ。

　映画の計画においては、脚本とともに、大量の絵コンテが描かれる。カメラがとらえるだろう構図を、カットやモンタージュという、のちの編集過程も考慮したうえで描いていく。それが絵コンテだ。『京都精華大学本館』も、そのような絵コンテを描くところから設計は始まった。

　設計に先立って僕が考えたシーンは、[fig. 32]（p. 303参照）のスケッチのようなものだ。映画制作における絵コンテに、この建築スケッチは相当する。映画のように、ある物語をシーンとして表現しようとしている。その物語とは、次のようなものだ。

　　——傾斜地から建物が見えている。巨大な三角形のガラスが光って
　　いる。照らし出された広場にひとが集まってくる。入口を抜けると、
　　黒い塔のなかだ。塔は上方に抜け、私はその底にいる。上を見上げる。
　　あそこに空があるのか、と私は思う。

　　あそこに行ってみよう。
　　階段を昇る。そこにも上から光が差し込み、壁の色とともに、空間
　　を青くあるいは赤く染めている。
　　階段を昇り切ると、小さな庭がある。先ほど見上げた塔が、小さく
　　頭を突き出している。しかしここにあるはずと思っていた空は、ない。

　　西に山が見える。その向こうに、それはあった。夕日に染められて
　　いく空が——。

　こうしたシーンの展開をつくり出すために、建物内外に動線を想定した。

　これによって、実際に、[fig. 33]（p. 303参照）のようなシーン展開が実

I used five architectural elements in realizing the development: a huge triangle of glass, a black tower, a blue staircase, a red staircase, and a court on the top floor.

First, I came up with the idea to design a black tower (as previously discussed in Chapter Two). The empty space inside the tower is the core of the story about the sky. That is the function of the tower.

The story functions in another space than that of the office. "Another world" appears where "another time" flows in the story.

3. Hidden Possibilities — *"Expressionism Debate"*

In such a case, what kind of relation is there between function and space? Shouldn't form follow function in architecture? In modernism, they made such claims.

"Function" was to be the most important reason to design architecture in modernism. Architects believed that the design of architecture would be focused solely on function after Louis Sullivan[2] said that "Form Follows Function" at the end of nineteenth century. It means that the idea was conjured up by modernism, and is not by any means universal in any region or era.

It was not sole origin of modernism. It was just one of the origins of modernism which each had their various potential.

The story of "religion" ended and modernism began. No style or ornaments were needed in modernism. This change brought freedom to architectural space, but on the other hand, it erased a reason for designing architectural space. If no spires towards a world of god are needed, what do we need to design architecture?

238   Chapter 4———*Architecture*

現した。

このシーン展開を実現するためにここで要した主な建築的な仕掛けは5つある。

巨大な三角形のガラス壁／黒い塔／青階段／赤階段／屋上庭園

これらによって風景は形づくられる。

このなかで、空が見える黒い塔を、僕は最初に思いついた。それは既に第2章で書いたとおりだ。この塔の吹抜け空間が空をめぐる物語の軸になる。そしてこの塔は、それ以外の、どんな機能も持たない。

オフィスという機能空間以外の場所で、この物語は成立している。この物語のなかに「もうひとつの時間」が流れ、そこに「もうひとつの世界」が表れる。

3. 埋もれた「可能性」──「表現主義論争」

だがこの時、機能と空間との関係はどうなるのか？ 建築の形態は機能が決定するのではなかったのか？ 少なくとも、近代建築の教科書には、そう書いてあった。

近代建築にとって、機能は何にもまして重要だった。ルイス・サリヴァン[2]が「Form Follows Function（形態は機能に従う）」というテーゼを発してから、まるで機能こそが建築の始原であるかのように捉えられてきた。だがサリヴァンがこれを言ったのは19世紀後半のことで、つまりはモダニズムとともに始まった考えかたにすぎない。

そしてこれは、モダニズムの唯一の根源というわけでもない。様々にあったモダニズムの源流のひとつだったという程度だ。

宗教という名の物語の現前としての建築は、近代の始まりとともに終わった。建築は様式を捨てなければならなくなった。それは空間の自由を意味したが、同時にそれをつくる根拠を失わせた。神の世界に向けてそびえる尖塔が必要ないのなら、いったい何を必要として建築をつくればいいのか。

建 築──第4章　*239*

Various groups appeared, such as "Expressionists" who seek intensity of expression, "Futurists" who want to break away from the past, and "Constructivists" who try to find aesthetics in compositions with simple geometry reduced to straight lines and flat squares. What reason should architects have for designing? Architects argued about the issue, and artists, novelists, poets, stage directors and critics joined to the debate to seek reason in their respective arts.

The "Expressionism Debate[3]" that was held and developed in Europe in the beginning of twentieth century is still worthy of reference. Gottfried Benn,[4] a poet and expressionist, professed that he would espouse Nazism. Benn, who bet on violence of expression, sympathized with the Nazis in exploring the future through violence.

Georg Lukács[5] criticized it. He was a literary critic of realism,[6] and a communist revolutionary. He criticized artists who didn't show interest in "reality" or the age of war and revolution. His critics targeted not only expressionists, but also all formalists, because Formalists erased contents of expression which should be real and focused only on forms of expression.

We can clearly see two streams of art here. Artists lost their reason to create, which had been rooted in religion until the modern age began. They found two reasons as alternatives to religion. One is realism. This group argued: you can forget God, but observe real society and express its problems through your content. Another is formalism. They claimed: you can forget God, and the contents may relate to reality or not, as long as you focus on how to express.

Various branches grew from formalism. This was happened because forms of expression have to be various. Constructivism, expressionism, futurism, minimalism and so on. Functionalism[7] in architecture was not a big branch, just a part of minimalism.

Why did functionalism become main stream? What situation led many

形態の強さを求める表現主義、過去からの決別を第一義とする未来派、面や線などに還元された単純な形態を用いる構成主義者など、様々な主張を成す者たちが現れた。建築はその造形の根拠として何を必要とするか？　建築家たちはそれを考え、論じ合った。いや、建築だけではない。あらゆる芸術家が、文学者が、その表現の根拠について模索した。

　20世紀初期にヨーロッパで行われた「表現主義論争」[3]は今でも十分に参照の価値がある。それは詩人ゴットフリート・ベン[4]が、表現主義者としてナチズムを支持すると公言するところから始まった。ベンは、表現の「力」にかけるものとして、未来を「力」によって開拓しようとするナチスに、共感したのだ。

　これに対して最も根源的な批判を行ったのはジェルジ・ルカーチ[5]だ。ルカーチは共産主義革命家にして、リアリズム[6]の文芸批評家だ。戦争と革命の時代に、現実（リアル）と向かい合おうとしない芸術家を批判し、それは表現主義者のみならずフォルマリスト全般へと向かった。なぜならば、フォルマリストこそが表現の内容（リアル）を消し去り、表現の形式（フォルム）ばかりに関心を寄せるからだ。

　つまり、こういうことだ。建築や他の表現は、近代の到来とともに、宗教という根拠を失った。そこでまず2つの主張が現れる。ひとつは、社会の現実を直視しその問題を内容として表すことが重要だとするリアリズムと、内容はどうでもいい、どのようにそれを表現すべきかが重要だとするフォルマリズムと。

　フォルマリズムから、さらに様々な主義主張が現れた。当然といえば当然だ。表現の形式（form）などいくらでもありうる。構成主義、表現主義、未来派、そしてミニマリズムなど。機能主義はここにおいて未だまったく主流派ではなく、せいぜいがミニマリズムのなかの小派閥にすぎない。

　ではなぜ、機能主義がその後、力を得たのか？　とりわけ建築において

建　築──第4章　　*241*

people to think functionalism is a standard of modernism?

Because economics, or the basis of the substructure of Marx[8], required it. They believed that architectural rationality would be brought forth by economical rationality which is sometimes mistaken for functional rationality. The truth is that there is no reason that economical or functional rationality will bring about architectural rationality. We might be able to say that mechanistic rationality will produce architectural rationality.

Monism which asserts that function will design everything is a kind of religion, or could be superstition. The pursuit of only economical rationality has brought environmental crisis, and has hidden the essence of the life of man.

However, the reasons other than function to shape architecture are not that obvious. We should not agree with any philosophy of monism which asks for a sole reason.

In recognizing it, we better refer precisely to architectures by expressionists surrounding the "Expressionism Debate."

Bruno Taut[9] was an expressionist who taught "new architecture" with Mies Van der Rohe and Gropius[10], themselves minimalists or functionalists a la Bauhaus[11].

He drew a famous drawing titled *Alpine Architecture*.

A structure of glass shines on the top of a mountain in the Alps.

That's it. Taut presented it as a utopia, and illustrates the function in his other drawings. But economics or function are not important in this drawing. He showed us just what architecture can do for a man's life in the drawing.

The shining huge triangle of *Kyoto Seika University Main Building* that I designed owes greatly to the imagination of Taut.

242   Chapter 4———*Architecture*

は、唯一の正統モダニズムのようにすら思われたのはなぜだろう？

　経済が——マルクスの用語でいえばすべての上部構造を規定する下部構造が、それを求めたからだ。建築においては経済的合理性が——それは機能的合理性と見間違えやすい——建築的合理性に見えたからだ。だが実のところ、経済的合理性あるいは機能的合理性が建築的合理性を保証するという根拠はどこにもない。多く見積もっても、力学的合理性こそが建築的合理性だと主張する程度にしかない。

　機能がすべてを決定するという一元論は、今や迷信と同じような「宗教」だと言ってもいい。経済的合理性の追求が今日の環境破壊をうみ、ひとの生の本質を見失わせた。

　かと言って、機能に変わる何が建築の根拠となるかは自明ではない。むしろ、根拠をただひとつのものに求めるような一元論こそを否定すべきだろう。

　その自覚の上で、「表現主義論争」時の表現主義者たちの建築は、今なお参考になるべきものだ。

　20世紀前半のドイツの芸術学校バウハウスで、ミースやグロピウスらミニマリスト（機能主義者）らとともに新しい建築のための教育を行ったブルーノ・タウトは、表現主義者だった。

　タウトが描いた有名な絵がある。『アルプス建築』と題された建築ドローイング。

　アルプスの山の頂上で、ガラスの建築が光っている。

　それだけの絵だ。タウトはほかのイラストで、ユートピアとしての機能も提示してはいる。だがこのドローイングでは経済や機能が重要なのではない。タウトはただ、ひとの生のために、建築がなし得ることを描いた。

　『京都精華大学本館』の光る巨大な三角形は、このタウトの構想を引き継いでいる。

建　築——第4章　*243*

4. The Story of the Formalists

Zaha Hadid, an architect who led the design scene in the beginning of the twenty-first century, has sought reasons for expression by returning to the roots of modernism.

Her proposal for the *New National Stadium* for the Tokyo Olympics 2020, which was unfortunately not realized, could be called an architecture of expressionism with advanced technology (It doesn't matter if she accepts the labeling of expressionism or not).

She became famous through her proposal for an architectural design competition, *Hong Kong Peak* (1991). Arata Isozaki selected the proposals for the first prize.

Her proposal was a challenging idea to review the history of modern architecture and project the future through it, and Isozaki got her intention. She drew pictures for the competition by tracing the ideas of drawings by Russian Constructivists, for example, *Architectural Fantasies* by Chernikhov.[12]

In the beginning of modernism, artists dreamed about the future. Chernikhov drew architecture which cannot be realized through contemporary technology. Hadid inherited the future, and tried to realize it with the technology of today. She drew her projects so as to extend ever further into the future. Even the architects of Realism were interested in what kind of future could be achieved by the reality they were looking at, so that they dreamed of revolution.

The future was the most important concept of modernism.

Function or economical rationality was not so attractive to them.

What can we say about the situation of the modernism of today? We have already seen the negative effects brought by Functionalism and Rationalism. We know, of course, that function and rationality are always

4．フォルマリストたちの「物語」

　21世紀初期のデザイン・シーンを牽引した建築家ザハ・ハディドもまた、モダニズムの根源に遡って表現の根拠を模索していた。

　不運にも実現しなかった『2020東京リンピック・スタジアム計画案』は、現代の最新技術を駆使した表現主義建築と評して間違いがない（「表現主義」というラベリングをザハ自身が好むか嫌うかは、批評上は大きな問題ではない）。
　ザハのデビュー作は『香港ピーク計画コンペ案』だった。審査員だった磯崎新がこれを最優秀に選んだ。

　磯崎が見抜いた通り、この建築案は近代建築の歴史を見返し、そこから未来を照射しようとする野心作だ。ザハがここで提示したドローイングは、近代初頭のフォルマリスト、とりわけロシア構成主義者たちが描いたドローイング（例えばチェルニホーフによる『建築的幻想』）を、発展的にトレースしたものだった。
　モダニズムの初期において、表現者たちは未来を夢見た。チェルニホーフが描いたのは、当時のテクノロジーでは実現不可能な建築だ。ザハはその未来を引き継ぎ、現代のテクノロジーで実現させようとしていた。そしてそれをさらなる未来に送り出そうとするドローイングを描いた。リアリズムの建築家ですら、目の前のリアルよりも、今ある現実がどのような未来を生み出すかにこそ価値をおいたはずだ（だからこそ革命を夢見た）。

　モダニズムにおいて、もっとも重要な概念は、未来だ。
　機能や経済的合理性などは、未来に比べれば瑣末なものであったに間違いない。
　今日における「モダニズム」の状況はどうだろうか？　機能主義や合理主義がもたらした弊害はわかっている。むろんだからといって、すべての機能性や合理性は否定されるものではない。それでも私たちが、機能や合

important. On the other hand, we are surely groping for a value other than function or rationality. We cannot have a future if we find nothing by groping around. We are losing the future.

That is why we are now reviewing what kind of future they dreamed of in the beginning of modernism.

Let's look at Hadid's architectural drawing in detail and compare it with the drawings of the dawn of modernism.

Hadid's drawing of a bird's eye perspective of *Hong Kong Peak*, a painting titled *Desk and Room* by Kazimir Malevich[13] who advocated "Suprematism," and another painting, *Stables* by Franz Marc,[14] an Expressionist.

Two common themes in the drawings include segmenting, and motion.

Next, let's refer to a painting, *Untitled #1 2003* by Agnes Martin,[15] a Minimalist.

In the Painting of Minimalism, the segmenting is inhibited, and no apparent motion is found though you might find a silent buzz of motion. Meanwhile, they are not afraid of segmenting too much in Expressionism or Suprematism, although Malevich is sometimes labeled a Minimalist. Motion supports the shape there.

For better understanding about the relation between motion and shape, we better watch a painting titled *Nude Descending a Staircase no.2* by Marcel Duchamp,[16] who was a representative artist of Dadaism.

Motion means dynamism here.

Many artists in the beginning of modernism tried to express dynamism. They presumably did so because they thought that the dynamism could be a reason for living after religion could not.

An architecture of expressionism from the so-called *Goetheanum* school was designed by Rudolf Steiner. He was an esotericist and an intellectual.

理以外の価値を模索していることは確かだ。なぜなら、その模索への答え
が見つからないかぎり、人類は未来を持ち得ない。未来が失われかけてい
る。

　だからこそ、今もう一度、近代の最初期においてどのような未来が夢見
られていたかを検証することには意義がある。

　ザハの建築ドローイングをもう少し詳細に見て、それを近代の黎明期と
比較してみよう。

　ザハ・ハディドの『香港ピークコンペ案』の全体鳥瞰ドローイング、
「シュプレマティスム」の画家マレーヴィチの絵『机と部屋』[13]、表現主義者
マルクの絵『馬小屋』[14]を見てみよう。

　これらの絵に共通する性質を乱暴にふたつの言葉でくくるなら、「分節
化」と「運動」だろう。

　これらの絵を、ミニマリズムの画家アグネス・マーティン[15]の作品（例え
ば『無題＃1 2003』）と比べてみる。

　このミニマリズムの絵画では、「分節」は抑制され、あからさまな「運
動」もない（「運動」のざわめきを見つけることはできるが）。

　表現主義や「シュプレマティスム」（マレーヴィチはミニマリストに分類さ
れることもあるが）においては、「分節」が過多になることも恐れられてい
ない。「運動」こそが形態を支えている。

　「運動」と形態との関係についてより良く理解するためには、ダダイズ
ムを代表するマルセル・デュシャンの絵『階段を降りるヌード No.2』[16]を
見れば足りるだろう。時間によって変化する「運動」を、重ねて描くこと
で画面を「分節」し、その「分節」が「形態」を生み出す。

　「運動」とはつまりダイナミックな「力」のことだ。

　近代初期の多くの芸術家たちは、こうした「力」を表現しようとした。
それは、宗教という後ろ盾を失ったあとの、「生」の根拠になりうると、
彼らが考えたからではなかったか？

　『ゲーテアヌム』という表現主義的な学校建築を設計したシュタイナー[17]
は、神秘主義者でもあったが、理智的な人物だった。シュタイナーは生き

He reformed education in order to give dynamism as a reason for living to young people, and designed a structure for the place with expressionism.

These adventures in the dawn of modernism must have been re-excavated by Zaha Hadid and the other architects and artists, but the essence has yet to be realized. As proof of this, many people thought Hadid's the *New National Stadium* for the Tokyo Olympics 2020 would be nothing more than an exhibitionistic architect's wasteful way of having fun with shape. Nobody can deny the problems of Hadid's Stadium. It might have been difficult for people to understand the shape by connecting it to "dynamism for living." However, expressions in the dawn of modernism must have had a desire for dynamism, and Hadid surely tried to inherit it. Nevertheless, few architects or critics provide evidence for it.

Even minimalists had the desire for dynamism. We can see it in the works by "Mono-ha" which means "Just-Material School," and can be called a descendant of Minimalism, for example, *Trieb⇔Void* by Toshikatsu Endo. Minimal shape and minimal material can surely have the power of dynamism. Mies must have imagined the power—dynamism in transparency —when he drew *Glass Skyscraper*.

Unfortunately, or out of historical necessity, expressionism and futurism got the side of Nazism and fascism, while minimalism borrowed the idea of functionalism joined to another side of capitalism. According to the necessity of economic history, there is no other way for minimalism to become mainstream. It is not sure if minimalism required it or not. Minimalism and functionalism would never be combined if the combination did not generate economic efficiency.

Another interesting theory can be found in those days which Trotsky,[17] a Russian revolutionist and literary critic argued for an "expressionism debate." While most of the revolutionists of communism advocated the

る「力」を若者に与えるための教育を構想し、その場所を表現主義的に造形した。

　これらの近代初頭の冒険は、ザハ・ハディド等によって再発掘されているはずだが、その本質はまるで顧みられていない。その証拠に、ザハの『2020東京オリンピック・スタジアム計画案』は、ただ自己顕示欲の強い建築家の、無駄遣いの形態遊びだと多くの者に捉えられた。むろん、『2020東京オリンピック・スタジアム計画案』には問題がなかったとはいえないし、その造形を「生きる『力』」にいきなり結び付けられても理解はされない。だが近代の表現の根源に、その力への欲望があり、ザハがそれを受け継ごうとしていたのは確かだ。しかし建築家や批評家で、そう証言したものはほとんどいなかった。

　ミニマリズムにも、そうした力への欲望はあった。ミニマリズムの末裔とでも呼ぶべき「もの派」の作品（例えば遠藤利克『Trieb⇔Void』）を見ればそれはわかる。ミニマルな形態、ミニマルなものがもつ力は、確かにある。ミースが『ガラスの摩天楼』をドローイングとして描いた時も、その力を──透明な力を、思い描いていたはずだ。

　不幸だったのは──それこそが歴史の必然というべきものに違いないが──表現主義や未来派はナチズムやファシズムと結びつき、ミニマリズムは機能主義という名で資本主義と結びついたことだ。経済史の必然からすれば、ミニマリズムが勝利するしか他になかった。それがミニマリズムの求めていたものだったかどうかは別にして（「経済性」が媒介しないのであれば、ミニマリズムと機能主義とが一意に結びつくルートはどこにもない）。

　この近代黎明期を振り返って興味深いのは、「表現主義論争」に「参戦」したトロツキー[18]の論理だ。トロツキーはロシア革命期の文芸批評家にして革命家。1960年代の、世界中の若者たちの革命願望に影響を与えた思

idea of realism and were offensive to the other movements extending from formalism, Trotsky presented another point of view. He insisted that formalism would be a very effective method if it was only used for the right purpose, and as such there would be various ways to avoid Nazism and fascism.[18]

Now we can review the possibility of the theory of Trotsky. Actually, we have been deducing the possibility of modernism from late twentieth century to early twenty-first century. We have been throwing away not only the ideas presented by expressionists or futurists, but also what minimalists truly desired. We have been trying to preserve ourselves through advocating significance of function, but in actuality only thinking about economics.

Architecture is strongly and directly related to economic activities much more than other art or literature in that it is very "realistic." Its drawback is that it is faced by the reality of economics. As the result, a sort of functionalism sometimes appears as a compromise between economics and expression.

Malevich, a suprematist, made some architectural models titled *Arkhitektons.*

Honestly, these architectural models are considerably less attractive than his paintings. The models are segmental like the paintings, but have no motion. The motion that the drawings had might have been gone after facing a reality which include not only economics, but also scale, technology and so on. I don't assert it, but can say something similar about Futurism as well.

Filippo Marinetti,[19] an Italian poet, led the futurist movement. Past meaning stains any language. They insisted they needed to release the language from its usual usage in order to get rid of the stain. "*We declare that the glory of the world has been enriched by a new beauty : the beauty of speed...*"[20] That was what Marinetti advocated. For that purpose, Marinetti

250   Chapter 4——*Architecture*

想家としても有名だ。共産主義革命家たちがおしなべてリアリズムを擁護しフォルマリズムに連なるあらゆる芸術思想を否定したのに対し、トロツキーは別の視点を提示した。つまりトロツキーは、使い方を間違えなければフォルマリズムは芸術のために有用だし、それをナチズムやファシズムに結びつけない道はいくらでもあると言ったのだ。[19]

　そして今、あらためて思うのは、このトロツキーの理論の可能性だ。実のところ私たちは、20世紀後半から21世紀初頭にかけて、モダニズムの可能性を不当に縮小してきていた。表現主義者や未来派のみならず、ミニマリストたちが本当に欲望していたものを切り捨て、ただ経済と結びつき、それを機能と呼ぶことで、自己保身を試みてきただけではなかったか？

　建築は他の芸術、つまり絵画や小説などと比べて、圧倒的に強くそして直接に経済行為と結びついている。そしてその故に、強く「現実的」だ。経済という「現実」を突きつけられると途端にたじろぐ。その結果、「経済」と「表現」との妥協点として現れる「機能主義」もある。

　「シュプレマティズム」のマレーヴィチは、『*Arkhitektons*』と題した建築案も残している。

　率直に言って、これらの建築案は、彼自身の絵画に比して魅力的ではない。同じように「分節」的ではあるが、運動がまるでない。

　建築という「現実」——そこには経済だけではなく、スケールや技術という問題も含まれる——を考慮した結果、絵画が持っていた「運動」が消えていったか。それをここでは断言しないが、同じようなことは未来派においても起こっている。

　未来派はイタリアの詩人フィリッポ・マリネッティ[20]によって主導された。言語には過去の意味がこびりついていて、それを払拭するためには、一旦言語を日常的な使用法から開放してやるしかない。それがマリネッティの主張で、そのためにマリネッティはトランス状態になって言語を綴る方法を使った。結果からすれば、マリネッティの試みは、大きな成果を得たと

建築——第4章　*251*

chose a way to write words under trance. We cannot tell if Marinetti's attempt bore fruit or not after reading his poetry. However, the intent to transcend reality is still interesting to us.

What about Antonio Sant'Elia, an architect who wrote *Manifesto of Futurist Architecture* following Marinetti's *Futurist Manifesto*? Sant'Elia is well known for his drawings titled *Città Nuova (New City)*. I have rarely observed severe criticism of Sant'Elia, but I will offer some. The future Sant'Elia drew was poor, I think.

Sant'Elia tried to share the future that Marinetti imagined. However, Sant'Elia was an architect, so he attached his mind to the actual possibility of realizing architecture. He was too concerned with the fact that function and economics might realize his idea. Accordingly, the dynamism for the future became weak.

It might be possible to tell what was lost in the possibility of realizing architecture by looking at Sant'Elia possibility of Modernism. We can read drawings by Zaha Hadid as an attempt to revive this lost possibility. We are going to visit Moscow, which used to be a center of social and artistic revolution in order to confirm it.

5. Learning from Moscow

Few cities other than Moscow are filled with multilayered enchantments. Everyone knows of the word "revolution," but only a few cities have spaces where their memories are engraved. Moscow was the first scene of the communist revolution throughout the world, and also a scene for experiments of expression.

Let us quickly review the history of thinking about the spatial structure of Moscow.

In the thirteenth century, Muscovy (Grand Principality of Moscow) was established. Kremlin and Red Square, where historical incidents

は言いがたい。だがそれでも、現実を越えようとした意志は今なお興味を引く。

　マリネッティの『未来派宣言』にならい『未来派建築宣言』を著した建築家サンテリア[21]はどうだろう。サンテリアは未来都市のイメージ『チッタ・ヌオーヴァ（新都市）』のドローイングで知られている。サンテリアを酷評した言葉というのを寡聞にして知らないが、あえてここで言ってみたい。サンテリアが描いた未来は、あまりにも貧弱だったのではないか？
　マリネッティが夢想した未来を、サンテリアも共有しようと試みた。しかし建築家であるサンテリアは、この時代における建築の実現可能性にも拘泥していた。機能や経済が、自らの建築を実現させてくれるかもしれないことに、強く自覚的だった。そのぶん、未来への力は薄れた。

　サンテリアの現実可能性において失われたものこそが、実はモダニズムの可能性だったのではないだろうか？　ザハ・ハディドのドローイングは、それこそを回復しようとする目論見だったのではないだろうか？
　そのことを確認するために、かつての革命——政治的なあるいは芸術的な——の中心都市、モスクワを訪ねてみよう。

5．モスクワから学ぶこと

　モスクワほど重層的な魅力に満ちた都市は、世界中に他にない。
　誰もが「革命」という言葉を知っている。しかしその言葉が刻まれた空間は、モスクワの他には少ない。モスクワは世界初の共産主義革命の現場であったと同時に、表現の実験のための空間だった。

　その空間構造を考えるために、少し歴史を振り返っておく。

　13世紀にモスクワ公国ができると、そこから徐々にモスクワ都市構造が決まり始めていく。20世紀のざまざまな世界的事件の舞台となったクレム

建　築——第4章　　253

happened in the twentieth century were built through the fourteenth to the sixteenth century. The outstanding Russian Orthodox Church has been giving the city color. Imperial Russia moved the capital from Moscow to St. Petersburg. In the eighteenth Century, St. Petersburg got influenced by Western Europe because of its geographical situation. Compared to St. Petersburg, Moscow had less influence, so it could foster a unique culture of its own.

As the twentieth century which was an age of war and revolution began, idea and confusion rushed into the space and scenery of Moscow. The Red Square became a space for red revolution. Soviet moved the capital back to Moscow. Kremlin took the Communist Party as a kind of ruler that no one in the world has ever seen.

Revolution also occurred in architecture. The "Expressionist Debate" got a physical shape in Moscow.

Architects related to realism designed housing for workers based on the principle of revolution. Dining halls where workers could enjoy meals together, recreation rooms where they could enjoy culture and a central heating system that could erase the fears of winter in Moscow. There is no doubt that they designed these not only as a solution for the real problem, but also as the ideal for the new epoch.

The existence of these buildings is on the decline. Historical research has never been enough, but the Russian Museum of Architecture is currently researching this topic.

Some architecture of formalism and Russian constructivism exists in Moscow.

Konstantin Melnikov[21] is one of the representative architects of Russian constructivism. We can see his works there.

Melnikov House informs us that the form follows not only function, but something just when we glance at the exterior. The cylindrical shape looks like it is refusing to assimilate into its surroundings. Hexagonal

254   Chapter 4———*Architecture*

リンと「赤の広場」は14世紀から16世紀にかけてつくられたものだ。目を引くロシア正教会の教会建築が多く建設され、モスクワの街を彩りだす。18世紀に入ると帝政は首都をサンクトペテルブルグに移す。位置的な関係もあって、サンクトペテルブルグは西ヨーロッパからの影響を強く受ける。モスクワはそれと比較して西ヨーロッパからの影響は弱く、だからこそ独特の都市文化ができた。

そして20世紀、戦争と革命の時代が始まると、モスクワの空間と風景に理想と混乱とが一気に押し寄せる。「赤の広場」は革命のための場所に変わった。ソヴィエト政府は首都をモスクワに定める。クレムリンは共産党という、今まで誰も見たことがない権力者を迎え入れる。

建築においても革命は起こった。「表現主義論争」はモスクワにおいては物理的な形態を伴った。

リアリズムに連なる者たちは、革命の理念に基づき、労働者たちの住居を設計した。労働者たちがともに食事を楽しむ食堂、文化に興ずる娯楽室、そしてモスクワの冬の恐怖を一掃するセントラル・ヒーティング。これらが単にリアルな問題への解決案としてだけではなく、新しい時代の理想として生み出されたことに、疑問の余地はない。

こうした「理想の労働者住居」については、現存するものは少なくなり、また歴史的な研究も十分とはいえない。だが近年、「ロシア建築博物館」がこれらの調査を進めているようで、その成果を待ちたい。

これに対して、フォルマリズム、とりわけロシア構成主義に分類される建築も、数多いとはいえないものの、モスクワで出会うことができる。

コンスタンティン・メーリニコフ[22]はロシア構成主義の代表的な建築家のひとりで、実作がいくつか残る。

『メーリニコフ自邸』は外からひと目その姿を見ただけで、形態が機能のみから現れたのではないことが知れる。シリンダーの外形は外部に溶け込むことを拒絶し、六角形の窓は機能的とも様式的とも呼べない。内部に、

建築──第4章　*255*

shapes of windows would not be made for function or style. The exterior makes us imagine that an unexpected space would be inside.

Gosplan Garage was also designed by Melnikov [fig. 34] (p. 303). The dynamism of expression doesn't need to be categorized into a school anymore. We can understand his intention after a hundred years which was toward something not framed in function or rationality. He was designing a root of modernism.

Rusakov Worker's Club [fig. 35] (p. 303). This architecture which is now being revived as a theater gives out a dynamic power to its surroundings, although smaller than the usual theater of today. The dynamic power is also present on the inside. The stage is surrounded by some volumes of spaces that have seats in them. These spaces were designed not only to make the function of the theater work. We can feel the dynamism of Dionysus there, in the modern age which God has left.

Melnicov's design method has been emulated and developed later in the history of modernism, as well as in Minimalism. It has influenced Brutalism with bold design, Post-Modernism with playful forming and so on. However, the methods which originated in Melnicov's works did not become mainstream until late modernism.

Two reasons why it did not: Architecture is an economic activity, as we discussed, and as such is restricted by a rule named economic rationality. The invisible rule exists in capitalist society, and also in a communist society like the USSR.

It is also because no one has logically sought out the possibilities of dynamism. Dynamic forming is attractive, so no one has called it anything other than "attractive." Someone might have a talk about how to dynamically form it. We cannot transcend architectural activity based on economic rationality if we don't have the logic regarding what is possible with dynamism.

We should say that we have always built on the wrong logic. As for the

見たことのないような空間が閉じ込められていることを予感させる。

　あるいは『ゴスプラン・ガレージ』[fig. 34]（p. 303参照）。この表現の力を、もはや何々主義とカテゴライズする必要すらないかもしれない。ただメーリニコフという近代の根っこに位置する建築家が、機能や合理という枠に収まらないものを目指していたことが、100年の時を超えて伝わってくる。

　そして、『ルサコフ労働者クラブ』[fig. 35]（p. 303参照）。今は劇場としての再生を待っているこの建築は、現代の劇場に比べればずっと小さいはずなのに、巨大な力を周囲に発している。そしてその力は内部にも向かう。ステージを取り囲むボリューム、そのなかに配された客席。この内部空間は、ただ「観劇」という機能を可能にしようとしたものではない。「神」が退場した「近代」において、演劇にまつわる「神々」がその覇を競い合うかのような迫力がある。

　メーリニコフの造形手法は、ミニマリズムなどと同様、その後の近代建築の歴史のなかで模倣され、発展形も示された。荒々しさを強調したブルータリズムや、形態の遊戯的冒険が盛んだったポストモダニズムなどに、その影響は及んだ。しかしやはり、ここに起源を持つ建築手法がモダニズムの後期までに主流になったことはない。

　その理由は2つある。ひとつは既に述べたことで、建築は経済行為でもあり、だから「経済的合理性」という名の規制が常に強く働いた。それは資本主義社会においても、ソヴィエトのような共産主義社会においても同じだ。

　もうひとつは、こうした力にどんな可能性があるのかを、誰も論理的に探ろうとしなかったからではないか？　強い造形はそれだけで魅力的だし、だから「魅力的」の一言で済まされてしまう危険性もはらむ。魅力的な造形を成すべきための理論は語られてもきただろう。だがそれで一体何ができるのか？　その論理がなければ、経済合理主義としての建築行為を超えることはできない。

　あるいは、その論理構成を常に誤ってきた、とも言えるのかもしれない。

建　築──第4章

intensity of shape, it is not Melnicov or any formalist who have a lot of opportunities to realize it in USSR. There remain many Stalinist architectural works scraping the sky in Moscow. The forms have intensity, but no feeling of freedom that the modern age must have brought, because the forming is just a ruled as "style." Those are the impressions we get as we go back to the previous age. The possibilities that the intensity of the form would bring was lost there.

It was the same in Western Europe during the period. Adolf Hitler in Germany, who paid close attention to the contributions of architecture, tried to abolish expressionism and the other new movements of art, and named it "Degenerate Art." He wanted to build Berlin, the Capital of The Third Reich with huge Neo-classical architecture. Albert Speer[22] designed and realized a part of the idea. So, most of the works by Speer could not get beyond Neo-classicism, but only *The Cathedral of Light* can be called a great Expressionist work.

When we walk around in Moscow, we can see its history all the way back the dark ages, adventures of modernism, and the effects of Stalinism as multiple layers. Interestingly, the days immediately after these periods seem to have been lost. Economic growth came to Russia, and has been changing the scenery of Moscow since the beginning of the twenty-first century. However, the scenery from the end of Stalinism until the end of the Cold War slipped out of there.

The scenery that slipped out might be another possibility for architecture.

6. Formative Design in Literature

The "Expressionism Debate" was opened with a controversy between a poet and a literary critic. An essential conflict between realists and formalists was revealed through the "debate." Expressionists, futurists

建築の力ということで言えば、それを実際にソヴィエトで展開させたのは、メーリニコフのようなフォルマリストではなかった。モスクワには空にそびえるスターリン様式の建築が多く残る。そこには確かに強い造形があるが、「様式」と呼ばれているとおり、規則化されて、近代の自由は見出し難い。時代のねじを逆に巻いてしまったような印象だ。造形の強さがもたらすはずの可能性は、ここでも失われた。

　同時代のヨーロッパ諸国においてもそうだ。ドイツでは、やはり建築の力に着目していたヒトラーが、表現主義などを「退廃芸術」の名に一括りにして排斥し、ただ巨大な古典主義的建築によって首都ベルリンを建設しようと夢見ていた。シュペーアがその一部を実現した。シュペーアの建築はだから概ね全て古典の模倣の域を出ないが、ただ『光の大聖堂』だけは、表現主義の優れた例だと評していい。

　モスクワの町を歩くと、中世からの歴史と、近代の冒険、そしてスターリニズムがもたらしたその結末とが、重層的に見えてくる。興味深いのは、そこから先の時代が、唐突に途絶えているように感じることだ。21世紀に入り、ロシアにも経済成長の波が押し寄せた。それがモスクワの風景を変えてもいる。だが、スターリン様式の終焉から冷戦終了までの風景が、そこからすっぽりと抜け落ちている。

　その抜け落ちた風景こそが、建築のもうひとつの可能性だったのではないだろうか？

6．文学における「造形」の力

　先に書いたように、「表現主義論争」は最初に、詩人と文芸批評家との間で口火が切られた。この時の大きな対立は、リアリズムとフォルマリズムとのあいだにあった。フォルマリズムのなかに、表現主義、未来派、後

and minimalists appeared on the side of formalists in the "debate."

In the fine art scene of today, simple realism seems to have almost disappeared. Already before the school of impressionism emerged, painters were interested in light, color and composition in paintings more than the object itself that they would draw. Impressionists accelerated this tendency. Fruits or vegetables in paintings by Paul Cézanne[23] were not concerned with reality. Through emerging artists of cubism and dadaism, and Mondrian[24] or Kandinsky,[25] formalism guided the direction of art.

In literature, compared to fine art, strange or distorted realism can be still found. Some "novelists" or "critics" are not even interested in the methods they unconsciously use because of ignorance or innocence.

The novel of the modern mass society was asked to reflect its time. For example the Akutagawa Prize in Japan has been working to ask novels to mirror it so that the most recognizable novel of realism wins the prize. And in Japan, some people want to ask for "Realism" not only in the novel, but also in the novelist. They get the information of the "real life" of the novelist from the internet and think that means that they have discovered the "truth" of the novel. It's not a sin or crime, but it says nothing about the reality or value of the novel.

Looking over literature in the world of today, we know simple realism already ended its role in history. Literature can have no value for men who have witnessed the scene of 9/11 if it cannot picture what is beyond reality. The situation became apparent at 9/11, but had begun before it. It began in the age of the "Expressionism Debate," in the dawn of the twentieth century when media suddenly began to cover the earth.

Expressionism and futurism as schools didn't continue so long. But the idea appeared in the novel with an uncanny form like it appeared in Melnicov's architecture. The form of "grotesque realism."

のミニマリズムなどが現れる。

　現代のファイン・アートの分野では、素朴なリアリズムは姿を消しているように思われる。印象派が現れる以前から画家たちの関心は光とか配色とか構図に寄せられ、描かれる対象の重要度は減っていた。印象派がその傾向を加速した。セザンヌの静物画に現れる果物や野菜が、現実として特に重要なわけではない。キュビズムやダダの画家たち、そしてモンドリアンやカンディンスキーの抽象画によって、フォルマリスティックな方向は定まった。

　それに比べると、文学においては、リアリズムは奇妙な——あるいは歪んだ——かたちで今なお続いているように見える。時には無邪気とも呼べる無知のために、そうした手法に無自覚な「作家」や「批評家」もいる。

　大衆社会における小説は、その時代をわかりやすく映し出す役割をも求められた。例えば「芥川賞」はそのような小説を創りだそうとする装置であり、そのためにしばしばわかりやすいリアリズム小説が賞をとる。さらに日本では、「リアリズム」を小説の内容にかぎらず、作家に求めようとする。つまり作家の「実像」をネットで知ることが、小説の「真実」を探り当てることだと考える。別にそれ自体は罪でもないが、小説のリアルとも、あるいは価値とも何の関係もない。

　世界の現代文学を見れば、素朴なリアリズムはとうに歴史的役割を終えている。9.11のテロを生放送で見てしまった人類にとって、文学はリアル以上のものを描き出さなければ価値はない。そしてそれは9.11に始まったことではない。始まりはやはりあの「表現主義論争」の頃、つまり、メディアが突如として全世界を覆い始めた20世紀初頭だ。

　派としての表現主義や未来派は長くは続かなかった。しかしその思想が建築でメーリニコフの異形の力として現れたように、小説でもいくつかの別の形式を伴って現れた。そのうちのひとつが、グロテスク・リアリズムだ。

建　築──第４章　　*261*

I have discussed "grotesque realism" in Chapter Two. Here we try to think about it again as an "uncanny form" in a novel.

In novels titled *The Game of Contemporaneity* and *M/T and the Narrative about the Marvels of the Forest* by Kenzaburō Ōe, a canny character named "**the One who destroys**" appears. Ōe describes the character as a giant who is tall over ten feet. His description about "**the One who destroys**" is real but not imaginary. We have never seen such a giant in real, and we surely know "**the One who destroys**" exists only in the novelist's imagination of course. Nevertheless, we can recognize "**the One who destroys**" as a real uncanny existence.

Adoration for dynamism of form in the dawn of modernism made Grotesque Realism in literature kind of mainstream throughout the world.

The reason why I wrote "kind of" is because we have a different situation in Japanese society. It only accepts things that are connected to the meaning of real life. Or it has only playful metaphors in the space. These are illnesses that the modern society of Japan suffers from.

It is clear that grotesque realism in modern literature could successfully express what Expressionism or Russian formalism wanted to express, although it seems to be more of a confrontational approach.

Or to put it in other words:

Literature holds a possibility which architecture might have lost.

7. *Alpine Architecture* and *Terrain of Future*

In a novel titled *Terrain of Future*, I described a "Guru, ex-classmate" who leads a cult. (Please see Chapter Two) The Guru explains that to "Try to Change the Terrain" is a core teaching of the cult as is specified in the following:

262   Chapter 4——*Architecture*

グロテスク・リアリズムについては、すでに第2章でも述べた。それを
ここでは、小説における「異形の形態」として捉え直してみる。

　たとえば大江健三郎の小説『同時代ゲーム』や『M／Tと森のフシギの
物語』には、体躯3メートルを超えるという巨人「**壊す人**」が現れる。
「**壊す人**」についての記述はほかの登場人物同様にリアルで、特別に想像
的な様子でもない。私たちはもちろん、そのような巨人を見たことがない
し、「**壊す人**」は間違いなく作者の想像のなかにしかいないことを知って
いる。にもかかわらず、私たち大江の読者は「**壊す人**」を、リアルな異形
の存在として認知するだろう。

　近代芸術の勃興期における「形の力」への憧憬は、世界文学においては
グロテスク・リアリズムという、ある種の主流派を形成した。

　「ある種の」という断りをつけるのは、日本的な社会においてはそうで
はなかったからだ。すべてを目の前の意味に結び付けなければ我慢ができ
ないような社会。あるいは逆に、遊戯的なメタファーのみが漂う社会。そ
れは日本のような近代社会がかかった病気のようなものだった。

　ともあれ、近代文学が表現主義あるいはロシアン・フォルマリズムを、
グロテスク・リアリズムという対立するようにも見える形式して、表現し
たのは間違いがない。

　あるいはこの事態を、このように言うこともできる。

　建築が見失ったもうひとつの可能性を、文学が別の形式で守ってきたの
だと。

7. 『アルプス建築』と『未来の地形』

　『未来の地形』という小説で、僕はカルト集団を束ねる「同級生の教祖
様」を描いた（第2章参照）。「同級生の教祖様」はその教義の中心をなす
「地形を変える試み」について次のように説明している。

建　築──第4章　　*263*

—The first "Try to Change the Terrain" was executed in 1917. It suddenly happened in a remote corner of Austria. Farmers began to excavate a land that suffered terrible drought which made the crops into garbage. They dug, dug and dug, like they were insane. A psychiatrist in Switzerland researched this behavior as a case of mass hysteria. The psychiatrist reported that the farmers just rushed blindly to dig in the area where no groundwater could be expected to exist.

The research conducted by the psychiatrist is definitely wrong, however. A drawing like a scrawl by a farmer was found. The drawing can be seen in the book, "Try to Change the Terrain" (12). The area was drawn like a sunken bowl that has diameter of two miles and a depth of 3,000 feet at the center. A small church was drawn at the bottom of the bowl in the center. All houses and farms were located for them to be able to see the church. A simple caption was written in the drawing of the church, "It shines at night."

I came up with the idea of "Try to Change the Terrain," while inspired by a drawing by Bruno Taut. It is the *Alpine Architecture* that I have previously mentioned.

Taut fled to Japan with the rise of the Nazis. He fled again to Turkey and died there. The drawings reflected the ideal architecture of Taut who had few opportunities to design real projects. The scene only shows alpine forms and architecture shining on the top.

Only a genuine scene has the power of a scene. The scene would stick to people's minds for long time. The power is the potential motivation.

1917年には、最初の『地形を変える試み』が行われた。オーストリアの片田舎でそれは突然に行われた。農民たちが、たまたまその年の干害で作物がめちゃめちゃになってしまった土地を、直径3キロにわたる範囲で、突然に掘り下げ始めたのだ。猛然と彼らは掘った。異常に見える行為だった。実際、後にスイスの精神分析学者が、この行為を集団ヒステリーの実例として研究している。農民たちは、地下水などがあるはずがないことがわかりきっている土地を、それを忘れてやみくもに掘っただけだというのだ。

　だがこの精神分析学者の研究は誤っている。なぜなら農民のひとりが描いたなぐり書きのようなスケッチが見つかっているのだ。そのスケッチは『地形を変える試み』の12ページで紹介されている。直径3キロに渡る範囲が、中央部がマイナス300メートルの深さになるようにして、楕円のボウル状に掘り込まれている。ボウルの底、つまり直径3キロの中心部には、小さな教会が描かれている。農民たちの家や畑からは、どこからでもその教会が見えるようになっていた。教会の絵には簡単な説明文も記されている。それは『夜になると光る』というものだった。

　この「地形を変える試み」も、僕はブルーノ・タウトの一枚の建築ドローイングから発想した。本著でもすでに言及した『アルプス建築』と題されたドローイングだ。

　ナチズムの台頭から逃れ、タウトは日本にやって来た。タウトはその後さらにトルコに逃れ、そこで客死している。実作の機会にあまり恵まれなかったタウトの、ひとつの理想の建築像がこのドローイングに描かれている。アルプスの山上にあるガラスの建築が光るという、ただそれだけの風景。

　純粋な風景こそ、ただ風景としての力を持つ。ひとの意識に永く留まり続ける風景、行動の隠れた動機になりうる力。

　僕はこの『アルプス建築』を反転する形で、「地形を変える試み」として描いた。アルプスの山は、楕円に掘り下げられた場所として仮想された。

建　築──第4章　*265*

"Try to Change the Terrain" is fiction. An "attempt" of these sorts has never been true in history. Nevertheless, we can say it could be called a real "architectural attempt" by Bruno Taut.

8. "The Magic Mountain" in Ronchamp

We can see a small wall on the top of the mountain in a little town in the east of France. On a sunny day, the white wall shines between the blue sky and the vivid green of the woods.

Chapelle Notre-Dame du Haut looks like that in Ronchamp.

A masterpiece of modernism that everybody knows was designed by Le Corbusier in his late life. It has the function of a chapel, but the function is not the only reason for its shape. The religion of Christianity is also not the only reason for the form. The reason is not even explained by geometry. *Chapelle Notre-Dame du Haut* got out of the Principles of Modern Architecture by sympathizing with the Functionalism which Le Corbusier himself had shown in his theory and projects. The forming of *Chapelle Notre-Dame du Haut* is like that of the expressionists. The paintings capture 3-dimensional objects into two dimensions.

Le Corbusier was also a painter and a Cubist. His style was close to Picasso's works like *Weeping Woman*, among others. Cubists adopted a method called "assemblage" which drew various sides of objects as flat surfaces. It proceeds in a way formalism has explored, which is to emphasize how you draw, more than what you draw. Capturing objects from multiple view-points gives us a sense similar to that of Duchamp's *Nude Descending a Staircase no.2*, and also to that of Expressionist's paintings involving motions. Rather, paintings by Le Corbusier were distinct from geometric formations like "De Stijl" or paintings by Mondrian.

266   Chapter 4——*Architecture*

頂上ではなく、窪みの中心に「夜になると光る」建築を配した。

　「地形を変える試み」はフィクションである。歴史上にそんな「試み」はなかった。だが、こうも言える。それはブルーノ・タウトによって実際に構想されていた「建築的試み」であったのだと。

8. ロンシャンの「魔の山」

　フランス東部の小さな村から山を見上げると、その頂上に小さな白い壁が見える。晴れた日だと、空の青さと木々の緑に挟まれたその壁は、さらに白く輝くようだ。

　『ロンシャンの礼拝堂』は、そんなふうに建っている。

　誰もが「モダニズムの傑作」として知るこの建築は、ル・コルビュジェが晩年近くに設計したものだ。それは礼拝堂という機能を持つが、機能によってのみ形態が決まっているわけでも、あるいはキリスト教という宗教によってのみ空間が決定されているわけでもない。それらの根拠は幾何学によっても示されない。ル・コルビュジェ自身がそれまでに著作と実作の両方で提示し続けてきた機能主義的な「近代建築の原則」から、『ロンシャンの礼拝堂』は脱出している。その造形は表現主義的であるといってもいい。

　ル・コルビュジェは画家でもあり、そのスタイルはキュービズム（立体主義）に属する。『泣く女』を描いていた頃のピカソの画風に近い。絵画は、立体（３Ｄ）としての対象を、画面（２Ｄ）上に描くものだ。キュービストたちは、立体の様々な側面をひとつの画像上にアセンブラージュするようにして描く方法をとった。それはフォルマリズムが切り開いた可能性、つまり描かれる内容よりもその方法を開拓する道の上にあった。複数の視点によって対象を捉える、という感覚は、デュシャンの『階段を降りるヌード №2』に近く、運動を内包するような画面構成は表現主義者たちの絵画と通底する。ル・コルビュジェの絵画はデ・スティル派やモンドリアンのような幾何学的な造形からはむしろ遠い。

建築──第4章　*267*

We cannot easily tell if *Chapelle Notre-Dame du Haut* is close to Cubist paintings, even if they are works by the same artist. However we can find various possibilities of modernism in Le Corbusier. Just parts of the possibilities, geometry and functionality for example, appeared in his early works. Later, Le Corbusier didn't change style, but focused on another possibility of modernism. The architecture shines white on the small mountain. It shares the dynamism and intensity of the *Alpine Architecture* by Bruno Taut.

And what shines on the top of the mountain is similar to the beginning of a story. For example, a sanatorium on a mountain in Davos, Switzerland. It's not *Alpine Architecture* by Taut. It's what Thomas Mann[26] wrote in his novel titled *Magic Mountain*, 1924.

Magic Mountain is usually labeled an "educational novel," not Grotesque realism or Expressionism. Mann described the sanatorium realistically, and the characters with idealistic conversation. Critics say that Mann came up with the idea of the novel when he actually saw a sanatorium in Switzerland. Nevertheless, we should not call it a novel of Realism. Several people suffering from illnesses give thorough thought to man and the world outside the sanatorium that is "another world" closed by snow. It's not a space in ordinary reality. *Magic Mountain* is a space in "Magic Reality."

9. Design Architecture in Fiction

I'm again talking about my own novel, *Perfect World*, this time in the context of *Magic Mountain*.

First, Greg Manos told me about his idea by e-mail: "It will be an SF film about the near future. This fear, brought by the huge meteor, balloons out of control. They plan to migrate to Mars because they have come to

268   Chapter 4———*Architecture*

『ロンシャンの礼拝堂』が画家ル・コルビュジェの作品に近いかといえば、直ちにそうとも言えない。ただ、ル・コルビュジェのなかには最初から、様々な近代主義の可能性があったことは確かだ。初期の建築群においてはそのうちのいくつか——幾何学と機能性——が大きく浮かび上がっていたということなのだろう。後期になってル・コルビュジェは、違う道に乗り換えたのではなく、ただもとから持っていた近代の別の可能性に焦点を宛てた。その建築は小さな山の上で白く輝く。形態も色彩も異なるが、ブルーノ・タウトの『アルプス建築』が示した建築表現の強度を共有している。

　そしてこの山の上で光るものは、小説の始まりを告げるものにも似ている。たとえばアルプス山脈のダボスの山頂のサナトリウム。それはタウトが描いた『アルプス建築』ではない。トーマス・マン[27]が1924年に上梓した小説『魔の山』に描いたものだ。

　『魔の山』は、文学史上の分類としては、「グロテスク・リアリズム」でも「表現主義」でもなく、「教養小説」に属するものとされている。確かに、ここに描かれるサナトリウムはリアルで、その場にいる者たちは高度に観念的な議論をする。トーマス・マンはスイスで類似の療養施設を見て、この小説を構想したのだという。しかしだからといって、この小説をリアリズムと呼ぶことはできない。雪に閉ざされた異世界で、病に冒された者たちが外部の世界と人間について徹底的に考察する。それは日常の現実に属する場所ではない。「魔」の山、まさに魔術的現実（マジック・リアル）の場所なのだ。

9.　フィクションで建築を設計せよ

　僕自身が書いた小説『パーフェクト・ワールド』に、『魔の山』との関連でもう一度ふれておきたい。

　最初、脚本家グレッグ・マノスはその素案を僕にメールで語った。「近未来を舞台にしたSF映画。隕石がもたらした恐怖が肥大し、地球が破滅する可能性を知ってしまった人類は、火星への移住計画を始める。そして

建　築——第4章　　269

realize the possibility of the demise of the earth. They build a preparation colony on the earth. It would be on the top of Mt. Everest. The Everest Colony becomes 'another world'..."

We could not discuss the details of "another world"="Everest Colony." We could only envision it after I'd written the novel. Greg asked me, a novelist, to write the original story, and requested me, as an architect, to design the colony. Greg became my client in more than one sense. It sounded like he was telling me to "design a sanatorium on the *Magic Mountain*."

In the novel, the name of the character who developed the idea of the colony is Ari'X, and the name of the architect who designed the colony is Taki.

In the final chapter of the novel, Ari'X stands before trial. I wrote their idealistic conversation in the closed world on top of Everest.

It is a debate about natural death, which was also one of the themes of *Magic Mountain*. It begins between Ari'X and the judges.

> *"A cicada can die while flying and fall to the ground. Man can't die like cicadas die. If you call it a natural death, we must say that we have been deprived of a natural death."*
>
> *(omission)*
>
> *"You say that Man has been expelled from nature so that we must give up natural death, right?"*
>
> *"No. That's wrong," answered Ari'X.*

The scene of judgment goes on for a while. "It won't work as well in a Hollywood film, as it does in the novel," Greg said. 'Action' is one of the keys required for a Hollywood film to become a hit. Seated debate is not

270   Chapter 4———*Architecture*

その準備のためのコロニーが地球上に建設される。エベレストの山の上に。『エベレスト・コロニー』はやがて『もうひとつの世界』として……」

　「もうひとつの世界」＝「エベレスト・コロニー」の詳細が、最初から明らかだったわけではない。それは、原作を書くのと同時に「設計」していかないかぎり見えてこない。グレッグは小説家である僕にその原作を書けと命じたのと同時に、建築家としての僕にこの「コロニー」の「設計」を委託したのだ。グレッグは二重の意味で僕のクライアントになった。このクライアントはまるで『魔の山』の「サナトリウム」を「設計」しろと言っているように、僕には聞こえた。
　小説のなかでは、このコロニーを計画した男の名はアリエクス、それをエベレストの山頂に設計した建築家の名はタキになっている。

　小説の終盤、アリエクスが被告として審判を受ける場面がある。エベレストの山の上、閉ざされた世界のなか。観念的な議論がそこで行われるさまを、僕は描いた。
　「自然な死」（これも『魔の山』のテーマのひとつだ）についての議論が、アリエクスと審判者とのあいだで始まる。

　　「……セミが飛びながら死に、地に落ちるようなことは、人間にはできない。それを自然な死と呼ぶなら、人間はあらかじめそれを奪われていると言うしかない」
　　（中略）
　　「人間は自然から追放されているのだから、それは断念するしかない、と？」
　　「それも違う」アリエクスは答えた。

　審判における議論の場面は長く続く。小説ならそれもいいが、ハリウッド映画ではだめだとグッレグからは言われている。ハリウッドのSFでは、アクション・シーンこそが生命線だ。登場人物が座ったままで議論をして

建　築──第4章　　*271*

exactly a 'money shot.'" I will think about it another time.

The scene of the Judgment changes "Everest" into the "Magic Mountain."
I described the "Everest Architecture" as inheriting something from
Alpine Architecture.

> *The Himalaya Mountains are there like a great white wall reaching the
> sky. Everest sticks into the sky steeply from its surroundings. A huge
> tower penetrates white clouds towards space from the top of Everest. The
> tower is changing color every minute.*
>
> *The upper part of the huge cylinder narrows like a bud. The material
> cannot be produced by the earth, the shape cannot be formed by man and
> the architecture cannot hide its own intention. A strange existence built
> by man occupies a scene in the mountains of the myth of great nature.
> The colors are changing, reflecting the landscape and the light in the sky.
> The fragments of the surface always jiggle like waves.*

The Architect, Taki, who designed the huge tower answered the
following to a question about what his first idea for the tower was:

> *"Emptiness." Taki answered. "I told Ari'X at first. "It will be on the top
> of Everest. A huge cone will be built first. 4,000 feet high, the diameter of
> the base of the cone will be 600 feet." I enjoyed Ari'X's face in amazement,
> and continued. 'However, the cone is invisible. It's just emptiness. A
> world will arise from the emptiness. So we will make it at first."*

> *Taki stared at a point in a space in front of him then folded the point by
> his palms. "I designed the space in my palms just before it was folded by
> them.*

272   Chapter 4——*Architecture*

も、「マネー・ショット」にはならない、そうグレッグは言う。その問題は別に考えるとしよう。

この審判のシーンによって、「エベレスト」は「魔の山」に変身した。

そして『アルプス建築』ならぬ「エベレスト建築」を、僕は小説のなかでこのように描写した。

　空まで届く白い壁のような山脈。ひときわ急角度で空に向かうエベレスト。そしてその山頂から白い雲を突き抜け宙に向けて伸びる巨大な塔。塔はその表面の色を刻々と変えている。
　（中略）
　巨大な円筒は上のほうで蕾のように窄んだ形になっている。この地球上にあるはずがない物体、人間がつくりえるわけがない造形、そのもの自体が意図を持っているかのような建築。自然の神秘としか思えないような雄大な風景の一角を、人間がつくり出した奇妙な物体が占めている。その色が、光と風景を映しだして変化を続ける。さらにその表面がいつもざわざわと揺れている。

　一方、この「巨大な塔」を設計した建築家「タキ」は、最初に何をつくろうと考えたのかと問われてこう答える。

　「『無』だよ」とタキは言った。「僕はアリエクスに最初に言った。『敷地はエベレストの山頂だ。そこにまず巨大な円錐形を、エベレストの山頂に立てる。高さは約4000フィート、円錐形の底円の直径は約600フィート』あっけにとられた様子のアリエクスの表情を楽しみながら僕は続けた。『とはいえこの円錐形は目に見えない。それはただの「無」だ。だがそこから世界が始まる。つまり、最初にこれをつくるのさ』」
　そう言うと、タキは自分の目の前の一点を凝視し、それから手のひらで今まで自分が凝視していた一点を包み込んだ。「手のひらに包み込まれるより先に、手のひらのなかの空間をつくるんだ」

建　築──第4章

Taki designed a space of emptiness without function before a story began in it.

Taki named the "emptiness," which was huge cone-shaped void, "Aura." "Aura" is what Walter Benjamin defined in his book *The Work of Art in the Age of Mechanical Reproduction*, as we will discuss in the next chapter.

Taki was probably inspired by Bruno Taut, although he has yet to tell anyone.

10. The Real "Another World" in the Ocean

"The Perfect World" on the top of Everest has a closed system of equilibrium. The people are born there, and die there. They grow crop there, and eat there as we do on the earth. Everything must be perfectly recycled there.

The "Everest Colony" is a facility for simulation of a world on Mars. All conditions for the "Colony" are designed like it would be on Mars. However, the "Everest Colony" has one thing that a world on Mars will never have. It is the "future," as someday we will transfer our world to Mars. Once we execute to transfer, the "future" will be gone. The "Everest Colony" is a world that depends solely on solar energy, wind energy and the "future" from the outside.

This is the world in architecture that only exists in SF. It can only be built in novel and film. Is that really the case? Could not such a world be built in our real world of the present?

Reality as another world is now imagined by global IT companies in Silicon Valley.

It is named *Techie Island*.[27] It is an instance of "seasteading," a portmanteau of sea and homesteading, on an artificial island. One might think it would be too small to call "another world." But remember that they have

274   Chapter 4——*Architecture*

機能よりも先に、あるいは物語が語られる瞬間よりも早く、「無」の空間をつくる。

　「建築家タキ」は、この「無」すなわち巨大な円錐状の吹抜け空間を「アウラ」と名付けた。アウラとは次章で論じるだろう思想家ワルター・ベンヤミン[28]がその著書『複製技術時代の芸術』で定義づけたものだ。

　「タキ」は自分の口ではそうは言わないが、おそらくブルーノ・タウトの思想を受け継いでいる。

10. 現実の「もうひとつの世界」

　エベレスト山頂の「パーフェクト・ワールド」は、閉ざされた平衡系を内部に持つ。この地球がそうであるように、そこでひとは生まれ、死ぬ。そこで食物をつくり、そこでそれは消費される。そこではリサイクルは完璧になされなければならない。

　「エベレスト・コロニー」は火星世界のシミュレーション施設だ。条件は火星と全く同じに設定される。ただ一点、「エベレスト・コロニー」にあって、火星世界にはないだろうものがある。それは、いつの日かこの世界は火星に移行するという「未来」だ。実際に火星に移行してしまえば、その「未来」も失われる。太陽光エネルギーと風力エネルギー、そして「未来」だけを外部に依存する世界。

　これはむろん、SFのなかの世界であり、建築だ。小説と映画だけがそんな建築をつくりうる。だが、本当にそうだろうか？　今、そんな世界をつくる可能性はまったくないだろうか？

　例えば、シリコンバレー[29]に集まるITのグローバル企業たちが思い描いている「もうひとつの世界」がある。

　Techie Island[30]と呼ばれるそれは、人工島の形をした海上都市だ。「もうひとつの世界」にしては、ずいぶんと小さいと思う人もいるかもしれない。だが彼らには地球上を覆いつくすネットワークがあり、ARすなわち拡張

建　築——第4章　275

networks that cover the entirety of the earth and AR: technology of Augmented Reality. It means that the reality which has the same large augmentation as the world on the earth will exist on the island.

It becomes difficult for establishments in Silicon Valley to find significance in paying tax. They seem to pay taxes to the state or the federation because Silicon Valley is a region of California and the United States, however, they are considering other possibilities. Google, Facebook or any other IT company produces no physical materials and import nothing but information though their offices which are casually located on the West Coast of North America. Their consumers are not domestic, but international. They don't care about their consumers' nationalities. So why do they need to pay taxes to the states just because their offices are there?

Modern society can only tax someone who works or lives there.

Of course, IT companies in Silicon Valley get benefits from the infrastructure of the regions. That might be the only thing they get. They might have an obligation to pay just for that. If they build and use their own system for health insurance, pension or even security like police and army, the logic for them to pay tax becomes invalid.

This logic inspired them to draft a destination like "another world." It is a place unlike the tax payment place of the homeland; it is a city floating on the sea.

This "another world" will have a territory that has the same area as the entire world in the augmented reality. All information, communications and scenes over the world will enter "another world" and be able to synchronize with the entire world.

Techie Island is designed not to be as closed as the "Perfect World." If *Techie Island* is built, it has no other way to sustain itself than to import

現実と呼ばれる技術がある。地球と同じ大きさの拡張を持つ現実が、想像上はその島のなかに畳み込まれることになると考えてもよい。

　シリコンバレーの「支配者」たちは、税金を支払うことに意味を見いだせなくなってきている。シリコンバレーはカリフォルニア州の、そしてアメリカ合衆国の一地域なのだから、州や連邦に税金を収めることは当然のように思えるが、「支配者」たちは別の可能性を考える。たまたま地理的に北アメリカ大陸の太平洋岸に位置しているとはいえ、グーグルもフェイスブックも、そこでどんな物質も生産してはいないし、情報以外の何も輸入してはいない。顧客は世界全体に分散し、国内外の区別はない。なのになぜ、社屋がそこにあるという理由だけで、その国に税金を払わなければならないのか？

　ある場所が納税を要求する対象は、現代社会では二通りしかない。その場所で稼いでいる者か、その場所で生活をしているか。つまり、その場所から何らかの恩恵を受けているかどうかだ。
　シリコンバレーのIT企業も、その地域のインフラストラクチャーの恩恵を受けている。だがそれだけかもしれない。彼らはそれらの使用料を支払えばいいだけなのかもしれない。健康保険も年金も、あるいは警察や消防のような安全保障すらも自前で用意すると言うのなら、彼らが税を支払う根拠は消えていく。
　そしてその論理の行き先として、彼らは「もうひとつの世界」を構想し始めた。それは租税地としての国土にとらわれない場所、つまり海上に漂う都市だ。
　そしてそれは拡張現実^{AR}のうえでは、全世界と同じ広がりを持つ。あらゆる場所の情報、コミュニケーション、風景が、そこには集まり、それらは世界上の時間とシンクロして、刻々と変化していく。

　彼らが構想しているTechie Islandは、「パーフェクト・ワールド」ほどには、自閉していない。もしTechie Islandが実現したとしても、食料や

建　築──第4章

food, medical care, cars or any industrial products from the outside. However, it's only logical for them to pay tax. *Techie Island* can't exactly be called a city-state if it has an independent legislature and judicial organ. Who can say that they have no right to such organs?

Techie Island was designed to depend on the outside for a lot of things. Any country of today needs a lot of things from other countries, and the military force as well as security is often interdependent. Thus, we have no reason not to call *Techie Island* a new city-state.

And if *Techie Island* has a farm, hospital, army and everything else inside, except only informational communication with the outside, it will be a kind of *Perfect World*.

Nevertheless, the establishments in Silicon Valley suppose that it's a good idea to depend on the outside for food and security because it costs less. *Techie Island* can be designed like a huge ship. It can move itself close to any existing country as it finds optimal, and get anything needed in trade with the country.

It is very rational and efficient. Still, there is only one thing that they can never have inside and get from the outside.

It is the "future."

11. Necessary Conditions for the Future

"No kidding" you might say. "The 'Future' is the best thing it can produce, isn't it?"

No.

They always and accurately show "tomorrow." It's their business. However, "tomorrow" cannot replace "future." "Tomorrow" will surely, or maybe come. On the other hand, "future" is "what has not come yet." "Migrating to Mars from the Everest Colony," or death to all of us. That

278   Chapter 4———*Architecture*

医療、車やその他の工業生産品を、その「外部」から「輸入」するより他に、持続の手段を持たないだろう。ともあれ租税の根拠はそれだけだ。金にまつわる行政の問題だけではない。Techie Islandが、独自の立法組織や司法機関を持つのなら──「それを持つ権利は彼らにはない」と誰が言えるか──そこは「独立した都市国家」以外の何ものでもない。

　Techie Islandは現在の構想上では、外部に多くのものを頼っている。だが現代では、どのような国家も多くのものを他国に依存し、軍事力も「安全保障」の名のもとに相互依存する。ならばこのTechie Islandを、新しい都市国家と呼ぶのはきっと何ら間違いではない。

　そして、もしも農場も病院も軍隊も、すべてを内部に持ち、外部との交通は「情報」以外になくなるのなら、Techie Islandはある種の「パーフェクト・ワールド」になるかもしれない。

　もっともシリコン・バレーの「支配者」たちは、食料やら安全保障などは外部に頼るほうがよほど安上がりだと、おそらくはそう考える。Techie Islandは巨大な船のようにデザインされることも可能で、そうなれば最適な外部となりうる既存の国家の近くに移動し、その国家と交通することで必要な物を得るだろう。

　とても合理的で、効率的だ。それでもTechie Islandがその内部に持たず、外部からも得ることができないものがひとつだけある。

　それは「未来」だ。

11.「未来」のための必要条件

　「何を馬鹿な」というものがいるかもしれない。「『未来』こそIT企業が描きうる最上のものではないか」と。

　違う。

　「明日」の世界ならば、彼らは確かに見事に描いてみせるだろう。それが彼らのビジネスだ。だが「明日」は「未来」と同義語ではない。明日は必ず、あるいはたぶん、やってくる。だが「未来」とは、「つねに未だ来ないもの」のことだ。「エベレスト・コロニー」にとっての「火星移住」、

is the "future."

What is the "future"?

At one time, "future" was a story narrated by religion. In most of the stories, "future" means "end."

When the end of life in this world comes to a man, his spirit goes to heaven or the Pure Land of Amitabha. The end of time will come to this world which is called the Last Judgment or Final Dharma. It is regarding the "future" that it unknown when it will come for a man. So a man must have a repetitive daily life, enjoying tiny happiness and misery until the "future."

The "Terrain of the Future" is what people have been imagining as the end of life or the world. It changed dramatically when modernism began. Or should we say that the "Terrain of future" has not changed, but begun to eternally change. It didn't begin changing for the "end," but for "progress."

The perspective of the progressive history of modernism is compatible with evolution, the natural law Charles Darwin[28] "discovered" in the nineteenth century. Of course there is no connection between evolution and the progress of technology. However, they seemed to believe that progress was a kind of providence of nature. With the "faith" in progress and technological advancement, military weapons became rapidly stronger, and society required dialectic evolution and revolution.

Technology still rapidly advances even after the illusion of progress and revolution has almost vanished. The pace of development in the field of terminal information devices becomes faster and faster. Nobody can imagine a scene today where all of the passengers in the subway aren't touching their smartphones, and we can hardly imagine how it will be in a few years.

Google, Facebook and Twitter revolutionized not only the medium of

あるいはすべてのひとにとっての死。それこそが未来だ。

「未来」とは、何か？

かつて「未来」とは宗教が語るもの、という時代があった。その多くで「未来」は「終末」を意味していた。

ひとがこの世界での生の「終末」を迎えると、その魂は極楽浄土か天国へ向かう。そしてやがては、この世界自体が末法あるいは最後の審判の時を迎える。それが「未来」だが、いつやってくるのかわからないほどには遠い。それまでは、悲惨とささやかな幸せを味わいながら、同じことを繰りかえす毎日を過ごしていくしかない。

生あるいは世界の終末の姿、それが長いあいだひとびとが思い描いてきた「未来の地形」だった。「未来の地形」が音を立てて変わったのは近代が始まった時に違いない。いや、正確にいえば「未来の地形」は「変わった」のではない。「常に変わり始めた」のだ。そしてそれは「終末」に向けて「変わり始めた」のではなかった。その変化は「進歩」に向かっていた。

ダーウィンが19世紀に「発見」した新たな自然法則「進化論」[31]と、近代の「進歩」史観とは相性が良かった。実際には進化とテクノロジーの進歩とは何の関係もない。それでもこの時代のひとびとは、「進歩」は自然の摂理の一種だと信じこむ様子だった。「進歩」という名の新たな信仰に根拠を与えるように、実際にテクノロジーは進化し、戦争兵器は急速に強力化し、社会は弁証法的な進化と革命を求めた。

革命や「進歩」の幻想がほぼ全壊した今でも、テクノロジーの急速な進化は続いている。情報端末機器の革新のスパンは短くなる一方だ。地下鉄のすべての乗客がスマホをいじっている風景を想像できた者はいなかったが、それが数年後にどうなっているかを今また想像することは難しい。

グーグルやフェイスブック、それにツイッターなどは、技術を進化させ

建築──第4章　*281*

communication but also its contents. Who wanted to pass on what they saw to someone they don't even know, before Twitter or Instagram appeared as information devices?

In the past, no live broadcast from war scenes had been made until CNN did it from Gulf War in Iraq and Kuwait. Lag times and regional differences were largely present in communication before the Gulf War. And the lag and the difference provide a critical eye and a strong motivation in the quest for truth. But now the situation has changed. The internet make people believe that truth must be conveyed without distorting real time. Consequently, the quest for truth and a critical eye have vanished. "Reddit geeks" believe information just because it exists on the monitor in front of them.

Techie Island must believe in a progress of information. Information will form their "world," they believe. The value of the information of tomorrow is so different from that of yesterday. Is it in progress that modernism believed? It must be almost the same, but a little different.

We can assume that the default of the world is in the system of equilibrium. The evolution of Darwin, the dialectic revolution, innovation of technology, all of those are what broke the default. In those ideas, they presumed that a positive vector can and should be bigger than a negative vector. They also believed that it would be solvable if the unbalanced vectors caused some problems. Modernism worked with this wishful conviction. But today, the world is thought to end because of the explosive population growth and global warming will exceed the level of risk, and if it continues, the equilibrium will break. We have built a prosperous world, beyond the scope of imagination for people living in the nineteenth century. The cost for the progress is being paid with the crisis of sustainability of the world. The situation seems to be at a conclusion as the equilibrium system will defend the system.

コミュケーションの方法に革命を与えたばかりか、コミュニケーションの内容までも変えた。ツイッターやインスタグラムが現れるまで誰が、自分が今見たものを同時に、遠く離れた見も知らぬ誰かに伝えようとしただろうか？

　かつてCNNがイラク・クエートの「湾岸戦争」を同時中継するまで、戦争の実況放送はなかった。「湾岸戦争」が起こるまで、コミュニケーションには遅延や地域間差異が生じるのが当然だった。そしてそのような時差や地域間差異こそが真実の探求への強い欲求を生じさせ、批評的な視点をつくり出した。だが今は違う。インターネットはひとに、真実とは同時に歪みなく伝わるはずのものだと信じさせ、その結果、真実への探求も批評も消えた。だから「２ちゃんねらー」のように、いま目の前のモニターに映る情報だけを信じる者もあらわれる。

　Techie Islandは、きっと情報の「進化」を信じている。情報が彼らの「世界」を形づくる、と考えている。たしかにそれは「進化」しているだろう。昨日の情報と明日の情報では、価値がまるで違う。それは近代が信じた進歩だろうか？　もちろん、そうだ。だが、異なる点がある。

　世界の初期設定は平衡系だったと仮定してみる。ダーウィンの進化論も、弁証法的革命も、テクノロジーの革新も、その平衡系を破るものとして現れた。それらのどれもが、プラスのベクトルを、マイナスのベクトルを上回るべきものとして想定し、それで何かの問題が生じたとしても解決可能なはずだと信じた。近代はその希望的確信の上に成立した。だが今では、この平衡系を破り続ければ、人口の過多や地球温暖化はすぐにでも危険水準を超えて、世界は壊れるだろうと予測されている。世界は２世紀前には思いもよらなかったような豊かさを得た。「進化」の代償として、地球は存続の危機を迎えた。それは平衡系が自己を守ろうとしている結果にも思える。

建　築——第4章　　*283*

Meanwhile, progress that doesn't necessarily break the equilibrium system has emerged. That is progress of information. Information has no mass or energy. That is why inflow and outflow of information doesn't need to follow the logic of the equilibrium system.

Now we imagine a world "A" and world "B" which are independent from one another. When "A" sell commodities to "B" and get money in return from "B," the quantity of the commodities decrease but currency increases in "A." In that case, the equilibrium system of each world is unbalanced.

On the other hand, when they trade information, it will be a different story. The quantity of information will never decrease in "A" even if "A" sells the information to "B." Marketability of the information will be reduced, but the quantity will not. It is a pretty big difference. Because the trading can eternally continue if "A" donates the information to "B" without asking for anything in return.

Of course not—*Techie Island* never wants relationships made up of donations. They must suppose that the marketability of information should be exchanged for currency, because it cannot be sustained without getting outside resources with currency. In this sense, *Techie Island* is not so different from real tiny countries.

We should imagine what would happen if the default for *Techie Island* is reset in another condition. What if *Techie Island* becomes independent without asking for food, education and security from the outside? What if it needs nothing but solar and wind-mill energy from the outside in the same way as the "Everest Colony" does? If it does, *Techie Island* can be a perfect "another world," and even export its information unlimitedly.

Of course establishments in Silicon Valley, and such kinds of "another world" means nothing. But for us, "another world" that is economically and ecologically independent from trade with the outside is worth

ところが、平衡系を必ずしも破壊しない「進化」が現れた。それが情報の「進化」だ。情報には質量もエネルギーもない。情報の「流出」や「流入」は、だから平衡の論理に必ずしも従わない。

　Ａという世界と、そこからは独立したＢという世界がある。ＡがＢにある商品を売り、対価としてＢから貨幣を得たとすると、Ａの内部においてはその商品の量が減少し、貨幣の量が増える。この場合、Ａ，Ｂいずれも内部の平衡系は、一時的に崩れる。

　だがその商品が情報の場合には事情が異なる。ＡがそれをＢに売ったとしても、Ａの内部においてその情報はなくならない。情報の商品価値は減るだろう。それでも情報量は変わらない。それは大きな違いだ。なぜなら、もしもＡとＢとが商業的な交換を行うのではなく、無償の贈与を行うのなら、その関係は永続的になりうるからだ。

　もちろん、Techie Islandは贈与関係など欲してはいない。情報の商品価値こそが貨幣と交換されるべきと考えているだろう。Techie Islandは、その貨幣で外部の資源を獲得しないかぎり、生き延びることはできないからだ。しかしそれならばTechie Islandは現存する極小国家とさして変わらない。
　それならば、Techie Islandの初期設定をもう一度設定しなおしたらどうだろう？　もしも、Techie Islandが、食料や教育や安全保障などを外部に頼ることなく自立できるとすればどうなるだろうか？　「エベレスト・コロニー」と同様に、太陽光と風力エネルギーの他に外部から取り入れるものがないとしたら？　その時にはTechie Islandは、たとえその外部に情報を無償で際限なく輸出したとしても、完璧な「もうひとつの世界」になりうる。
　もちろん、繰り返すが、シリコンバレーの「支配者」たちにとっては、そんな「世界」が目的なのではない。しかし私たちにとっては、外部との交換に頼らずに経済的あるいは環境的に自立する「世界」を、思考実験上

建　築──第4章　*285*

simulating for our thought experiment. We can find another future there different from what modernism has shown.

12. Information, Imagination and the Instant City

The Modernists believed that the world must keep growing physically. Mass product / mass consumption, and the earth's resources / fossil energy supporting them brought growth to the world. Most of the architecture and cities were imagined as an embodiment of the physical growth. Nobody doubts that architecture is nothing but physical.

An "incident" happened in 1970 which informed us that architecture can be something other than physical. A series of drawings titled *Instant City* caused the incident.

Instant City means a city which appears suddenly and disappears after a while.

An airship carries a big screen beneath it which projects some images. A new city can be realized by it. Peter Cook and Archigram declared so with the drawings. It's not a city that needs lots of years to be physically built and developed. It's a city which only exists while new information is carried there and stays there.

While perspectives of *Techie Island* are not as attractive as architectural images, the drawings of *Instant City* are very imaginative and attractive.

The images of information technology, *Instant City*, are rudimentary if compared to those of today, however, it can make us see the fantastic "future" more so than what we actually get today.

Were the other architects not interested in information? Of course, they were. But their interests were mostly in information that exists in physical architecture as a receptacle. The drawings by Archigram reversed the relationship between architecture and information so much so that it should have been called an "incident." Information is not in architecture.

286   Chapter 4———*Architecture*

でシミュレーションしてみることには意味がある。なぜならそこから、モダニズムが示したのとは異なる「未来」が見えるかもしれないからだ。

12. 情報、想像力、インスタント・シティ

モダニズムが信じた、世界の「成長」。それは身体的／物理的つまりはphysicalなものだ。大量生産／消費が「成長」を生み出した。それを支える地球資源／化石エネルギー。ほとんどの建築や都市の姿も、このphysicalな「成長」の体現として描かれた。建築自体がphysicalなものであるという常識を誰も疑わなかった。

この常識をくつがえす「事件」が、1970年に起こる。それは『インスタント・シティ』という名のドローイングが引き起こした。

『インスタント・シティ』とは文字通り、即興的で一時的な都市のことだ。

飛行船がスクリーンを運んできて、そこに映像が映し出される。それだけで新しい都市はできる、とピーター・クックと彼が率いるアーキグラムはこのドローイングで宣言した。長い年月をかけてPhysicalに建設され成長する都市ではない。情報が一時的にそこに運ばれてくることで出来上がる都市だ。

Techie Islandの「完成予想図」が建築としては魅力が乏しいのに対して、『インスタント・シティ』の絵は夢幻的で、ひとを惹きつける。

現代のIT技術に比べれば原始的とすら言える情報技術を描きながら、しかしそれは遥かに豊かな「未来」を私たちに「予感」させる。

このドローイングが現れるまで他の建築家たちは情報には無関心だったのかといえば、そんなことはないだろう。だがその関心は、Physicalな建築が容器として受け入れる情報という辺りにとどまった。アーキグラムのドローイングはその関係を逆転させたという意味で「事件」だった。建築のなかを情報が行き来するのではない。情報それ自体が、建築なのだ。

建築──第4章　*287*

Information is architecture as Archigram drew.

"Archigram" is a neologism coined by combing "architecture" and "telegram." They added the word "telegram," which was an old information technology even in the 70's, but was brought forth by modernism to their own name.

They were not indifferent to physical architecture. Walking City, another work by them, showed too much physical emotion as the physical verb "to walk" was put in the title.

Architecture hardly flees from many restrictions. A city that is a field of architectural sets must have more restrictions. They are anchored to certain places with heavy chains. "Chains" meaning the restriction by gravity, infrastructure, economics and height. That is why architecture doesn't move. Movable parts of architecture are only doors, windows, chairs and toilet seats.

A trailer can move, and function as a small house. However, we cannot expect it even with the maximum possible progress of technology that an entire city move, or even walk on huge legs.

Why did they draw images of such architecture and cities which cannot be realized? I have already answered the question. They did not choose physical architecture, but looked at it as information. Images of architecture and cities on drawings are information. If the images are too physical, drawings are media of information.

What information can we read about in the media? It is "The City Moves!" It might be a message like "you can cut 'chains.'" Or we can read it as "architecture is what we imagine and draw."

These messages have been surely delivered to architects of the same and the next generation. To me, for example.

I came up with the idea that I would write a novel when I began to

288   Chapter 4———*Architecture*

アーキグラムはその様子を描いた。

　そもそもアーキグラムという名前自体architectureとtelegramを組み合わせた言葉だ。Telegram＝電報という、当時でもいささかクラシックだが、確かにモダニズムが生み出した情報技術の名を彼らは自らにつけた。

　彼らがphysicalな建築に無関心だったわけではない。「ウォーキング・シティ」は、歩くという身体的動詞が加わっているぶん、むしろ過剰にphysicalだ。

　建築とは不自由なものだ。その集合体としての都市なら、なおさらに。それはその場所に、いくつもの「鎖」で縛りつけられている。「鎖」とは例えば重力、交通などのインフラストラクチャーあるいは経済や法律などだ。これらの「鎖」のせいで、建築は動かない。可動部分はドアや窓の建具、いす、それとトイレの便座くらいのものだ。

　それでも小さな住宅程度の機能なら、車のなかに詰め込んで移動するということもある。だが都市が丸ごと地上を動く、しかも足が生えていてそれで歩く、などということは今後のテクノロジーの進歩を最大限に見積もってもなお難しい。

　まるで実現不可能な都市と建築の姿を、なぜ彼らは描いただろうか？これに対する答えは、すでに書いた。彼らはフィジカルな建築ではなく、情報としての建築を選んだ。ドローイングに描かれる建築や都市は、情報だ。たとえ過剰にフィジカルなものを描いたとしても、ドローイングは情報メディアである。

　それではこのドローイングに描かれた情報とは何か？　「都市よ、動け！」というメッセージだ。「『鎖』は断ち切れる」というメッセージかもしれない。あるいは「建築とは、構想され、描かれるものだ」というメッセージにも読み取れる。

　こうしたメッセージは、同世代そして次世代の建築家たちに届いた。そのひとつの例は、僕自身だ。

　僕が建築を学びながら、小説を書こうと思い立ち、そしてそれはひょっ

study architecture. Architectural adventures by Peter Cook and Archigram taught me that it's possible.

The space you imagine, the scene you draw, that is architecture. You can build architecture with images and words. They told me so through books that were the best media at the time when I was a student.

I have luckily become one of Peter's friends now, but that is another story. Others besides me have received the message as well.

The message has also been delivered to *Techie Island*. It has the possibility to move freely on the sea, escaping from the existing economic system, tax and regulations imposed by a country. It will not walk, but it might swim.

13. The Technology of Literature and Space

Techie Island can develop to be "another world." Meanwhile, such city states have been realized on the internet.

Everyone knows of a "city" named "Facebook." I have hundreds of friends in the "city" and my friends tell me that it's a pretty small number in that "city." Less than twenty percent of those hundreds are friends in Japan, so I communicate with them in English in the "city." They come from varying nationalities. Some of them became friends with me just recently, and others are old friends from ten years ago or more. I meet my friends from LA there and five minutes later, I look at scenery on a monitor which a girl in Moscow is looking at.

What internet and SNS caused was not the first revolution for media. The world in the twentieth century was drastically and rapidly changed by photography, film, radio and TV.

Chapter 4——*Architecture*

として可能なのに違いないと考えることができたのは、アーキグラムの、そしてそれを率いたピーター・クックの「建築的冒険」があったおかげだ。

　空間を、そして風景を構想し、描くことができるのなら、それこそが建築だ。ドローイングであれ、言葉であれ、建築はできる。アーキグラムとピーター・クックは、まだ学生だった頃の僕に、そう教えた。本という、その当時の最上のメディアによって。

　今では僕は、この尊敬すべき、そしていかに感謝しても足らないピーター・クックの友人のひとりになることができた。だがそれは一旦置こう。僕以外にも、もちろんピーターとアーキグラムのメッセージは受け継がれた。

　Techie Islandにもそのメッセージは届けられた。それは既存の経済＝税制や、国家という規制の間をすり抜けて、海上を自由に動き回る可能性を保持している。歩きこそしないが、それはやがて泳ぐかもしれない。

13.　空間と文学のテクノロジー

　Techie Islandは「もうひとつの世界」になる可能性がある。しかしそのような「都市国家」はインターネット上には、とっくに実現している。

　誰もが知っているフェイスブックという「都市」がある。僕もこの「都市」に数百人の「友人」がいるが、その数はほかの住人たちの「友人」数よりはだいぶ少ないらしい。僕の「友人」たちの８割以上は日本人ではなく、だから僕はそこでは英語でコミュニケートする。「友人」たちの国籍は多様で、知り合った時期も10年以上の幅がある。僕はこの「都市」で、ロサンジェルス時代以来の友人と再会し、その５分後にはモスクワの女性がいま目にしている風景をモニター上で眺めている。

　メディアの革命は、インターネットやSNSが初めてだったわけではない。写真、映画、ラジオそしてテレビ、それらは20世紀の世界を猛スピードで変えていった。

Andy Warhol appeared there. He alleged that his arts are color copies (screen printings) of Marilyn Monroe's portrait and mentioned that art is just something like that. His attitude represented the essence of modern art and the desire of people living in the age of media.

"In the future, everyone will be world-famous for 15 minutes," said Warhol. Such as Marilyn. Some people would say, "I don't want be famous like that." However, that's not the point. "Media" and "famous" are just metaphors. They are the metaphors which create the desire for people living today and dying someday to carve their identity somewhere.

Marshall McLuhan[29] wrote *Understanding Media: The Extensions of Man* in 1964. It was in 1961 that a TV camera captured the moment of J. F. Kennedy being shot. The touch of the world was changing. McLuhan realized this situation, not as media infiltrated our life, but as our physical sense extended into the world. That is exactly why people felt as if they watched the moment of Kennedy's assassination on scene. They felt that they were involved in history. McLuhan thought that TV showed us a power which we had never seen before, to involve the audience in a process of history when Kennedy's funeral was broadcasted.

It was in 1991, thirty years after the JFK case that CNN broadcasted war live, and in 2001, forty years after JFK, we watched live skyscrapers in New York collapsing after two airplanes crashed into them. We can say that the evolution of McLuhan's theory has been confirmed every ten years. We have seen war and terrorism on scene, even if we have never been there. However, it is difficult for us to feel it through physical reality. We always feel déjà vu. As Baudrillard mentioned[30], we can say that nothing might have happened.

Now we are living in the world where nothing is happening. Of course, a lot of things are happening, a lot of scenes that someone actually watches prevail on Facebook and Twitter. No one can doubt this reality.

292   Chapter 4——*Architecture*

アンディ・ウォーホルがいた。カラーコピーしたマリリン・モンローの顔がアートだと言い張り、あるいはアートなどその程度のものだと示唆した。ウォーホルの態度は確かに現代アートの本質を、そしてメディアの時代を生きる者たちの欲望を表している。

「誰でも世界的に有名になれる、ただし15分だけなら」とウォーホルは言った。マリリン・モンローのように有名に。自分は別に有名になどなりたくない、と言うものは多いかもしれない。だがそれは問題ではない。「メディア」も「有名」も、メタファーに過ぎない。今日を生きるもののすべてが、自らの固有の生——今を生き、やがて死ぬべき自分——をどこかに刻み込みたいと願っているその欲望の、メタファーだ。

マーシャル・マクルーハンが『メディア論——人間の拡張の諸相』[32]を書いたのは1964年だ。J・F・ケネディが狙撃されたその瞬間をテレビカメラがとらえたのが1961年。世界の感じかたは確実に変わりつつあった。マクルーハンはこれを、メディアがひとびとの生活に侵入してくるというよりも、人間の身体感覚が世界に延伸していくという方向にとらえた。確かに人々は、自分の目が、ケネディ暗殺の瞬間を見たように感じた。私たちがそこに参加しているかのように感じたのだ。マクルーハンによれば、ケネディの葬儀の時、テレビは視聴者を一つの過程に共同参画させる比類のない力を発揮した。

CNNが戦争の生中継をしたのはJFK事件の30年後の1991年、ニューヨークの摩天楼に旅客機が突っ込む様子を私たちが見たのは2001年つまりJFK暗殺からぴったり40年後だ。10年毎にマクルーハンの理論は進化が確認されている、と言ってもいい。私たちは戦争を、テロを、その場にいなかったにもかかわらず、確かに見た。ところが逆に、私たちの皮膚感覚は、それをどうにもリアルにはとらえなかった。戦争にもテロにも、既視感があった。ボードリヤールが言ったように[33]、それらは「起きなかった」とすら評することができるのかもしれない。

今や私たちは、さらに「起きてもいない」世界に生きている。もちろん、多くのことは起き、フェイスブックやツイッターで、誰かの目が実際に見た風景が大量に垂れ流されている。その事実性は、疑いようもない。9.11

建築——第4章 293

That is why we feel as if nothing has happened. Everything has been overlapped with déjà vu. How can we feel it as something happening here and now, if it is so similar to the scenes we have already seen in TV or film?

We cannot escape from such a sense of déjà vu because we live in this kind of "city" which exists on the internet.

Should we just be pessimistic while faced with this situation? Can architects based in real space and cities do nothing for the situation? As I wrote by quoting the logic of Shinji Miyadai in Chapter One, we are living in the world where information has much more value than real space does. On the other hand, as we have been discussing, architecture and cities surely exist in fictional spaces such as novel and film. A "city state" with "establishments" in Silicon Valley might build it, but it can also be completely imagined by an architect. The "Future" that Peter Cook and Archigram pictured has definitely predicted the situation of today. We must have learned from them, about another possibility of architecture.

Architecture and Literature must be facing a crisis. I don't think I want to defend them from the question we put forth in Chapter One. "Architects" or "novelists," whoever needs existing labels for their authenticity loses any influence in the world. On the other hand, we can consider another possibility. It must be found if we can put up a possibility which modernism showed us in architecture and literature on the technology of today.

The "future" will be different from what we have imagined as "future."

With cognition, we have to design the "future." We cannot give up designing it because we have cognition.

So, what can we design?

Chapter 4——*Architecture*

の風景のように、それは事実だ。だからこそ、それは「起きなかった」と
すら感じられる。すべてが既視感に包まれている。映画やテレビやほかの
どこかで見たような風景を、どうして今、目の前で初めて起きたものだと
感じることができるだろうか？

　だからといって、私たちはもはやその既視感を否定して生きることはで
きない。私たちは、確かにその「都市」のなかで生きているからだ。イン
ターネット上にある都市のなかに。

　それは、悲観すべき事態だろうか？　リアルな建築や都市にその基礎を
置く建築家は、もはや無力だろうか？　序章に引いた宮台真司の論理の通
り、情報がリアルな場所よりも上位を占める時代を僕たちは生きている。
だがこれまで論じてきたように、小説や映画という、フィクショナルな空
間に、確かに建築はある。都市もそこに存在している。IT企業が作り出
すかもしれない「国家」も、建築家が構想し得る範囲内に、やすやすと収
まる。ピーター・クックやアーキグラムが構想した「未来」は、今日の状
況を確かに予感していた。そして私たちはそこから学んでいたはずだ。建
築のもうひとつの可能性を、確かに。

　建築も、小説も、危機に瀕しているのは間違いない。序章で組み立てた
問いに、無理やりな弁護で答える気はさらさらない。既存の枠組みを自ら
の基盤として頼ろうとするものたちなど、21世紀半ばには完璧に息絶える
だろう。それは間違いないのだが、別の言いかたもすぐにできる。初期の
モダニズムが示した「建築」や「文学」の可能性を、現代のテクノロジー
下に置くことができるのなら、突破口も見えてくる。

　「未来」は、これまでの私たちが夢見てきた「未来」とは、異なるだろ
う。

　そのことを自覚したうえで、私たちは「未来」を「設計」しなければな
らない。自覚してしまったからには、「設計」しないという選択肢は、も
はやない。

　だがいったい、私たちは何を設計することができるだろう？

建　築──第4章　　*295*

＊ notes

1 Novelist. Japan. Born in 1959.

2 Architect. United States. 1856-1924.

3 I could not find English book that covers the entire of the debates developed in a magazine, *Das Wort*, and the others in 1930s. For more, see: *Of Critical Theory and Its Theorists*, by Stephen Eric Bronner, Psychology Press. Or in German, *Die Expressionimusdebatte*, by Hans-Jürgen Schmit, Suhrkamp Verlag. In Japanese, *Hyogen-Shugi Ronso*, by Hiroshi Ikeda, Renga Shobo Shinsha Publishing, 1988.

4 Germany. 1888-1956.

5 Hungary. 1885-1971.

6 We should know that "Realism" contains two meanings of "real" which are "real description" and "description about the real."

7 Function is not content in functionalism. "What" function the architecture has cannot be a criterion when we say, "Form follows function." Jail, church, or whatever it is, function itself is not a criterion but "how" form follows it is important.

8 Functionalism appeared with realism in housing for workers in Moscow. Meanwhile, architecture in the so-called Stalinist style has a sense of expressionism that communists have found offensive, so they refer to it as realism.

9 Architect. Germany. 1880-1938.

10 Architect. Founder of Bauhaus. Germany. 1883-1969.

11 School of art and architecture. Founded in 1880 and closed in 1938.

12 Yacov Chernikhov. Architect. Russia. 1889-1951.

13 Painter. Russia. 1878-1935.

14 Painter. Germany. 1880-1916.

15 Painter. United States. 1912-2004.

16 Painter, Sculptor. France, naturalized American. 1887-1968.

❖注

1　小説家。日本。1959年生まれ。

2　建築家。アメリカ。1856〜1924

3　主たる論争は、池田浩士編訳『表現主義論争』れんが書房新社、1988年にまとめられている。

4　ドイツ。1888〜1956

5　ハンガリー。1885〜1971

6　「リアリズム」は日本語では「写実主義」と訳されてきた。対象をリアルに描くという趣旨と取れば、文学や絵画においてはその訳語で理解しやすい。だが建築や思想の場合だと「現実主義」と訳さなければ意味を成さない。「リアル」は今や日本語化しているのだから、今後はどのような書物でもリアリズムと日本語で表記されるべきだろう。

7　機能主義において、機能は「内容」ではない。「形態は機能に従う」というとき、その機能が何であるかは批評の対象にはならない。刑務所であれ教会であれ、機能自体が問題なのではなく、形態がどのようにそれに従うかが重要なのだから。

8　モスクワの労働者住宅には、機能主義とリアリズムが結合して現れている。ただ、スターリン様式と呼ばれる建築群は、リアリズムを標榜していながら、共産主義者たちが攻撃した表現主義的な感覚すらある。

9　ドイツの美術・建築の学校。1919年開校、33年閉校。

10　建築家。バウハウス創立者。ドイツ。1883〜1969

11　建築家。ドイツ。1880〜1938

12　建築家。ロシア。1889〜1951

13　画家。ロシア。1878〜1935

14　画家。ドイツ。1880〜1916

15　画家。アメリカ。1912〜2004

16　画家、彫刻家。フランス、のちにアメリカに帰化。1887〜1968

17　思想家、教育者、建築家。オーストリア。1861〜1925

18　ロシア。1879〜1940

建　築——第4章

17 Russia. 1879-1940. After losing the power struggle against Stalin, he exiled himself and was finally assassinated in Mexico.

18 *Literature and Revolution*. Orig. 1924, Haymarket Books (2005).

19 1876-1944.

20 *Futurism*, by Sylvia Martin, TASCHEN, 2005.

21 Architect. Russia. 1890-1974.

22 Architect, Reich Minister of Armaments and War Production for Nazi Germany. 1905-1981.

23 Painter. France. 1839-1906.

24 Painter. Nederland. 1872-1944.

25 Painter. Russia. 1862-1944.

26 Novelist. Germany. 1875-1955.

27 The Seasteading Institute, a Non-Profit Organization, drew the picture.

28 Naturalist, biologist. UK. 1809-1882.

29 Philosopher. Media theory. Canada. 1911-1980.

30 *La Guerre du Golfe n'a Pas eu Lieu*, 1991.

19 トロツキイ（桑野隆訳）『文学と革命（上・下）』岩波文庫、1993年

20 1876〜1944

21 建築家。イタリア。1888〜1916

22 建築家。ロシア。1890〜1974

23 建築家。ドイツ。1905〜1981。ナチス政権において軍需大臣を務めた。

24 画家。フランス。1839〜1906

25 画家。オランダ。1872〜1944

26 画家。ロシア。1862〜1944

27 小説家。ドイツ。1875〜1955

28 哲学者。ドイツ。1892〜1940

29 サンフランシスコ湾の南岸、サンノゼ市他のいくつかの都市を含む地域の呼称。

30 The Seasteading InstituteというNPOが、その姿を描いている。

31 博物学者、生物学者。イギリス。1802〜1882

32 哲学者、メディア理論。カナダ。1911〜1980

33 ジャン・ボードリヤール（塚原史訳）『湾岸戦争は起こらなかった』紀伊國屋書店、1991年

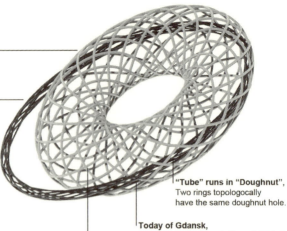

"Doughnut"=past.
It is "closed time".
Nothing can be changed there.
It can only repeats.

"Tube"=present.
It is "flowing time."
Nothing can be stopped here.
It will even metamorphose.

Travel for past through "Tube".
We will get into "Doughnut"
where Second World War
eternally repeats.

"Tube" runs in "Doughnut",
Two rings topologocally
have the same doughnut hole.

Today of Gdansk,
we will come back again through "Tube"
after experience of the War.

Future will apear on surface of the reseptacle,
if we succeed to contain the past in it,
as the glitter of the brass "Doughnut".

[fig. 26]

[fig. 27]

300   Chapter 4——— *Architecture*

[fig. 28]

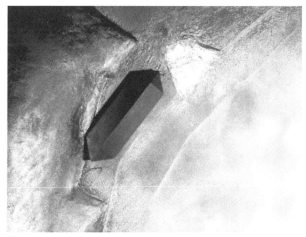

[fig. 29]

建　築――第4章　　*301*

[fig. 30]

[fig. 31]

[fig. 32]

[fig. 33]

[fig. 34]

[fig. 35]

建　築——第4章　　*303*

Chapter Five

Future

1. We Might Have Known from the Beginning

The Truth is always hidden in the beginning of a good detective or spy novel in such a way that the readers or the protagonists cannot figure it out.

What "future" can we design instead of what is lost?

The answer might have been written in Chapter One.

—A train was running through a forest. I sat by the window looking at the raindrops falling through the gaps between the branches. The high school students on the train sometimes laughed and talked in high voices, but I was not listening. I was only looking at the raindrops. The raindrops fell silently into the dark pond in the bottom of my mind. I was looking up at the forest from the bottom of the pond, and the train was still running.

—Facing the window, I asked myself. "So, what should I do? I suddenly took off on a journey because I didn't want to do whatever I was doing.

第 5 章

未　来

1.　最初からわかっていたはずだった

　推理小説やスパイ小説では——とりわけそれが優れた小説の場合、答え
は最初のほうに書かれている。主人公にも読者にも、そうとはわからない
方法で。

**「失われた未来」に対し、僕たちはどんな「別の未来」を設計すること
ができるのか？**

　答えは、この問いを立てた第 1 章のどこかに、実は示されていたのかも
しれない。

　列車は森のなかを走っていた。僕は窓際の席に座り、木々の隙間から落
ちてくる雨粒を眺めた。列車のなかでは登校途中の生徒たちが時おり嬌声
をあげていた。だが僕は聞いていなかった。ただ、雨粒を眺めた。雨粒は
僕のなかに静かに落ちていき、そこに暗い池をつくり出した。池の底から
森を見上げているような僕を乗せて、列車は走り続けた。

　窓の外を睨みつけながら、僕は考えた。——いったい何をしたらいいの
だろう？　何もかも嫌になって旅に出たのはいいけれど、ただ森から零れ

But I knew I could still do nothing but look at the raindrops leaking through the forest." I supposed that it would keep raining until the train would arrive at its destination, and that the journey would end without me noticing and leaving everything unchanged.

—I found at the time that the scenery outside of the window began to change slightly. The raindrops leaking between the gaps of the branches gradually lessened. Instead of raindrops, weak sunlight began to leak through. The sunlight fell on the window of the train, the raindrops were disappearing. I stared at it, trying not to blink.

A few minutes later the rain was gone, and clear light in the morning filled the forest. It was a blinding light.

—"I will never forget this scenery for my entire life," I predicted. "I will surely remember these raindrops, and the light until death comes for me."

I was just around twenty years old when I had a vision. I had grown up physically, but was just beginning my spiritual growth. I imagined my future at the time. I began to think about the possibility of writing a novel, and designing architecture in my life. Nevertheless, this is not a "coming-of-age story." I looked at my death before "coming-of age." Growth was not on my mind. I looked at my life from the end of time.

"Eternal growth" as a myth of modernism was ending. Only "eternal repetition" and "death as the end" remained for us. Literature and architecture as "adolescence" became impossible.

On the other hand, I felt the possibility of literature and architecture at the time just when I thought about the time until death. I began thinking about literature and architecture as my life work because I had unconsciously noticed the impossibility of literature and architecture as "adolescence."

One day, every society or city must end its growth. The word "progress"

落ちる雨粒を見つめていて、何ができる？　僕はこの雨が、終着駅まで
ずっと降り続けるのだろうと思う。何も変わらぬまま、旅はいつか、知ら
ぬ間に終わるのだろう、と。

　その時、僕は気がついた。列車の窓からの風景が、微妙に変化を始めた
ことに。森の枝葉の隙間から落ちる雨粒は少しずつ減っていた。その代わ
りに零れ始めたのは、日の光だ。頼りない光が、隙間から差し始め、その
量は雨粒が減るのにつれ増えていった。僕はそれを、瞬きの時間まで惜し
むほどに見つめ続けた。
　木々の隙間から落ちる雨粒はやがて完全に姿を消し、午前の鮮やかな光
が、森のなかを満たした。その光に僕の目は眩んだ。
　——この風景を、生涯忘れることはない。そう僕は予感した。——やが
て死ぬときには、この光のことを思い出すのだろう。

　こんなことを考えたとき、僕はまだ二十歳そこそこだった。身体的な成
長こそ終えていたかもしれないが、精神的にはまさにその途上だっただろ
う。僕はこの時に自らの未来を考え、そして小説と建築の両方をやろうと
構想を始めた。だが、この旅は僕にとって「成長の物語」だったろうか？
　違う。なぜなら、僕は自らの「死」を先に見ていたからだ。「成長」が
目的だったのではない。「終わり」から現在までの時間を遡って眺めてい
た。
　「永遠の成長」という近代の神話は消えつつあった。私たちの「未来」
に残されているのは、果てしない繰り返しと、その先の「終わり」＝
「死」だけだ。「青春」としての文学も建築も、不可能になった。
　だが僕が建築と小説の可能性を予感したのは、まさにその「死」からの
時間を考えた時なのだ。「青春」としての文学も建築も不可能だと無意識
のうちに悟ったから——推理小説の主人公同様、僕自身そのことに気がつ
いていなかったが——僕は建築と小説のことを同時に考えようとしていた
のだ。
　社会や都市は成長を終える。進歩という言葉は「死語」となるか、そう

未　来——第5章　*307*

must change its meaning, or become obsolete. "Architecture" must get independency from physical buildings or lose its meaning. "Authorities now depend on no real space," to quote the logic of Shinji Miyadai in Chapter One. That was why I thought of designing architecture in a place that can be free from physical "buildings."

We can say the same thing about literature. Adolescence supporting the modern novel has ended, to quote the logic of Masashi Miura in Chapter One. That was why I wrote my first novel as not in accordance with the chronology of events, and by mixing the present with the past. So the timelines made space as a structural diagram. Thus, the novel after *The End of Adolescence* became close to architecture as I argued in Chapter Two by quoting from several novels.

Experience in architecture resembling literature becomes close to it in film. The architectural novel can be translated into film to create new expression. In Chapter Three, I showed some examples of film as "place" where architecture and literature can be designed.

After the discussions in Chapter Four, I have shown how architecture can change itself in the "future." I have pointed out that architecture and the other forms of expression have as yet unrealized potential. I also showed the germination of the possibilities that emerged in various genres in the beginning of modernism.

The answer always lies in the beginning.

The answer was there when I predicted that I would never forget this scenery for the entirety of my life and surely remember the raindrops and the light leaking through until the time when death comes for me.

2. Aura and Copy-Paste

We have not discussed thoroughly enough the concept of future. We need to think about future in the age when the meaning of "future" has

ならないためにはその意味を変えるしかない。建築という言葉も、物理的な「建設」という意味からの独立性を獲得しなければ、やがて意味を失う。第1章で宮台真司の言葉を引いたように「権力は空間に依存しなく」なった。だからこそ僕は考えたのだ。物理的な「建設」からは自由な場所に、建築を考えてみよう、と。

　小説についても同じことが言える。第1章で三浦雅士が指摘しているように、近代文学を支えた「青春」は終わった。だからこそ僕は最初の小説を、時系列に従わないものとして書いた。出来事を入れ替え、記憶と現在とを混在させた。そうすることで、時間は構造的に空間化した。つまり、『青春の終焉』という事態後の小説は、必然的に建築的になるのだ。それは第2章で様々な例を挙げて論じたとおりに。

　小説的な建築の経験は映画のそれに近くなる。建築的な小説は映画として新しい表現の力を得る。建築や小説が「設計」されるべき「場所」としての映画があることを第3章で示した。

　そしてこうした考察をへたのちに、建築がどのように変わりうるかを先の第4章で書いた。建築には、あるいはほかのすべての表現形式に、いまだ実現されていない多様な可能性が潜んでいたことをも指摘してきた。その萌芽は近代の最初期にはいたるところにあったのだということも確認した。

　答えは最初にあった。

　列車の窓に降り注ぐ雨と光を眺めながら、死の前にはきっとこの風景を思い出すだろうと予感した、あの時に。

2. アウラとコピペ

　それでも、まだ到底、未来について語り尽くしてはいない。「未来」の意味が変わってしまった時代に、私たちは未来を考えなければならない。

totally changed.

We need to look more carefully at the situation which appeared in our discussion at the end of Chapter Four. We should consider how the information has changed and how it will continue to change space and story, in order to be able to tell what kind of architecture, novel and film there is demand for today.

Walter Benjamin[1] speculated about the change of information and the world in the beginning of modernism. He wrote an essay titled *The Work of Art in the Age of Mechanical Reproduction*[2] in 1936.

Benjamin did not predict the situation of today, the twenty-first century. He was looking at photography and film as "mechanical reproduction" which prevailed rapidly in the beginning of the twentieth century. Now, the "mechanical reproduction" has made great progress, and become increasingly convenient. "Copy and paste," "C&P," is now part of our daily language. "C&P" gives us a negative impression like that of "plagiarism," "falsification," or "cheating," however, it might be more than just that.

We already had a technique for reproduction before photography was invented. Artists learned techniques by reproducing existing great paintings or sculptures. Some famous pictures have been works of forgery. Architects were renowned for their ability to reproduce certain styles. However, these reproductions in art and architecture were so different from photography. Only gifted and skilled artists could reproduce the arts. On the other hand, photography was produced and reproduced by a lens, film and developing fluid. Mass reproduction could be made at the same time as the original was produced. The masses became viewers of the "new art."

Art got accepted by the general public and lost something, said Benjamin. A sole art work, a sole architectural space and a sole music performance listened which can only be listened to as it is performed. It had "aura"

310   Chapter 5———*Future*

それらを十全に考えるためには、第4章の後半で浮かび上がってきた今日の時代の諸相を、もう一度よく見ておく必要がある。とりわけ「情報」が空間や物語をどう変えてきたか、そして変えていくかを考察したい。そしてそこから、これからの建築／小説／映画が何を求めて創作されるかが見えてくるはずだ。

　近代の初期に、情報と世界の変化について深く考察していた思想家がいた。ワルター・ベンヤミン[1]。1936年に「複製技術時代の芸術」[2]と題した論文を書いた。

　ベンヤミンは、21世紀の今日の事態を予言していたわけではない。ベンヤミンがその時見ていたのは、映画や写真といった、20世紀初めに突如普及した「複製技術」だ。世紀を隔てた現代、「複製技術」ははるかに進歩し、そして容易になった。コピー＆ペースト、すなわち「コピペ」は日常語になった感すらある。盗作や捏造、そこまでいかなくても「ズル」といったネガティブな意味に付き纏われる「コピペ」だが、ひょっとしたら他の可能性もあるかもしれない。

　写真が現れる前にも、複製の技術はあった。絵画や彫刻では模写をして学び、優れた絵画には贋作も多くある。建築家には、すでにある様式（スタイル）を再現できる能力こそが第一に求められた。だがそれらと写真とのあいだには、絶対的な違いがある。絵画や建築における複製は、才能に恵まれたものが訓練された手でつくる。しかし写真では、レンズやフィルム、現像液といった工業製品が作製／複製する。オリジナルの作成と大量の複製が同時に可能になり、さらにその数の何倍もの「鑑賞者」を生み出した。

　アートが幅広い層の人々のものになっていく一方、失われるものがあるとベンヤミンは言う。唯一のものとしての作品、その場所だけにある空間、そのとき限りに聞こえてくる音楽。それらはその唯一性のゆえに、アウラ[3]

未　来──第5章　　*311*

because of its singleness. Gift, technique and representations like miracles moved people and inspired awe. The "miracle" was what Benjamin called "aura." An "aura," like a miracle, can never be reproduced.

Benjamin called the value of art "cult value" which was given by "aura." And he said that the "cult value" was replaced by "exhibition value" after the "age of mechanical reproduction." An "art museum" as a building type or a system was established after modernism. We go to a museum to appreciate art works, but not to worship them, even if someone might do so. Most of people today go to an exhibition of Gogh or Monet after having looked at their works as reproductions or images.

Of course, paintings and sculptures as original singularities have been painted and carved since the "age of mechanical reproduction." But we cannot go back to the previous age. Today, "aura" comes back only when an auction is held. A painted canvas of one square-foot is traded for one million dollars. Now people find "cult value" only in money. Besides the irony, some artists like Marcel Duchamp and Andy Warhol opened a new era by utilizing reproductions. Benjamin had thought about art by Duchamp and Dadaism as well. The famous series of works by Duchamp was titled "Ready Made." He brought a urinal, a window and a wheel and "converted" them into art works. These works were positively accepted by Benjamin.

Benjamin didn't lament the loss of "aura." He also didn't promote the change from "cult value" to "exhibition value." He only observed the changes of the times and sought a logic which he thought should come with change:

> *One might generalize by saying: the technique of reproduction detaches the reproduced object from the domain of tradition. By making many*

を持っていた。奇跡のような才能、技術、現前にひとは感動し、畏怖の念すら覚えた。その「奇跡のような」ものこそが、アウラだ。奇跡の大量生産は不可能なように、アウラもまた複製されえない。

　アウラに基づくアートの価値を、ベンヤミンは「礼拝価値」と呼んだ。そしてそれは、複製芸術以降においては「展示価値」にとって替わられるという。「美術館」というビルディング・タイプ、あるいは制度が出来上がったのも、近代以降のことだ。美術館に展示された作品を、私たちは鑑賞しに行く。その霊性を礼拝しに行くのではない（なかにはそのようなことを期待して行く者もいるだろう）。ゴッホやモネの展覧会に、それまでその複製や画像を見たことがないというものが出かけることはめったにない。
　もちろん「複製技術時代」以降にも、唯一の絵画は描かれ、彫刻が彫られた。だがそれで時代が逆戻りするわけもない。現代のアートの「唯一性」にアウラが現れる瞬間があるとすれば、それはオークションの時くらいだ。１メートル四方の絵の具のついた布（キャンバス）が、数億円で取引される。ひとが今、「礼拝価値」を見出すのは金だけだ。皮肉はともかく、これまでにも見てきたように、マルセル・デュシャンやアンディ・ウォーホルなど、むしろ複製性を積極的に取り込むことで新しい時代を開いたアーティストたちも多かった。実際、ベンヤミンはデュシャンらダダのアートも意識していた。デュシャンには「レディ・メイド（既製品）」シリーズと呼ばれる作品群がある。デュシャンはそこで、小便器や窓や自転車の車輪をどこかから持ってきて、それをアートとして「流用」した。ベンヤミンはそんなダダを肯定的に見ていた。
　ベンヤミンはアウラの喪失を嘆いていたわけではない。とはいえ、「礼拝価値」から「展示価値」への変化を推進していたわけでもない。ただ思想家として時代の変化を観察し、その変化の下にあるはずの論理を探していた。

　　複製技術は──一般論としてこう定式化できよう──複製される対
　象を伝統の領域から引き離す。複製技術は複製を数多く作り出すこと

未　来──第5章　　*313*

reproductions it substitutes a plurality of copies for a unique existence. And in permitting the reproduction to meet the beholder or listener in his own particular situation, it reactivates the object reproduced.

—*The Work of Art in the Age of Mechanical Reproduction*

Art had moved its address from the "domain of tradition," church, and aristocracy to the art museum and film theatre. Art would be reproduced and exposed to the masses so that the "cult value" was reduced, and "exhibition value" emerged. A urinal that Duchamp took out of a toilet became an art work titled "Fountain," because an art museum assigned the "exhibition value" to it. The "exhibition value" of "Fountain" would disappear if it was returned to the toilet. It could become art or urinal in order to meet the beholder or listener in his own particular situation.

Does it mean that any value must be relative? That might be the case only if a place gives a value to it.

The value can abruptly reverse, vanish or rise. How can we keep believing in such a value, which is a technique brought forth by mechanical reproduction?

Today the high-technology of mechanical reproduction which has progressed much more than Benjamin expected, has been realized. Everybody uses "C&P" for any purpose. Mediocre pictures change into something worth seeing through Photoshop. "Selfies" by smartphones can be retouched easily, and Instagram is filled with pictures of "Kawaii me" which means "Cute me." The "I" has got an "exhibition value" on the internet. In the "place" where everything is relative, the "I" has the "exhibition value" as high art works.

The value of "I" has not increased, and the value of art has not decreased. However, the space of the internet changes anything within it into the

314   Chapter 5——*Future*

によって、複製の対象となるものをこれまでと違って一回限り出現させるのではなく、大量に出現させる。そして複製技術は複製に、それぞれの状況のなかにいる受け手のほうへ近づいてゆく可能性を与え、それによって、複製にされる対象をアクチュアルなものにする。

――『近代の意味』

　芸術はその所在（アドレス）を教会や貴族の邸宅など「伝統の領域」から美術館や映画館などに移した。複製されて大衆の目にさらされることで「礼拝価値」は薄れたが、「展示価値」が生まれた。デュシャンが「トイレ」から持ち出した小便器が芸術作品となったのは、確かに美術館の「展示室」がもたらした「展示価値」のゆえだ。それは同じ美術館内でも、「トイレ」に返却すれば価値は消える。「それぞれの状況のなかにいる受け手のほうへ近づいて」芸術にもなり、便器にもなる。

　そうであれば、あらゆる価値は相対的だということになるだろうか？置かれる場所によって価値が生じ、あるいは失われるなら、それは確かに相対的なものかもしれない。
　価値は逆転することもあれば、無化することもあるし、反対に突然高騰することもある。だとすると、複製技術がもたらしたそのような価値を、私たちはどうして信じ続けることができるだろうか？
　今日、ベンヤミンが観察し予感もしていた「複製技術」よりもはるかに進化した「高度複製技術」が到来した。「コピペ」は日常化し、凡庸な写真も「フォトショップ」で見るべき価値のある映像へと変化する。SNS「インスタグラム」ではスマートフォンで撮った写真をインスタントにリタッチでき、結果「かわいい私」の「自撮り写真」で溢れている。インターネット上では「私」こそが「展示価値」を持った。すべてが相対的なこの「場所」では、「私」は「芸術作品」と同等の「展示価値」を持っていると言ってもいい。
　「私」の価値が上がったわけではない。「芸術作品」の価値が低下したわけでもない。ただインターネットという空間は、すべてを「展示価値」に

"exhibition value" and partially erases the substance just before it is exhibited. The "I" retouched in Instagram is not the same as what I am. Nevertheless, everybody begins to believe that the retouched "I" is what I am.

The myth of "growth" is based on trust in an identity that grows. If the "I" or society looks like it is changed after growth, it must keep its identity. Or trust the identity. Literature, architecture, film or any expression of modernism thematized the issue of identity. They looked for the identity and expressed the crisis of it. It was the age that was losing the "aura" that guaranteed the identity. The "Technique of mechanical reproduction" rendered probable the eventual nullification of identity. The issue of identity or nothing became their theme.

On the other hand, we can talk about another kind of logic.

Identity had not been the theme for expression before the "technique of mechanical reproduction." It was the issue that the "technique" brought. Nobody cares about the "original" when they have no idea about the "copy." Our identity is the concept that modernism has brought.

What about today and the coming age? Would the problematique of "identity" still be significant for the "I" that depends on the "exhibition value" attained through the internet?

3. A Nightmare Called "Identity"

The twenty-first century began with terrorism by Al-Qaeda. Then ISIS, another Islamic fundamentalist group, took over and continued the terrorism. In the 2010's, they devastated Paris with their terrorist attacks. The shooting in the Bataclan Theatre in November 2015, left the world in shock. In 2014, they also attacked the magazine company "Charlie Hebdo," and they announced that "Charlie Hebdo" had insulted Islam and that was why they committed the crime. But the Bataclan Theatre

316   Chapter 5——*Future*

変えると同時に、「展示」直前の主体をなかば消去する。インスタグラムでリタッチされた「私」は私そのものとは微妙に違う。だがやがて誰もが、リタッチされた「私」こそが私そのものだったのだと思い始める。

　「成長」という神話は、「成長」する主体の同一性^(identity)への信頼に基づいていた。「私」や「社会」が「成長」して変化を遂げたように見えても、その主体はアイデンティティを保つ。あるいは保つと信じる。文学にせよ建築にせよあるいは映画にせよ、近代の表現はそのアイデンティティこそをテーマに据えた。アイデンティティを求め、それが失われそうな危機を描いた。アイデンティティを保証するアウラが失われつつある時代だった。「複製技術」はアイデンティティの無効化を宣言する可能性があった。その問題こそが主題化されたとして、不思議はない。

　だが一方で、こうも言えるのだ。

　アイデンティティとは、「複製技術」以前のテーマではない。それは「複製技術」こそが生み出した「問題」なのだ。コピーという概念がない時代に、だれもオリジナルなどを気にしない。私たちのアイデンティティとは、近代が生み出した概念に違いない。

　現代そしてこれからの時代においてはどうだろうか？　インスタントにリタッチされ、ネット上での「展示価値」に頼る「私」に、果たしてアイデンティティという問題構成はなおも有効であり続けるだろうか？

3. 「アイデンティティ」という悪夢

　21世紀はアルカイダのテロとともに始まった。テロはその後ISISという、アルカイダとは同根別系のイスラム過激派によって受け継がれた。2010年代には、パリがISISによる忌むべき攻撃を受けた。

　特に2015年11月の、Bataclan劇場他での銃撃テロは衝撃的だった。それに先立つ2014年の「Charlie Hebdo」襲撃テロは、イスラムを侮蔑している雑誌社という、テロリストなりの攻撃目標があった。だがBataclan劇場はイスラムとも反イスラムとも一切の関係はない。劇場がある地域は、

未来──第5章　*317*

had nothing to do with neither Islam nor anti-Islam. The area around Bataclan was a multicultural district with the diversity to accept the differences. The young attackers were born in France. They grew up in the culture of France, however they were Muslim and children of immigrants.

Did these young people become terrorists because they have nowhere they live in society? Is it because there is few job opportunities for sons of immigrants? To these questions, Le Clézio[3] answered, "The problem is not if they can find jobs. The problem is if they could find their identity. The key for all problems is education.[4]"

What did Le Clézio mean with the word "identity?" It is difficult to grasp in the short interview.

Self-fulfillment in the society established selfishness as the result. This kind of "identity" has been criticized as a European or modern capitalist idea.[5] Some critics pointed out that the idea could be an origin of violence.[6] Others said that everyone would live by switching between plural identities.[7]

I don't think Le Clézio, who has been charmed by the cultures of Asia and Central and South America, and criticized European society from the outside, would regard self-fulfillment in society as an identity. I suppose that he would mention diverse identities in society that they should design for young people to be able to choose plural identities. Actually in his early novels, it is difficult to even identify the characters. The end of *War*[8] (1970) contains the following sentences:

Someone has made an attempt to understand. One day, someone who began to think about war, wanted to find out what war was all about, and

むしろ異質なものでも受け入れようとする多文化的、多様的な場所だった。そこが攻撃の対象とされ、しかも、テロ遂行者はフランスで生まれ育った若者だった。移民の子でモスリムだったとはいえ、フランス文化のなかで生まれ育った人間だったのだ。

　こうした若者は、ひょっとして自分の居場所が見つけられないがためテロリストになるのだろうか？　時として、移民の子であることを理由に仕事にすら就けないから？　そうした趣旨の質問を受けて、フランスの作家ル・クレジオ[4]は、こう答えている[5]。「問題は、そこで仕事が見つかるか見つからないかということではない。問題は、アイデンティティを見つけられるかどうかということだ。すべての問題への鍵は、教育にある」。
　ここでル・クレジオは、どのような意味で「アイデンティティ」という語を使っているのだろうか？　短いインタビューからそれをくみ取るのは難しい。
　社会のなかでの自己実現、その結実としてのゆるぎない自我。そのような「アイデンティティ」はヨーロッパ的な、あるいは近代資本主義的な概念であると批判されてきたし[6]、あるいはそれこそが「暴力」を生み出してきたと批判する者もいる[7]。私たちはだれも複数のアイデンティティを行き来しながら生きているのだという主張もある[8]。
　アジアや中南米の文化にひかれながらヨーロッパ社会を外から観察し批判もしてきたル・クレジオが、安直にヨーロッパ社会のなかでの自己実現こそアイデンティティだと考えているとは思えない。もっと多義的なアイデンティティのことを言っていたはずで、それこそを若者が選択的／複数的に獲得していけるようにすべきだと、主張はそのような意味なのだと推測する。そもそもル・クレジオの初期の小説では、登場人物の人格さえあいまいだ。『戦争』[9]（1970年）はこんな文章で終わる（正確には、文章のあとにル・クレジオ自身が撮ったパリのスナップショットが数ページ続く）。

　　誰かが理解しようと試みた。誰かが、ある日、戦争の何たるかを、
　　いかにしてそれが終わるものかということを知ろうとした。誰かが、

未　来──第5章　*319*

how it would come to an end. Someone wanted to break windows in order to breathe, wanted to launch words in quest of this kind of peace. Then, vanished.

Those who will see peace are not yet there, have not even been conceived.

I myself am not really sure that I am born.

This "war" is not referring to the terrorism of today, nor the Vietnam War in the time when the novel was published. It's not about the war broadcasted by mass media, but actually and secretly proceeding between individuals and cities. "I" who "am not really sure that I am born" tells about the "war." Characters such as "Monsieur X" or "Bea B," with unspecified identities, enter the story. Substance who has consciousness to narrate the story are switched between the characters so that it is difficult to be specified. "*I shall no longer be called Bea B, nor you Monsieur X, and Pedro will no longer be called Pedro. [...] We shall all call ourselves by one identical name, something tender and genuine, a name that will launch our bodies in unison, in swift particles, in an assault upon the glass bubble. We shall call ourselves ELECTRICITY, for example.*" The characters who share an identical name have "war" with the city described as "*Bea B had seen the city take shape around her head.*"

"Bea B," or "*ELECTRICITY*," talks about what annoys her:

WHY DO ALL PEOPLE WANT TO EXPRESS THEMSELVES? They are so intelligent, all of them, and there they are, trying to keep things together. They all want to do something. You see, they don't want to disappear. They want to assert their existence.

"We," or "*ELECTRICITY*," accept wavering identity and give affirmation

320   Chapter 5———*Future*

呼吸するために、窓ガラスを割ろうとし、一種平和のようなものを見出すがために自分の言葉を発そうとした。それから姿を消した。

　平和を目の当たりにするであろう者たちはまだ存在していない。生まれてさえいない。
　僕自身、生まれたということが本当に確かなわけではないのだ。

　この「戦争」はもちろん今日のテロのことではないし、出版当時のベトナム戦争でもない。マスメディアに報じられる戦争ではなく、個人と都市との間で密かにしかしはっきりと進行している「戦争」だ。その「戦争」が、生まれたことが確かでもない「ぼく」によって語られている。ムッシューXやベア・Bといったアイデンティティ不詳の登場人物がそれに絡む。セリフや意識の主体は時に登場人物の間で入れ替わり、特定ができない。「あたしの名前はもはやベア・Bではないだろうし、あなたもムッシュー・Xじゃなく、ペドロの名前はもはやペドロではなく、（中略）あたしたちはただ一つの同じ名前を名乗るだろう、（中略）それがあたしたちのそれぞれの体をともどもに、急速な分子としてガラスの球の襲撃に送りだすだろうし、あたしたちの名前は例えば**電気**であるだろう」（太字原著）。アイデンティティを分かち合う人間たちが、都市と戦争をする。「ベア・Bという名の娘は都市が自分の顔のまわりに形作られるのを見てきた」と描写される都市と。

　ベア・Bは──あるいは**電気**は──こんなふうに憤る。

　なぜ誰もかれも自分を表現したがるの？　みんなは実に賢いわ。誰もがよ。そしてみんなは物ごとに辻つまを合わそうと試みてるのよ。誰もが何かをしようとしている。わかる、あの人たちは消えてしまいたくないのよ。自分を肯定したいんだわ。（太字原著）

　アイデンティティの揺らぎを受け入れ、その複数性や共有性も肯定する

未　来──第5章　　*321*

to the plurality and the concept of sharing. On the other hand, they know some people "don't want to disappear" but "want to assert their existence." Those are splintered ways of identifying themselves. Actually, in our real world in the era after "technique of mechanical reproduction," all of us have no other way but to identify ourselves in the splintered ways.

There are no longer any unwavering identities. Our world itself has been divided into small fragments or multi-layers and is always wavering. Nation and class are also wavering. Even the idea of distance is changing a lot. We can see a landscape anywhere on earth, just by knowing the location. The number of worlds that every individual belongs to has increased since the emergence of social media. Everyone can give plural answers to such a question like "where are you now?" And "who are you?" might not be so easy to answer definitively. That might be why "people all want to express themselves." Forms of self-expression like pictures, illustration, music and manga fill the internet, and some people live broadcast motion pictures of their lives.

Not only Muslim immigrant children, but also all of us living today have problems finding our own identities. Nobody can picture a vivid self-portrait of themselves.

Young people from Europe who left Europe to be trained as terrorists must have been quite anxious. They have surely known what kind of identity would be important in European society. They are familiar with Twitter and Facebook, and they know that they live in various layers of the world. They were the same as us. We can metaphorically say that all people of today are a kind of "immigrant." They may have wanted to express themselves just like the other young people in the world. If they were in Japan, they may have drawn manga comics or something to express themselves. They could have tried to be professional manga

「あたしたち」あるいは**電気**。一方で「消えてしまいたくない」「自分を肯定したい」ひとびとがいることを認める。それらは一見、相反する様態の存在だ。そして私たちの現実の世界でも、「複製技術」の到来以来、だれもがその一見相反する様態の存在となった。

　　・

　単一の世界のなかでの揺るぎない自己などというものは、もはやない。世界自体が常に揺るぎ、多層的な、あるいは細分化された空間へと変化した。国家も階級ももはや確かなものではない。距離という概念すら揺らいで、世界のどこであれその住所を打ち込めばグーグル・アースでその周りの風景を直ちに見ることができる。自己が帰属する世界は、SNSの出現後さらに増えた。「私はどこにいるか」という問いに対して誰もが何通りも答えを用意できる。「私は何者であるか」は単純には確定しない。しかし、だからこそ、「誰もかれも自分を表現したがる」のだろう。インターネット上に、写真、イラスト、音楽、漫画の類の「自己表現」は溢れかえり、「ユーチューバー」「ニコ生主」として自らの姿を放映し続ける者たちもいる。

　「アイデンティティを見つけられるかどうか」という問題を抱えているのはヨーロッパで生まれ育ったモスリムの移民の子たちだけではない。現代を生きる者たちすべてがそうだ。誰もがはっきりとした自己像など描きえない。

　生まれ育ったヨーロッパを出てテロリストとしての訓練をうけた若者たちにとっては、確かにその不安は大きくそしてリアルなものだっただろう。彼らはヨーロッパの伝統的・正統的なアイデンティティの在り方にも確かに触れた。ツイッターやフェイスブックにも普通になじみ、だから複層的な存在としての自己も知っていた。そこまでは、彼らと私たちの違いは何もない。アイデンティティの単一性が揺らぐ世界では、世界中の誰もが移民のようなものなのだと比喩的に言うことだってできる。世界のほかの若者と同じように、彼らもだからこそ「自分を表現」したがったのかもしれない。日本であれば、そうしたければ漫画でも描いていたかもしれない。

未　来──第5章

artists, and tried to upload their works on the internet. But the situation is different for Muslim immigrant children in Europe, however it is only for a few of them. They may have believed that they could best express themselves through terrorism. Actually, many were recruited by ISIS on social media. This means they became Islamic fundamentalists not just because they were Muslim. They just chose it as one of their self-portraits. In fact, some of them converted in order to join the terrorists.

As a result, the twenty-first century began as the era of terrorism, and it will continue for a long time. When people who can't stand the heavy anxiety which unstable identity has brought, or meet the difficulty which economics and human relations impose, they might come up with the idea to use a violent system if they find it around them. It is not an unnatural way.

Today, the gap between where we are and violence is not so wide. Some people who have accustomed themselves to express assaultive emotions on the internet cannot stop using dirty words which express ethnic discrimination. There are several reasons for them to become terrorists, if it is easy to get their hands on weapons and find some comrades. They can find a space to hide themselves if they take on different identities. On the internet, many people are expressing themselves under a handle or anonymity. An identity on the internet is different from an identity in the real world. They do not need fundamentalism. If it appears possible to find an intriguing self-portrait through doing so, many will instantly become terrorists.

What can we do against such terrorism? Should we try to retrieve simple, unique identities by rejecting wavering identities, as some conservatives argue? No way. Such an identity is just an illusion, even a joke, in some ways. Some people might believe it to be cult-like; however, it cannot help us to rebuild the actual world. We must accept the way identity is

プロの漫画家を目指すか、そうでなくても同人誌やネットで、表現はできる。そこがヨーロッパの移民——といってそのごく一部だが——にとって少し違った。彼らがもっともよく「自分を表現」できるのは、テロリズムだと、彼らの目には映ってしまった。実際、彼らはISISに加わる意思をわざわざツイッターなどで発信している。つまり、彼らがイスラム原理主義者となったのは、彼らがモスリムだったからではない。自己像のひとつとして、目的的にイスラム原理主義を選んだだけで、その証拠に、テロの隊列に加わるために改宗したものも少なくない。

　結果として、21世紀はテロの時代として始まり、そしてそれは長く続くだろう。アイデンティティの揺らぎがもたらす不安に耐え切れなくなったものが、経済的にあるいは人間関係的に追い詰められ、その時身近に「暴力開放装置」があれば、「自己表現」としてその装置を操作しようと考える、それは当然の成り行きというものだ。

　今、暴力はそれほど高いハードルの向こうにあるのではない。例えばインターネットで攻撃的感情の吐露に慣れてしまった人々は、リアルな場所で民族差別の汚らしい言葉を使うことも躊躇しない。武器が手に入り適当な徒党が組めるのなら、彼らがテロリストに転化しない理由はあまりない。複数のアイデンティティを使い分ければ身を隠す空間などいくらも見つかるだろう。ネット上では匿名あるいはハンドルネームで「自分を表現」しようとするものも多い。その世界での「自分」は、本名で暮らす世界の自分とは、異なるのだ。宗教の過激な原理など、必要ではない。彼らにとって魅惑的な「自画像」がそこに描かれるのなら、インスタント・テロ集団は世界中のどこにでも出来上がる。

　そのテロに対抗しようとするなら、どうしたらいいのだろう？　アイデンティティの揺らぎを否定し、再び単一で単純なアイデンティティを取り戻さなければならないのだろうか？　保守主義者たちが言うように？　そんなことはありえない。そんなアイデンティティは幻想か冗談のようなもので、信仰する者がいるのは勝手だが、実質的な時代の構想力になりうる

未　来──第5章　*325*

today. We need to understand any desire people have to "express themselves." Then, we should consider how the journey of looking for an identity can be oriented to another point besides violence.

4. How to Draw Your Self-Portrait

Amartya Sen[9] wrote the following in his book titled *Identity and Violence: The Illusion of Destiny* (2006):

> *One of the oddities of the postcolonial world is the way many non-Western people today tend to think of themselves as quintessentially "the other" as Akeel Bilgrami, the philosopher, has beautifully discussed in a paper called "What Is a Muslim?" They are led to define their identity primarily in terms of being different from Western people.*

Sen is discussing Muslims here and is clearly criticizing Euro-centrism. The logic can be applied to other identities as well. After the emergence of modernism, a given entity would discover or define its identity in terms of what an "other" opposed entity was not. For example, Japan tried to define "Japan" in terms of how it was different from Europe, and would overcome it when Japan was in the process of modernization.[10] Today too, individuals meet other people and find their identities to be "the other." We can see the same thing in bullies in school societies. Someone can claim the identity of "not bullied" through bullying the other one.

The idea of "identity" must be something like this. This word had not been familiar to Japanese people before modernization. In fact, we have not found an appropriate translation for the word in Japanese, so I have

326   Chapter 5——*Future*

はずがない。私たちは、現代のアイデンティティの在りかたを受け入れる
しかない。「自分を表現」しようとする誰もかれもの欲望も理解するしか
ない。そのうえで、これからのアイデンティティの在りかたを探る旅が、
暴力とは違う方向を目指すように考えていかなければならない。

4. 自画像の描きかた

　アマルティア・セン[10]は、『アイデンティティと暴力』のなかで、次のよ
うに書いている。

　　　独立後の社会に見られる奇妙な現象の一つに、今日、多くの非西洋
　　人が自らを根本的に「他者」とみなす傾向がある。哲学者のアキール・
　　ビルグラミは「ムスリムとはなにか」という論文のなかで、それについ
　　て見事に論じている。つまり彼らはおもに西洋人とは異なるという観点
　　から自己のアイデンティティを定義するように仕向けられているのだ。

（傍点原文）

　センがここで言うのはモスリムの例であり、ヨーロッパ中心主義的な世
界を批判するものだ。だが、こうした論理はアイデンティティ一般にもあ
てはまる。近代以降の主体は、自己以外の何ものかの「他者」として、自
己を発見する。例えば日本は近代化の過程で、ヨーロッパとは異なりさら
にはそれを超克するものとしての「日本」[11]を、見出そうとした。あるいは
現代を生きる個人も、絶え間なく自己以外と出会い、結果その自己以外の
ものにとっての「他者」としての自分を発見し続けている。「いじめ」も
そうだ。自己以外のものをいじめることで、いじめられる悲惨な存在から
逃れた存在になれる。

　アイデンティティとは本質的にそのようなものかもしれない。この語は
例えば日本人には、昔からなじみのある概念ではなかった。実際、今でも、
この語に適切な日本語訳はない。だからこの本でも、その発音をカタカナ

written it phonetically in the Japanese original of this book. For Japanese people, "identity" is the idea that emerged when Europe as "the other" appeared in modernization. Identity must be essentially something to be found as "the other" by someone else. Even if "I" travel alone in the cosmos, "I" would find the identity as "the other" for the cosmos, the space ship or the operating computer.[11] "I," as something different from them, has this consciousness and this body.

That is why the issue of "identity" has emerged in the beginning of the age of mechanical reproduction and is becoming invalid in the era of "C&P" of today. "I" is always similar to someone, and someone is only a copy of "I." In such a world, how can we strive towards a unique life?

I wrote about such a world in my first novel, *Portrait in Number*. I described how to draw self-portraits in a world where the "I" must resemble others. (Refer to Chapter Two)

"Identity" is not a simple idea. "Fulfillment in a society" has nothing to do with "identity." Even celebrities can feel that their identities are fragile if they have a sensibility for the situation of today. Wealth or fame doesn't work against the replication of self, but reinforces it through some evidence. Fame is like attention shares. The exchange-value is high but gives nothing for a unique life of "I."

Nobody is sure to have an identity. It is the same situation for Donald Trump[12] and illegal immigrants labeled as "criminal aliens"[13] by Trump. What we should do is to carefully draw portraits of "the others" then we might be able to see ourselves in the portraits. It is not so special. Many people would feel the significance of life when they see themselves in the child which resembles them. Some may try to identify a self-image reflected on the eyes of their lover. Those are important, but not enough. So we read novels, watch films, and build works of architecture.

表記している。日本人にとってアイデンティティとは、近代においてヨーロッパという他者が現れて初めて問題化した概念だ。つまりもともと、アイデンティティとは、自己以外にとっての「他者」として発見されるしかない。宇宙のなかをただ一人さまよっていたとしても、「私」は「私」を宇宙、飛行船あるいはそれを操るコンピューターにとっての「他者」として見出すだろう。私はそれらとは違う、この意識、この身体を持っているものとして。

だからこそ、複製技術勃興の近代においてアイデンティティは問題化され、コピペ全盛の今日では無効宣言すらされることもある。「私」はいつも誰かに似ていて、誰かは「私」のコピーでしかない。そのような空間で、一回きりの生を生きるとはどのようなことか？

僕が最初の小説『ポートレイト・イン・ナンバー』で書いたのは、そのような空間だった。「私」が常に誰かに似てしまう場所での、「自画像」の描きかたを僕は書いた（第2章参照）。

アイデンティティとは、ここに論じてきたように、それほど単純なものではない。「社会的な自己実現」などは、アイデンティティとはあまり関係がないか、あったとしてもそのごく一部でしかない。金持ちや有名人でも、今日への感受性を持つものなら、自らのアイデンティティがどれほどあやふやなものか感じているはずだ。金も有名性も自らの複製性に対抗するどころか、むしろそれを証拠付け補強する。有名性は注目銘柄株のようなものだ。交換価値は高いが、固有で一度きりの「私」の生に意味を与えるものではない。

誰もが確かなアイデンティティを持ちえない。ドナルド・トランプも、彼が「その多くが犯罪者」と罵倒する「移民」も、状況は等しく同じだ。私たちがすべきことは、せいぜい「他者」の像を丹念に描くことで、それでそこにかすかに浮かび上がる自己を感じることができるかもしれない。特別なことではない。例えば自分の子の姿に現れる自己への相似を確認して、生の意義を感じ取ろうとするものは多いだろう。恋人の目に映る自己に、アイデンティファイする者も珍しくない。そうした行為に価値がないとは言わない。だが、それだけでは不足なのだ。だからこそひとは小説を

People who write novels, shoot films and design works of architecture draw portraits of "the other." It would be an attempt to counter the "technique of mechanical reproduction" through help from the "technique." However, it lost the power to counter, and then the intention to counter.

For example, you can look at advertising copy for Japanese "pure literature" from the end of the twentieth to the twenty-first century. Most of them promise "a tiny feeling of strangeness in daily life." "The great other" has been lost. On the other hand, a tiny strangeness can be real and literary. Japanese literature has been trying to survive through "literary strangeness." Some critics insisted that the tiny feeling can picture "the lost great other." Actually, they were wrong. A tiny strangeness can only call itself "the tiny self." In conclusion, Japanese literature has become a kind of "taste" which hardly responds to the changing world.

As I wrote in Chapter One, boiling it down to "taste" might be inevitable in this age. "Future" has been lost, Ten'yo Kato has argued, and modernism has ended, as Kojin Karatani has argued, and as a result the possible world cannot stop shrinking. It is actually happening. Our sole and unique life is also shrinking, and some who cannot stand it become terrorists, finally everything will be suppressed in the real world.

Nevertheless, does this situation require a fictional world?

A fictional world is truly "the other." Future, insanity and death. That is why Dostoevsky[14] wrote *Crime and Punishment*, Tarkovsky[15] shot *Stalker* and Melnikov designed *Rusakov Workers' Club*. Those were "the strong others" with the power to show you your insane self-portrait.

We need to accept reality as everything has changed. We should not

読み、映画を見、建築する。

　小説を書き、映画を撮り、建築を設計する者も、そのような「他者」の像を描き、あるいは作り出そうとしてきた。それは「複製技術」の力を借りながら、それに対抗するはずのものだった。ところがまず対抗する力を失い、次に対抗する意思すら消えつつある。

　例えば20世紀末から21世紀初頭までの、日本の「純文学」の売り文句を調べてみればいい。それはおおむね「日常のなかの小さな違和感」だ。大きな「他者」は失われた。だが小さな「違和」にはリアリティがあるし、何より「文学的」だ。日本の文学はそのような「文学的違和」によって生き延びようとしてきた。その小ささが「失われた大きな他者」を描きうると主張してきた。だが実際は違った。小さな違和は結局小さな「自己」しか召喚しなかった。結果として、日本の「純文学」は世界の動きにごく「小さく」しか反応しない、「趣味」的なものになった。

　第1章で述べたように、こうした「趣味」的なものへの縮小は、時代の必然かもしれない。加藤典洋が言うように未来が失われ、柄谷行人が言うように近代が終わった後なのであれば、縮小は避けがたいものなのだろう。現実は、確かにそうだ。私たちの、それぞれの単独で固有の生は、ますます縮小し、そしてそれに耐えられぬ者たちが時にテロを起こし、結局は鎮圧されていく、現実の世界では。

　しかしそもそも、だからこそ必要とされたフィクショナルな世界ではなかったのか？

　フィクショナルなものこそが、本当の他者だった。未来であれ、狂気であれ、死であれ。だからこそドストエフスキーは『罪と罰』を書いた。タルコフスキーは『ストーカー』を撮り、メーリニコフは『ルサコフ労働者クラブ』を設計した。それらは「自画像」を危険な姿として映し出しかねない、強い「他者」だった。

　すべてが変わったことは、受け入れなくてはならない。「成長」が終わ

underestimate the change, as the time of growth comes to an end. It is a conclusive change.

However, we need to live.

We have to continue our unique life until our time of death.

There is nothing to do but to draw self-portraits. In order to do that, we need to imagine and create "the strong other" as fiction.

5. You Can Do Nothing but Travel

In the past, architecture used to be a space to meet "the other," God, the Pure Land, and the future and movement in the beginning of modernism which had intensity.

Then these "others" which had intensity were dismissed. They were oppressive and hazardous because of the intensity. Instead, the homogeneous space which did not stress intensity was asked. Economy and universality became the rational reason for the design. As a result, the functional space that any office buildings have today became the global standard of architectural space.

We definitely asked, and are asking for freedom. On the other hand, no one wants to die in a functional space such as an office.

We secretly want to encounter "the other" which has intensity, not God, nor future after "growth." However, we are still travelling to encounter what is called "the other."

Humans launched a rocket which has approached Pluto. Research into the cosmos will keep progressing. For some scientists, it is a kind of journey back in time to research the origin of the cosmos.

Another journey has been continuing, researching elemental particles. In the small world, nobody can tell if a cat is dead or alive[16] even after a moment because the uncertainty principle rules there.

We are travelling there to encounter the truth.

Chapter 5———*Future*

るという変化を、過小評価することは決してできない。それはあまりにも決定的な変化だ。

　それでも私たちは生きなければならない。

　死の瞬間までの、ただ一度の生を。

　私たちは「自画像」を描き続けるしかない。そのために、強い他者をフィクショナルに想像／創造するほか、生きるすべはない。

5．「旅」をするしか他にない

　かつて建築とは他者に出会うための空間だった。神や浄土と、近代黎明期においては未来や運動という、飛び切り強度のある他者と。

　やがてそれら強度のある他者たちは退けられた。それらは強度があるゆえに抑圧的で、自由を阻害するからだ。均質空間——強度によるストレスがない空間——が求められた。経済性と万能性がその合理的な根拠となった。結果として、現在のオフィス・ビルディングがもつような「機能的空間」が世界のスタンダードとなった。

　確かに私たちは自由を求めた、そして求めている。だが、機能的空間のなかで死にたいと願っているわけではない。

　私たちは、強い他者との遭遇を密かに願っている。それは神ではないし、成長の先の未来でもないかもしれない。だが何ものかと遭遇するための旅を続けている。

　人類は冥王星までロケットを飛ばし、さらにそのずっと先まで探査の感覚を延伸している。それは時間を遡る旅になるとも言われている。つまりは宇宙の起源を探る旅だ。

　別の旅もある。人類は、広大な宇宙とは真逆の微小粒子のなかを覗き込もうとしている。そこは一瞬後の命の状態すら確定できない不確実な空間らしい。[16]

　私たちはそのような場所で、真理と遭遇するための旅を続けている。

未　来——第5章　　*333*

In the film *2001 Space Odyssey*, Stanley Kubrick pictured such kind of a journey to encounter a mystic truth. After the "murdering" computer system called HAL, the protagonist encounters the origin.

The Monolith is depicted as the origin of truth in the film. Actually, we do not encounter "the Monolith," save for in fictional space. We can fictionally see, touch and hear it.

We will never know the origin of truth. We will die before knowing it. That is why we are so eager to travel.

In this sense, the journey by train running through the forest was "fictional" for me. I had actually gone, so it was not fiction. I surely saw that the raindrops leaking between the branches were depleting. I actually saw that the weak sunlight began to leak. It was fact. On the other hand, I can say without contradiction that it was what I imagined and created. I met a mystic truth there. And I created the truth at that moment. It was both fictional and real.

"Space travel," that is what we should draw and create for the next age in the twenty-first century. We can die in space travel, it means we can truly live there. The forest filtering raindrops and sunlight was my Monolith.

The Monolith is the same as the stones that Matsuo Basho saw on his trip in *The Narrow Road to Deep North*:

> *How still it is here—*
> *Stinging into the stones,*
> *The locusts' trill*

> (Translated by Donald Keene)

"The stones" causes emptiness=stillness by making the phenomenon sting into them. And just after the moment, the phenomenon comes back

映画『2001年宇宙の旅』ではそのような旅が描かれた。不可解な真理との遭遇のための旅だ。「ハル」という名のコンピューターを「殺した」後に、主人公はその真理と遭遇する。

　「モノリス」と名付けられた物体が、『2001年宇宙の旅』のなかでは真理の始原として示された。私たちは現実では「モノリス」と出会うことはないだろう。だが、フィクショナルな空間のなかでは、私たちはそれと出会う。フィクショナルにそれを見、触り、聞く。

　私たちは真理の起源と出会えないだろう。誰もがその遭遇の前に、死ぬ。しかしそれがわかっているからこそ、旅を希求する。

　僕にとって、森を通り抜ける列車での旅は、その意味でフィクショナルな旅だった。いや、確かに私は旅をした。雨が葉の隙間を縫って落ち、次の瞬間にそれが光に変わるのを現実に見た。それは事実として間違いがない。同時に、矛盾せずに、それは僕が想像／創造したものだった。僕はその風景に、得体の知れぬ真理を見た。真理を瞬間的に創作した。それはフィクショナルだが、リアルだ。

　私たちがこの21世紀に、次の時代のために描き、あるいはつくり出すべきものは、そのような「旅の空間」に違いない。私たちはそのような「旅の空間」のなかでなら、死ぬことができる。つまり、生きることができる。あの雨と光をろ過する森は、僕にとって「モノリス」のようなものだった。

　「モノリス」は例えば、松尾芭蕉が『奥の細道』への旅の途中で出会った「岩」とも同じだ。

　　閑かさや　岩にしみ入る　蟬の声

　この岩は、現象しているすべてを瞬間に吸い取って無＝「閑かさ」を呼び起こす。そして瞬間ののち、すべての現象をもとに戻す。芭蕉はそれを

from the stones. Basho felt it and wrote a haiku poem. It's fictional. Because no sounds can physically sting into stones. It's real. Because we can hear the stillness that Basho felt.

"Space travel" is generated in each era and vanishes in each era. The space and the time can be there only at once. While I was travelling, I came up with the idea to write a novel because I thought that the novel would be the best way to revive the unforgettable experience in the future. We already know that travel can be experienced by the other or "the other mind." All of us can relive experience of temporal and spatial travel through Basho. Travel is retouched every time and revived with new intensity.

One can do nothing but travel in developed societies. Travel can always renew something.

We will design architecture as "space travel," write a novel as a story of a journey, and shoot a film as time travel.

That is what we can do.

6. What is Possible with Architecture?

What can change "space" into "space travel"? Kyoto, Paris or Delhi which are famous travel destinations are just spaces for the residents who spend their daily lives there. And the cities are just physical compositions composed of various materials. However, that is not the case for travelers.

Hiroshi Hara wrote about the relation between man and material:

> *Man is the troublesome existence. Material can exist without error if there is no man. However, material presents misalignment. I assigned a concept as stories to the misalignment. It means that the existence of*

感じ、5・7・5という定型句としてそれを創作した。もちろん、それはフィクショナルである。なぜなら、物理的には岩は音を吸収したりしないのだから。そして同時にリアルである。芭蕉が感じた閑かさを、私たちも聞くことができるのだから。

　旅の空間は、そのつど生成し、そして消えていく。一回性の空間であり時間である。かつて僕が旅のさなかに小説を考えたのは、きっとその一回性をやがてよみがえらせるのに一番いい方法だと思ったからだ。私たちはすでに、旅が他者によって、あるいは「他我」によって経験されることも見た。芭蕉の『奥の細道』への旅の空間と時間を、私たちは誰もが繰り返し追体験している。その都度、旅はリタッチされ、新しい強度を持ってよみがえる。

　成長後の社会では、「旅」をするしか他にない。常に新しくよみがえる可能性を持つ「旅」。
　私たちは、建築を旅の空間のように設計し、小説を旅の物語のように書き、映画を旅の時間のように撮ろう。
　それが、私たちの可能性だ。

6.「建築に何が可能か？」

　それでは、空間を「旅の空間」に変えるものはいったい何だろうか？
旅の目的地として有名な京都もパリもデリーも、住民にとっては日常の空間だ。様々な物質がつくり上げる物理的な構成物にすぎないといってもいい。しかし「旅人」にとっては、それだけではない。

　原広司は人間と物質との関係について、こんなことを書いている。

　　……人間は、困った存在なのだ。人間がいなかったら、物質は十全な存在なのだ。物質は、人間の出現とともに、ずれを表出する。私はこのずれに対して、物語性なる概念をあてた。つまり物の在り方は、

未　来──第5章　　*337*

materials would transfer to stories when man is related to it. Stories are
meanings that existence gives to consciousness.

—*What is Possible with Architecture?* [17] (translated by Suzuki)

The "travel" to which I referred is the same as "stories" in Hara's thought. It is the *misalignment* that cities and nature show to a traveler. For example, the forest I looked at from the train used to be the existence as a forest without error. But once I, a traveler or "man" in Hara's words, or to all the other people on the train, the forest presents *misalignment*. Raindrops and sunlight leaking between the branches began to slip from the existence as material to narrate the stories of my life. Meanings that the existence of rain and sunlight gave to my consciousness are "stories" and "travel" by my logic.

Hara must have thought that designing architecture should include designing the stories, because no architecture exists without man. Material with errorless existence become architecture only after man is there. That is where "Stories" emerge.

Hara argued that "What is architecture?" is the wrong question. In that case, an answer must be "whatever meets condition A is architecture." And then the answer means that "what doesn't meet condition A is not architecture." This question can only function to reduce the potential or possibilities of architecture.

Hara insisted that we should instead ask "what is possible with architecture?" While man is there, misaligned stories appear on materials. Stories are meanings that materials give consciousness. Consideration about the meaning brings the question "what is possible with architecture?"

Hara wrote about the perception of essences by asking "what is possible?"

This dynamic perception of essences which appears in dialectic would be

人間の介入とともに物語性に転化する。物語性とは、存在が意識に与える意味である。（傍点原著）

——『建築に何が可能か』[17]

　僕が言う「旅」とは、ここで原広司が定義している「物語性」に他ならない。それは「旅人」にとっての都市や自然の空間が示す「ずれ」なのだ。

　例えば、かつて僕が列車の窓から見上げていた九州の森の空間は、ただ森という名の「十全な存在」だった。しかし僕という「旅人」（原の文章内の「人間」）が出現したことによって、「ずれ」を表出した。木々の葉の隙間から零れ落ちる雨と光は、その時ただの物質であることからずれ始め、私の生にとっては欠かせない物語を語り始めた。雨と光の存在が、私の意識に与えた意味、それこそが原の言う「物語性」であり、私の言う「旅」である。

　原は、建築を設計することを、そのような物語性に関わる行為だと考えたはずだ。なぜなら、人間が関わらない建築はありえないからだ。「十全な存在」の物質は、人間がそこにいる（あるいは、いた）ことによってはじめて建築になる。「物語性」は、必然的にそこに生まれる。

　原は、「建築とは何か」という問いは、問いそのものが間違っているという。この問いに対しては、「建築とは定義Aに合致するものである」という答えが想定されると同時に「定義Aに合致しないものは建築ではない」という答えも導き出してしまう。それはただ、建築の可能性を縮小するためだけの問いだ。

　「建築に何が可能か？」という問いこそをたてよと原は主張する。人間がいる限り、物質には「ずれ」＝「物語性」が表出する。それは物質が人間の意識に与える「意味」だと原は言う。その「意味」を考えることが、「建築に何が可能か？」という問いにつながる。

　原は「何が可能か」を問う「本質のとらえかた」について、次のように書いている。

　　こうした動的な本質のとらえかたは、弁証法の示す基本的な性格で

positive for the value of existence and time. It must be the only and most effective form of value judgment to restore the dignity of man. We should understand that we live in a world constructed of differentials. The study of change should be true philosophy. It is more important to have an attitude of giving high value to make change and direction than change for its own sake.

—*What is Possible with Architecture?* (translated by Suzuki)

"Misalignment" and "stories" are signs of the beginning of "change." As Hara mentioned, we live in "a world of differential" that could have no beginning or end. So to be precise, they are signs which point towards a change in the way of change. In terms of "differential," it is the change of "derivative function."

Travel is the change from "change" that our daily life has. "The derivative function" would be changed by travel.

Hara wrote that "It is more important to have an attitude which appraises high value to making change and choosing directions." For the sake of "restoring the dignity of man." Architecture and man are not just materials. Ideal figure ="Idea" is not anywhere. We are not "shadows of the Idea." We live, change and die. For us, who live in a limited time, the questioning of what we are, is similar to looking for the "idea of ourselves." We should think about "how we change" and "what we change for."

The change is "travel." Everything changes during "travel." Place, time and traveler's consciousness that relates to it changes.

What happened during travel where the train ran through the forest? In the train, I surely wanted change and felt the misalignment in materials and nature. When the raindrops leaking between the leaves began to change into sunlight, "stories" definitely existed there. However, I didn't know what the change was for.

340   Chapter 5——*Future*

あるが、時間と存在の価値を肯定するであろうし、人間の尊厳を回復するために有効な唯一の価値判断の形式であると思われる。私たちは微分学の世界に生きていることを了解しなければならない。変化についての学が真の哲学になるべきなのだ。しかし、この際重要なのは、変化することに価値のすべてをおくべきではなく、変化させること、さらにはある方向に変化させることに価値を置くという姿勢である。

——『建築に何が可能か』

「ずれ」や「物語性」とは、ここでいう「変化」の始まりの兆候だ。むろん原の言うように私たちは「微分学」の世界に生きているのだし、そうである以上始まりも終わりもない。したがってより厳密にいうなら、「ずれ」や「物語性」は、「変化」のしかたが「変化」し始めることの兆候だ。「微分学」の例に倣うなら、それは「導関数」の変化だと言ってもよい。

日常も変化を持つが、旅はそこからさらに変わる変化だ。導関数が変わる。

原は「ある方向に変化させることに価値を置く」という姿勢が重要だという。それこそが「人間の尊厳を回復する」と。建築も人間も、ただの物質ではない。どこかに理想の形＝イデアがあって、その影として私たちは存在しているというのでもない。私たちは生き、変わり、やがて死ぬ。その限られた時間を生きるものにとって、「私たちは何か」を問うのは、「私たちのイデア」を探すことに似て、確かに不毛だ。「私たちはどう変化するのか」そして「何に向けて変化するのか」を、考えなければならない。

そしてそれはまさしく「旅」のようなものだ。「旅」ではあらゆるものが変化していく。場所も時間も、物も、そこに深くかかわる「旅人」の意識も。

列車が森の中を通り抜けたあの旅は、どうだったか。確かに僕は変化を求め、そして物質や自然の「ずれ」を感じた。樹の枝を通り抜けるのが雨から光へと変わりつつあったとき、「物語性」は確かにそこに存在した。とはいえあの時の僕はその変化が「何に向けて」のものなのか、まるでわかっていなかった。

未 来——第5章　　*341*

What does it change for?

Here we return to this thesis.

And we can logically assume that it is an antithesis.

"Change" itself is much more important than "what the change is for."

We need to consider the contradiction between the thesis and antithesis. It is related with the end of the "myth of growth" and the "disappearance of future" as we discussed in Chapter One.

Answers to the question "What is possible?" should vary. "Possibility" has meaning only if the answers vary. The default is "everything is possible." So only that which serves to deprive us of freedom is excluded, for example, discriminatory opinions.

Then, what would be a reason to depart on our journey?

Should we know the destination of our journey before departure?

7. Once Ideology Tried to Lead

We already know one possible direction.

This world is going to stop growing. The sustainability can only be kept if it gets to a state of equilibrium in a sense, after it has shrunk a little. I'm not completely sure, but someday this world might try to grow again. Probably sometime after the twenty-second century, or perhaps even later.

So, should we say it like this? "Change for a shrinking world?" Would that be the goal for the thought of humanity?

Philosophy and thought should talk about purpose. They surely did by the end of modernism. But now the situation has become different. Philosophy has downsized its role to become smaller than any other role.

342   Chapter 5———*Future*

何に向けて変化をするのか？

ここでまた、私たちはこの命題に立ち戻る。

一方で、論理上は、私たちは反命題を仮定することもできる。

変化そのものが重要なのだ。それに比べれば「何に向けて」の価値は低い。

このふたつの命題の矛盾はよく考えておく必要がある。それは序章から繰り返し述べてきた、「成長」神話の崩壊や、「未来」の消滅にかかわるからだ。

「何が可能か」という問いへの答えは、多様に示されるべきだ。もしそれが多様でなければ、「可能性」はそもそも意味を持たない。「可能性」は、「私たちは何でもできる」という地点にある。そうである以上、自由を剝奪するような「方向」のみが、最初に除外される（例えば言論の自由を略奪する差別的言論のみが最初に除外されるように）。

だがそのあとに、私たちは「何に向けて」歩き出したらいいのだろう？

旅が何に向けてのものなのか、出発の前に私たちは予め知っておくべきだろうか？

7．かつては「思想」が導こうとした

私たちはすでに、可能なひとつの「方向」を知っている。

この世界はやがて成長をやめる。少し縮小したのち、ある種の平衡化を得るしか、その持続可能性はない。遠い将来、再び成長が目的になる時代が来るかもしれない。だがそれは、当面は——今この時代を生きているものが死を迎えるまでの時間内には——ない。

それで私たちはこう言うのだろうか？　「縮小する社会に向けて変化せよ」と？　それが人類の思想の結末なのか？

ほんとうは、哲学や思想こそが、「何に向けて」を語るはずだった。近代の終焉まで、それは確かにそうだった。だが、今はもう、そうではない。哲学は、ほかの何よりもその役割を縮小した。

未　来——第5章　*343*

I have talked again and again about the crises facing literature, art and architecture in this book. Now we see another severe crisis in philosophy and contemporary thought.

Philosophy is a study of man and the world. People still need philosophy after the explosive progression of science and clear elucidation of secret life and the cosmos. It might be because we can't understand ourselves even after understanding other people and the world. However, philosophy and contemporary thought cannot treat the painful mind.

Contemporary thought has gotten lost in the narrow path of logic and language. Or we got lost on the way. Brain science and genetics have inductively shown what a man is. Sociology and anthropology have followed the methods. The methods are scientific and inductive so that they could clearly picture man and the world of today. Philosophy and contemporary thought only translates the "picture" in terms of philosophy.

Yet, Quentin Meillassoux,[18] a brilliant thinker of the younger generation, wrote the following:

> *How are we to grasp the meaning of scientific statements bearing explicitly upon a manifestation of the world that is posited as anterior to emergence of thought and even of life —posited, that is, as anterior to every form of human relation to the world? Or, to put it more precisely: how are we to think the meaning of discourse which construes the relation to the world —that of thinking and/or living —as a fact inscribed in a temporality within which this relation is just one event among others, inscribed in an order of succession in which it is merely a stage, rather than an origin?*
>
> —*After Finitude : An Essay On the Necessity Of Contingency*[19]

While science reveals the secrets of the cosmos, life, and the enigmas of the self, it is also about the anguish of life and death. The role of

この本で、僕はたびたび文学や芸術、そして建築の「危機」について論じてきた。もっと危機的状況にあるものがあった。それが哲学、あるいは「現代思想」と呼ばれるものだ。

　哲学は、人間と世界について考察する学問だ。自然科学が爆発的に発展し、生命や宇宙の謎が大きく解き明かされてもなお、人間は哲学を求めてきた。自分以外のひとや世界に合理的な理解はできても、自分自身に対してだけは、なおも理解しきれない何かが残るからだ。だが今や哲学や「現代思想」は、その苦痛に満ちた感覚に対して、何も治療を行いえない。

　「現代思想」は言葉と論理の隘路に陥った。あるいは、人類がたどるべき隘路に陥ったといってもいい。脳科学や遺伝子学は帰納的に人間の姿を描き出した。社会学や人類学もその方法に追随した。それらは「科学的」かつ帰納的であるがゆえに明晰に、この時代の人間や世界を描き出してみせる。哲学や「現代思想」は、その明晰な描画を哲学用語で翻訳するだけになった。

　それでも最も新しい思想家のひとりであるメイヤスー[18]は、こう書いている。

　　世界に対する人間のいかなる関係よりも前であると想定される世界のデータを扱う科学的言明の意味を、私たちはいかに理解すべきなのだろうか？　あるいは世界に対する——生物そして／あるいは思考の——関係を、他のあらゆる出来事と同列でしかないひとつの事実として——すなわち時間的な継起の起源としてではなく、その途中の道標として——時間のなかに書き込むような言説の意味を私たちはいかに考えるべきだろうか？

　　　　　　　　——『有限性の後で——偶然性の必然性についての試論』[19]

　科学は宇宙や生命の謎を次々と解き明かしているが、それでも「私」自身への謎——生と死についての苦悩——はまだ、あるいはむしろ増えるだ

philosophy might be continual as to what "inscribes the relation to the world in temporality." But can only philosophy do it? Is there high value placed on "inscription" with logical language and no fallacy? Or should we say it in another way. What can be understood in science doesn't require philosophy, for example, the issue of "brain death and organ transplants," and what cannot be understood in science cannot be understood in philosophy, for example, the issue of "the meaning of life."

I must add an obvious fact that philosophy and contemporary thought would never lose its value. Philosophy and contemporary thought has clearly helped me a lot in writing this book. The era of modern architecture, literature and film was also the era explored by philosophy and modern thought. Thought had power, and will has power. When we try to change the world or ourselves, we must support the attempt. However, it would be correct to say that we can never explain the world and man in a way free of fallacy —and we don't need to do so. What is not revealed by science is what we cannot see clearly. Architecture, literature and film are expected to express what we cannot clearly see. Art can do it. Philosophy can give intensity to the various expressions, and relate them to each other. It would help the expression to discover a new possibility.

Not philosophy, but science is first to answer the questions such as "what is the world?" or "what is man?" But philosophy doesn't want to give up the questions. Then it gets lost in the logical labyrinth, and loses another power. It is a power that would be brought by the question as "what is possible with the world?" or "what is possible for man?"

Husserl posed the question "what is existence?" in the phenomenology which he established. Sartre re-fabricated the question to "what is possible with existence?" And we should re-fabricate it again into "what is possibility for?"

346   Chapter 5——*Future*

ろう。哲学の役割は、メイヤスーの言葉を借りれば、「世界に対する関係」を「時間のなかに書き込む」ものとして、今もあるかもしれない。だが、「世界を私という時間のなかに書き込むもの」は、哲学でなくてはならないのか？　それを誤謬なく、論理的な言語として「書き込む」ことに価値があるだろうか？　むしろ、これからの世界ではこう乱暴に言い切ってしまってもいいのかもしれない。科学として理解されうるものは哲学を必要とせず（例えば「脳死と臓器移植」の問題）、科学として理解されえないものは哲学でも理解されない（例えば「生きる意味」について）、と。

　むろんここで急いで付け加えておかなければならない。哲学や「現代思想」に価値がなくなるわけではない。そもそもこの本では構造主義や現象学の成果を多く援用してきた。建築・小説・映画の歴史自体が、哲学や思想が切り開いてきた時代と重なった。思想の力は有効だったし、これからもそうだろう。社会のありかたを変えようとするとき、あるいは自己のありかたを変えようとするとき、それはその行動を根底で支える。だがにもかかわらず、きっとこういって正しいと僕は思う。哲学で世界と人間のすべてを誤謬なく説明することはできないし、する必要もない。科学で解明できないことは、私たちは理解ができないのだと認めるしかない。その理解できないものを、建築や小説や映画は表現すべきだ。アートには、それができる。哲学はその時それらさまざまな表現に力を与え、関連付けることができる。建築や小説が新しい可能性を開くのを援護するだろう。本書でもその様々な例を挙げてきた。

　今や「世界とは何か？」「人間とは何か？」という問いに最初に答えるべきは哲学ではなく科学になった。しかし哲学はその問いにこだわった。そのための論理的迷路に迷い込むうちに、別の大きな力を失おうとしている。それは「世界には何が可能か？」「人間には何が可能か？」という問いの力だ。

　フッサールは現象学において「存在とは何か」を問うた。サルトルはその問いを「存在に何ができるか」という問いに組み替えた。私たちはその問いを今度は「何に向けて？」という問いに再構成すべきだ。

未　来——第5章

Contemporary philosophy tried to incorporate results of the latest science to be a sovereign of knowledge, but failed in the "Sokal Hoax."[20] But it might just be a case of ex-post facto. Philosophy had already lost the actuality and the reality before the "Hoax." It was not only because philosophy had stopped to talk about politics or social events. It might rather be because philosophy had lost the imagination, but also because contemporary literature and architecture was losing imagination.

Some philosophers and thinkers are also literary critics. Trotsky and Lukács, as well as Hideo Kobayashi[21] to Kojin Karatani and Ten'yo Kato from Japan. They tried to dismantle the age and the cognition with words, so it might be right to say that thought means literary criticism. However, the time of literary critics is also coming to an end. *Gunzo,* the Japanese literary magazine, has been giving literature prizes for two categories, "novel" and "critic." A lot of critics entered the scene after getting the prize for "critics," and they have sometimes presented discourses about society out of the flame of literature. But *Gunzo* abolished the literature prize for "critics" in 2015 and made new prize just for "critics" that was rid of the label of "literature." They noted that the "target of criticism is not limited to any genre" so critiquing such things as politics, crime or manners and customs is within their scope. Critics has left "literature" and in "reality" even left literary magazines. But how can the critics without literary imagination have actual power?

Critics of real issues might clearly reflect society like high-resolution images on a monitor. But it would need imagination to be thoughts.

We have a lot of real issues in the world. The problems of terrorism committed by ISIS, and the flood of refugees as a consequence, issues of religion, economics and humanism. The bloated growth of China gets continued threats for unbalancing the economy and the environment of the world. Meanwhile, Japanese society is shrinking and hundreds of

知の統治者であろうとした現代思想は、様々な現代科学の成果を取り入れようとしたが、それはいわゆる「ソーカル事件」[20]で大きく躓いた。しかしそれはむしろ事後的な「きっかけ」だったかもしれない。思想はすでにアクチュアルな手触りを失っていた。しかしそれは、思想が政治や社会的な出来事を語らなくなったから、というわけでは必ずしもない。むしろ、思想が構想力を失っていたから、そして同時代の文学や建築が構想力を失っていったからだ。

　かつて思想家は、文芸批評家を兼任することも多かった。トロツキーやルカーチがそうであり、日本でも小林秀雄から柄谷行人[21]、加藤典洋らに至るまで多くの思想家がそうだった。時代とその認識を言葉で解体しようとする点において、思想とは文芸批評のことなのだと言ってもさほど不正確ではない。しかし文芸批評も終焉を迎える。文芸誌『群像』は長く「文学新人賞」を「小説部門」と「評論部門」に分けて与えてきた。その評論部門から多くの批評家が生まれ、彼らは時に文学の枠を超えて時代と向き合う言説をなした。だが『群像』はそれを2015年に廃止した。代わりに16年から、「文学」の語を外した「群像評論賞」を設けた。「評論の対象は問わない」ということだから、政治や犯罪、あるいは風俗などの評論が賞を得ることもあり得るのだろう。批評は文芸誌の上ですら、「文学」を抜け出し「現実」の側に渡った。だが文学の構想力をもたない批評がアクチュアルな力を持つことがあるだろうか？

　現実への評論は、解像度の高いモニターの画面のように、この社会をクリアーに見せてくれるかもしれない。だが構想力を伴わなければ「思想」は生まれない。

　現代世界には多くの現実的問題がある。ISISによる世界的なテロ、それに結びついた大量の難民の問題は、宗教や暴力そしてヒューマニズムの問題と結びついている。中国の「肥大化」は経済と環境のバランスを大きく崩す要因になり続けるだろう。日本の社会は縮小化し、いくつもの都市が「消失」の危機を迎えている。これらはどれも極めて「物」的な具体性を

未　来──第5章　　*349*

cities are facing the crisis of vanishing. All of these problems are real and physical crises. We can understand why critics want to directly approach the issues, and not by going through literature.

Did literature, architecture and thoughts end their role because they got away from physical issues? We can say yes, and no.

As a word "literary" is often used to imply irony or to claim that it is obsolete. Literary words have drifted further away from reality. "The keen and high-pitched sound of the flute was overlapping with the rhythm of the Japanese drum which shakes the earth"—these words look like they would be typical "literary" words in the 1950's or 60's, but in truth, it is the first sentence of *Hibana (Sparks)* written by Naoki Matayoshi and awarded the Akutagawa Prize for best novel in 2015. Now novel does nothing but literary imitation. It is quite different from the rediscovery of another possibility of modernism by Zaha Hadid. Words of literature have now lost imagination.

Meanwhile, architecture became a part of an economic system after modernism. "Materials" became "commercial products" and then "something less valued than commercial products" after "the bubble economy." We have reflected on such situations as putting commercial value ahead of everything after the collapse of the "bubble economy" and several other disasters. However, instead of that, only innocent realism as pure communitarianism appeared, for example, sympathy for villages in northeastern Japan which suffered damage from the tsunami. Of course, it is in our nature for us to feel sympathy with small villages troubled by disaster. And architecture has lost the thoughts concerned with facing "our nature."

Today, we are far from "reality" and "thoughts." Is it still possible for us to ask "What is possible?" and "What is it for?"

帯びた危機だ。評論が、文学などを経由せず、直接に対象に迫りたがるのも理解できる。

　それでは文学や建築そして思想は、「物」から遠ざかってしまったがゆえに、その役割を終えたのか？　そうでもあるし、その逆でもある。
　「文学的」などという言葉が揶揄あるいは「死語」そのものでしかないように、文学の言語はいつの間にかリアルから遠く退いてしまった。「大地を震わす和太鼓の律動に、甲高く鋭い笛の音が重なり響いていた」これは「昭和的」な「文学的」言語のように見えるが、実際は2015年に芥川賞を受賞した『火花』（又吉直樹）という小説の出だしである。「文学」は「文学的」模倣しかできなくなってしまった。これは先に見たようなザハ・ハディドによる「近代のもうひとつの可能性」の再発見とはまるで別のものだ。文学の言語は構想力を失った。

　しかしその逆でもある。近代以降、建築は経済の運動に完璧に組み込まれた。「物」は「商品」になり、バブル経済期を経て、「商品」以下のもの（経済価値以下のもの）になり果てた。好景気の崩壊や様々な災害ののち、商品価値至上主義への反省は行われたが、代わりに生まれたのはあまりに素朴な、共同体主義的な「リアリズム」（例えば日本東北村落への無垢な共感）でしかなかった。災害に見舞われた小集落に、リアルな同情を感じるのは当たり前のことだろう。そしてその「当り前さ」を目前にして、建築は思想を失った。

　私たちは「リアル」からも「思想」からも遠ざかってしまった。今や私たちには、「何ができるか」つまりは「どこに向かって」を問うことは不可能なのだろうか？

8. Trotsky and "the Eggs"

"It reminds me of that old joke—you know," mumbles Alvy, the protagonist of *Annie Hall,* in the last scene of the film:[22]

> *A guy walks into a psychiatrist's office and says, hey doc, my brother's crazy! He thinks he's a chicken. Then the doc says, why don't you turn him in? Then the guy says, I would but I need the eggs. I guess that's how I feel about relationships. They're totally crazy, irrational, and absurd, but we keep going through it because we need the eggs.*

"The eggs" refer to something mystical that is left at our feet. "Man" is unraveled by science at the level of the gene, but it is still obscure around our feet. "The eggs" would probably be there in the obscure space. We feel a little warm when our feet touch it. It slightly shines when we shine light upon it. It will break if we handle it too roughly. Something hard to understand, crazy, irrational and absurd, but necessary. While "the eggs" are "relationships" in *Annie Hall,* we might find another "egg." Various eggs are at our feet, but just can't be seen.

We are hoping that something will be hatched from "the eggs." Something of a memory to be recalled, or a future to be dreamed. Reconciliation with nature or reunion with the other. What we need in the origin of our life will be born from "the eggs." We can only live by believing in that.

It is impossible to picture "the eggs" in reality. "The eggs" can exist only

8. トロツキーと卵

——それでまた、僕は古いジョークを思い出した。

映画『アニー・ホール[22]』のラストシーンで、主人公のアルビーがつぶやく。

　　精神科にやってきた男が言う。「先生、俺の弟が、おかしくなってしまって。自分は雌鶏だ、なんて言い出すんだから」「そう……それでどうして弟さんを連れてこないの?」精神科が訊くと、男は答える。「そうは言っても、卵は要るからね」……男と女の関係も、このジョークに似ている。いかれていて、理不尽で、ばかばかしい。それでもひとが恋することをやめないのは、きっと、卵がほしいからなのだろう。

（鈴木訳）

「卵」とは、人間の足元に落ちている、謎に満ちた何かだ。科学的には遺伝子レベルで解明が進んでいる人間だが、その足元は暗く、よく見えない。その暗がりに、おそらくは転がっているのだろう「卵」。足に触れると少しだけ暖かく、光を当てると微かに光り、乱暴に扱うとつぶれてしまう何か。決してわからないもの、いかれていて、理不尽でばかばかしいもの。それでも、あるいはだからこそ、私たちの生が必要とする何か。

「卵」は、『アニー・ホール』では「男と女の関係」だったが、別の「卵」もきっとある。足元には多種多様な「卵」が転がっているのに、ただ見えないだけだ。

私たちは「卵」からやがて何ものかが生まれることを期待している。それはいつの日か思い出すべき記憶かもしれない。かつて夢に見た未来かもしれない。自然との和解かもしれないし、他者との再会かもしれない。私たちの生が根源的に必要とするものが、やがてそこから生まれる。私たちはそう期待して今を生きることを続けている。

「卵」をリアルに描くことはできない。「雌鶏」がいかれた妄想である以

未　来——第5章　　353

as illusion, for the "chicken" is just a crazy delusion. However, illusion can be pictured in imagination only if we shine the light around our real feet by imaginary illumination.

It reminds me of the "Expressionism Debate" again. Most of all of what Trotsky insisted upon when he joined the debate.

Many communists advocated the idea of realism and tried to reject formalism. They tried to deny it and throw it away because it seemed like a dangerous expression for them. Trotsky was a little different from them. He argued that literary persons and artists must have an obligation to face the real issues, and formalism can be an effective method.

> *If the Futurist protest against a shallow realism had historical justification, it was only because it made room for a new artistic recreation of life, for the destruction and reconstruction on new pivots.*

—Literature and Revolution[23]

While "the eggs" in *Annie Hall* are absurd yet peaceful, "the eggs" called "futurism" which Trotsky quoted have the intensity that might cause "destruction." However, it could work against the "shallow realism" which had lost the real intensity of realism and could recreate life.

Philosophy must have been the best formalist method to face the real issues. Marx was the philosopher in this meaning, and Trotsky as well. The modern literature which many philosophers referred to is the philosophy in this meaning.

In the dawn of modernism, architecture, literature and film tried to tackle real issues and explore formalistic methods for it. They believed that they could express the touch of "the eggs" even if they couldn't see "the eggs" themselves.

上、「卵」もまた想像的にしか存在しえない。しかし想像的に存在し得るのなら、創造的に描くことはできる。私たちのリアルな生の足元を、想像的な光で照らしだしさえすれば。

　そこで僕は再び「表現主義論争」のことを考える。とりわけ、トロツキーがこの論争に加わった際にした主張のことを。

　多くの共産主義者たちがこの論争でリアリズムの立場に立ち、フォルマリズムをこき下ろした。単に認めなかったのではなく、危険な思想として否決しようとしたのだ。トロツキーは少し違った。文学者や芸術家はリアルな問題に向き合う義務があるとしながら、そのためにはフォルマリズムも有効な手段——あるいはそれ以上のもの——になりうると論じた。

　　　うすっぺらになっていた日常的リアリズムにたいする未来主義的抗
　　議が歴史的正当性をもっていたとするならば、それはまさに、日常生
　　活を新たに芸術的に再創造するために、すなわち日常生活を破壊して
　　新たな結晶軸にそって建て直すために、場所を用意したというかぎり
　　においてである。
　　　　　　　　　　　　　　　　　　　　　　　　　　——『文学と革命』[23]

　『アニー・ホール』の「卵」がいささか微温的であったのに対し、トロツキーが引き合いに出す「未来主義」という名の「卵」は破壊的な力を生みかねない危険なものだ。しかしそれこそが「リアリズム」を標榜しながらリアルな力を失ってしまった「日常的リアリズム」に対抗し、ひいては日常生活をも「再創造」するだろうとトロツキーは言っている。

　本当は、哲学こそ、リアルな問題に向き合う最高のフォルマリスティックな手段のはずだった。マルクスがそうであり、トロツキーもそうだ。哲学者たちがこぞって参照した近代文学も、確かにそうだった。

　近代の黎明期、建築も、小説も、映画も、リアルな問題に向き合おうとし、そのためにフォルマリスティックな手法を試した。「卵」という「物自体」は無理だとしても、「卵」の感触だけは描きだせるに違いなかったから。

未　来——第5章

In the dusk of the era of "growth," the obscure space at our feet became dark. It became hard to tell if "the eggs" are there or not, and what can be born from them. People looked away from the darkness at their feet. In the not so dark and not so bright space, all of the intensity was lost. Architecture lost the "future," the novel forgot the meaning of "fiction." Imagination disappeared. People stopped to think about what would be born from "the eggs," then forgot the existence of "the eggs."

We need to recall "the egg." We need to imagine it, describe it, shoot the image and design the fictive form. We need it to live.

I'm replacing one of Trotsky's words as the following.

Now you recall the tentative destination of the travel you had with the words.

If something fictive against a shallow realism had historical justification, it was only because it made room for a new artistic recreation of life, for the destruction and reconstruction on new pivots.

—Literature and Revolution

Something fictive means "the egg."

You are travelling to seek "the egg."

* notes

1   Philosopher. German Jewish. 1892-1940.

2   Translated by J. A. Underwood. Prism Key Press (Kindle version), 2012, original in German in 1935.

「成長」の終わりとともに、足元の闇は深くなった。「卵」が本当にあるかどうか、何を生み出してくれるかもわからなくなった。足元の暗がりからひとびとは目をそらし、明るくはないが暗くもない空間のなかで、すべての強度は失われた。建築は未来を失い、小説はフィクションの意味を忘れた。構想力＝想像力が、消えた。ひとは「卵」から何が生まれるかについて考えるのをやめ、次に「卵」の存在についても忘れた。

私たちは今、「卵」を思い出さなければならない。それを想像し、フィクションで語り、そのイメージを映し出し、そしてそのフィクティブな形態をデザインしなければならない。生きるために。
　このトロツキーの言葉のなかの一語を差し替えよう。
　あなたはそれで、あの旅の、とりあえずの目的地を思い出す。

　　うすっぺらになっていた日常的リアリズムにたいする「フィクティブなもの」が歴史的正当性をもっていたとするならば、それはまさに、日常生活を新たに芸術的に再創造するために、すなわち日常生活を破壊して新たな結晶軸にそって建て直すために、場所を用意したというかぎりにおいてである。

――『文学と革命』

フィクティブなもの。それは、「卵」である。
あなたは「卵」を探して、旅を続ける。

◈注

1　思想家。ユダヤ系ドイツ人。1892〜1940

3   Jean-Marie Gustave Le Clézio. France. Born in 1940. Nobel Prize in 1980. He stayed in Central and South America and was known for his critical attitude toward Europe

4   NHK "NW9" broadcasted the interview on January 6th 2016. The interview was in English and Le Clézio used a word "identity." The sentences are based on Suzuki's memory.

5   For example, Edward Said, *Orientalism.*

6   For example, Amartya Sen, *Identity and Violence: the Illusion of Destiny,* W. W. Norton, 2006.

7   For example, Chizuko Ueno, *Datsu-Aidentiti- (De-identity),* Keiso Shobo Publishing, 2005. Only in Japanese.

8   Le Clézio, *La Guerre,* translated by Simon Watson Taylor. Vintage Books, London, 1970.

9   Economist. Born in India in 1933. Nobel Prize in 1998.

10   For example, the well-known symposium, "Overcoming Modernity," held by critics and philosophers of the Kyoto School in 1942 with the proceedings published in magazine *Bungakukai.*

11   We can find the similar sense in the film *2001: A Space Odyssey* directed by Stanley Kubrick.

12   Businessman, Television Personality. 45th President of United States of America. Born in 1946.

13   Twitter, November 4, 2016

14   Novelist. Russia. 1811-1881.

15   Film Director. 1932-86.

16   Refer to the anecdote of "Schrödinger's cat."

17   *Kenchiku-ni Nani-ga Kanō-ka? (What is Possible by Architecture?),* Gakugei Shorin Publishing, 1967. Only in Japanese.

18   Philosopher. France. Born in 1967.

19   *After Finitude: An Essay On the Necessity Of Contingency.* Translated by Ray Brassier. Continuum Publishing.

Chapter 5———*Future*

2 邦訳は晶文社版他多数。本書での引用は、ヴァルター・ベンヤミン（浅井健二郎編訳、久保哲司訳）『近代の意味（ベンヤミン コレクション１）』筑摩書房、1995年

3 ドイツ語、英語ともに表記はaura。日本語化している「オーラ」の語源。

4 （Jean-Marie Gustave Le Clézio）小説家。フランス、モーリシャス。1940年生まれ。1980年ノーベル文学賞受賞。中南米の滞在が長く、ヨーロッパへの批判的視座も持つ。

5 NHK NW9が2016年１月６日に放送したインタビュー。インタビューは英語で行われ、ル・クレジオはidentityという語を用いた。ここでのセンテンスは、同放送での音声を鈴木が訳している。

6 例えば、E. W. サイード（今沢紀子訳）『オリエンタリズム（上・下）』平凡社、1993年。ヨーロッパはアジアを他者化することで、自らのアイデンティティを構築した。

7 例えば、アマルティア・セン（東郷えりか訳）『アイデンティティと暴力──運命は幻想である』勁草書房、2011年。

8 例えば、上野千鶴子編『脱アイデンティティ』勁草書房、2005年。

9 豊崎光一訳、新潮社、1972年（*La Guerre*, Gallimard, 1970.）

10 経済学者。1933年インド生まれ。1998年、ノーベル経済学賞受賞。

11 1942年「近代の超克」とタイトルされたシンポジウムが、京都学派の哲学者や、文学者たちによって行われ、『文学界』に掲載された。

12 映画『2001年宇宙の旅』（スタンリー・キューブリック監督、1968年）の感覚はこれに近い。

13 アメリカの実業家、大富豪。1946年生まれ。第45代アメリカ合衆国大統領。

14 小説家。ロシア。1811〜1881

15 ソ連の映画監督。1932〜1986

16 素粒子物理学の不確定性理論。「シュレディンガーの猫」は、その一瞬後には50％死に、50％生きている。

17 学藝書林、1967年

18 哲学者。フランス。1967年生まれ。

20 Lacan, Deleuze, Kristeva and the other contemporary thinkers quoted the latest results of mathematics or physics to support their theory. Alan Sokal (b. 1955), a professor of physics at New York University, doubted whether these thinkers understood math and physics well, so he wrote an philosophical article intentionally quoting faulty math and physics. He submitted the essay to Social Text, and it was accepted and published in the magazine in 1996. Sokal's doubt was verified. Sokal explained that he didn't intend to criticize philosophy but just its usage of terms of math and physics without adequate understanding.

21 Literary Critic. Japan. 1902-1983. He established Japanese modern criticism by looking not only at literature but at all arts. He also commented extensively on World War II.

22 Directed by Woody Allen, starring Diane Keaton. United States. 1977. Academy Award for motion pictures, actress, and the others.

23 *Literature and Revolution* in collected writings on *Literature and Art &* *Literature and Revolution*.

19 千葉雅也・大橋完太郎・星野太訳、人文書院、2016年（*Après la finitude : essai sur la nécessité de la contingence,* 2006.）

20 ラカン、ドゥルーズ、クリステヴァといった20世紀後半の「現代思想家」たちは、自らの理論を語るのに数学や物理学の最先端の成果を援用していた。ニューヨーク大学物理学教授のアラン・ソーカル（1955〜）は、「現代思想」は本当はまるで数学や物理学を理解していないのではないかと疑い、自らでたらめな数学や物理学を多用した「哲学」論文を書いた。これを哲学評論雑誌『ソーシャル・テキスト』に送ったところ、1996年にそれは採択掲載され、ソーカルの疑いは実証されてしまった。ソーカル自身は、自分は哲学そのものを批判したいのではなく、「現代思想家」たちがわかりもしない数学や物理学を援用したがることを批判している、と再三念を押している。

21 1902〜1983。文学のみならず芸術全般を見渡し、日本近代の批評を確立した。戦争についての言説は多く参照され、批判もされた。

22 ウディ・アレン主演・監督、ダイアン・キートン主演。アメリカ、1977年。アカデミー作品賞、主演女優賞他受賞。

23 トロツキイ（桑野隆訳）『文学と革命（上・下）』岩波文庫、1993年

Epilogue

Dedicated to Annie Hall

"Go on travelling,"

I say to myself while lying on the bottom of a bunk bed in a youth hostel in London. Someone turns over on the top of the bunk bed and I can hear it creak.

Two years have passed after I travelled through the forest by train. I open my eyes and notice that I am not on the train which I thought was the cause of the shaking. "But," I ask myself. "Where should I go next?"

I can't tell where I will be tomorrow, and I don't know the name of the hotel I will stay in tonight. That is the journey I am on. I will go on, or…I must go on.

I was in LA six weeks ago. It was my first trip abroad. I thought that I would travel around the US for four weeks or so and be back to Japan. It took a month to get from LA to NY by Greyhound and stopping in towns in the Middle America. I found a cheap hostel on the Westside of Manhattan, then stayed for two weeks and changed my mind.

—I won't go back. I will go on traveling somewhere.

—So I have come "somewhere," the frame of the bed creaks when the guy on the top rolls over. How do I decide where to go next?

I had not guidebook. There was no internet at the time. I became

終　章

アニー・ホールのために

　旅を続けよう。

　ロンドンのユースホステルの、二段ベッドの下段に横たわりながら、そう僕は決心する。上段の同宿者の寝返りを、スプリングの軋みで感じる。

　森を抜ける列車での旅から、2年が過ぎていた。目を開ければ、自分の体を揺らしているのは列車ではなく、二段ベッドなのだとわかる。しかし、と僕は考えた。旅を続けるとはいっても、いったい次にどこに行けばいいのか？

　明日いる町の名前も知らない、今晩眠る宿もたどり着くまでわからない。そんな旅を続けよう。というより、もはやそうするしか他に選択肢はなかった。

　その6週間前、初めての海外渡航でロサンジェルスまで来た。アメリカをひと月ほど回ったら、帰るつもりだった。グレイハウンド・バスで中南部をうろうろしてからニューヨークまで行き、ウエストサイドの安宿に予定を大幅に過ぎて居ついたところで、気持ちが変わった。

　帰るのはやめた。このままどこかに行こう。

　そうして僕は、とりあえずのどこかまでやって来た。二段ベッドの上の男が寝返りを打つたびにベッド全体がギシギシと鳴る。次のどこかを、どうやって決めよう？　ガイドブックはもっていなかった。インターネット

363

nervous. "Die in a ditch" was a reality which was often present in my mind. I did not have a ticket for the return flight, but just about enough money to live for a few weeks, and I was planning to stretch the money thin over a few months. Reckless and poor, my travel began—or restarted.

"When did I begin this travel?"
Annoyed by the heat, I asked myself this question in a cheap hotel in Old Delhi. The room was so dirty that I suddenly recalled the bunk bed in London as a utopia. The temperature would never be below a hundred degrees Fahrenheit, even after midnight. No fan, no air conditioner and no wind from opened windows. Finally, I emptied a bucket of water on the bed. The bed was dry in the morning.

Did my poor travel begin in London, New York or Narita Airport where I got on the plane bound for LA? The noise of cars in traffic began to reach my ears from a faint light outside the window. As I closed my eyes, my consciousness returned to the train running through the forest. My senses were hazy with heat and sleepiness, my ears registered the horn of a car as a train whistle, and my lids reflected the morning light of India as the light leaking between the branches. I couldn't fall asleep and was caught by a hazy idea. That the journey might …I said to myself.

"That the journey might still be taking place. I might still be on the train."

I'm still looking at the raindrops leaking between the branches in my imagination. I'm still traveling by train. The travel will never end. It will trace my memory forever.

I was tracing my memory in Delhi, London and in the train. I was tracing the affairs that made me travel. I was remembering *Annie Hall*, which I watched and fell in love with when I was a high school student. If I

364   Epilogue ——— *Dedicated to Annie Hall*

もない時代だ。不安だった。「野垂れ死」という言葉が現実感をもって、頭のなかをくるくると回った。帰りのチケットも持たず、数週間分の生活費を数か月分に引き伸ばして使うつもりの、とんでもなく貧乏で無謀な、旅の始まり——再開——だった。

　この旅を、いつ始めたのだったか？

　オールド・デリーの安ホテルで——ロンドンのベッドが理想郷のように思い出される不衛生な部屋で——暑さに苦しめられながらそんなことを思う。40度を超える気温の夜、部屋にエアコンはおろか扇風機すらなく、窓を開けたところで空気は全く動かない。やむなくベッドに水をぶちまけてその上に寝るという乱暴な行為を試みた。ベッドの水は明け方にはすっかり乾いた。

　貧しい旅の始まりはロンドンだったかニューヨークか、アメリカに向けて初めての飛行機に乗った成田空港か？　薄っすらと明るくなった窓の外から、早くも往来の車の音が聞こえ始める。目を閉じると、僕の意識はまた森を抜ける列車のなかへと戻った。暑さと眠さで混濁した僕の耳はクラクションを汽笛として聞き、インドの夜明けの光を木漏れ日として瞼の裏で見た。眠りに落ちきらぬまま僕は妄想ともつかない思いを続けた。ひょっとして、と僕は思う。

　この旅は、あの列車の旅の続きなのか？　僕は今も、あの列車に乗ったままなのだろうか？

＊

　きっと今も、僕は木の葉の隙間から零れ落ちる雨を眺めている。列車に乗って、旅を続けている。旅はいつまでも終わらないだろう。そして、始まりを遡り続けるだろう。

　デリーで、ロンドンで、そしてあの列車のなかで、僕はずっと始まりを遡り続けていた。僕を旅へと追い立てた出来事。高校生の時に見た映画『アニー・ホール』、そしてその主人公の「アニー・ホール」に恋をしたこ

hadn't seen that film –and Annie- again and again, and didn't learn a lot from it, I wouldn't have been able to write a novel, and let alone this book. I was thinking about Sartre, whom I read with shock when I was fourteen. And I was recalling Mr. Ito, a teacher who taught me how to think when I was just eleven. Mr. Ito died before he became thirty years old.

Every time I trace it, I'm astonished by how much they gave me. Nobody can say that it's enough, no matter how much praise I give them.

To my deceased parents who complained, but still gave me permission to go on my reckless journey, thank you.

I would also like to thank Noriko Yokobatake, a partner on my journey through life which began much later than days of India.

A lot of time has passed since the day I arrived in Japan via Karachi, Bangkok and other cities in Delhi. I got to know that travelling without a guidebook was really fun, but it left me very impoverished. I think that I won't be able to complete a journey where I lose twenty-five pounds in a few months ever again.

However, my mind is still stuck on one thing.

"I will go somewhere."

と。この映画を数十回と見、そしてそこから学ぶことができなかったのなら、僕は一片の小説も書かなかっただろうし、したがってこの本も書いていなかっただろう。あるいは中学時代に衝撃とともにむさぼり読んだサルトル。さらに遡って、まだ小学生だった僕に悩むことを教えておきながら、自身は30歳を前にして死んだ伊藤先生。

　今さらではあるが、彼らが僕に与えてくれたものの大きさに、僕は愕然とする。僕がどれだけ感謝しても、きっと誰もそれで十分だとは言わないだろう。
　貧乏で無謀な「旅」、つまりは僕のその後の生きかたにも、文句を言いながらも、結局は許容してくれた今は亡き両親にも、できることならありがとうと伝えたい。
　そしてインドよりもだいぶ後、ずっと僕の「旅」の同伴者であり続けている横畠倫子に、感謝したい。
　デリーからカラチやバンコックそのほかの都市を経由して帰国した日から、だいぶ長い時間がたった。ガイドブックのない旅は愉快だったが、飢餓に近い空腹は本当につらいものだとあの時知った。体重が数か月で十キロ以上減るような旅を、僕はもうできないかもしれない。

　それでも僕はまだ思っている。
　どこかに行こう、と。

アニー・ホールのために──終　章

鈴木隆之 (すずき・たかゆき)

1961年生まれ。建築家、小説家。聖ジョセフ大学（マカオ）訪問教授、元京都精華大学教授。元南カリフォルニア建築大学客員教員。京都大学卒業。1987年群像新人文学賞受賞。主な著書に、『パーフェクト・ワールド』（論創社、2014年）、『ポートレイト・イン・ナンバー』（現代企画室、1988年）、『未来の地形』（講談社、1992年）、『「建築」批判——空間をめぐる光芒』（生国舎、1995年）、『不可解な殺人の風景』（風塵社、2002年）など。建築作品として、「EXCES」「京都精華大学本館」など。

英訳監修　ヨーナス・エンゲスヴィーク
　　　　　ジョーダン・スミス（城西国際大学准教授）

Takayuki Suzuki

Born in 1961. Architect, novelist, visiting professor, The University of Saint Joseph. Ex-professor, Kyoto Seika University. Ex-instructor, Southern California Institute of Architecture. Graduated from Kyoto University.

Translation Editor :　Jonas Engesvik
Editional Assistance : Jordan A. Y. Smith
(associate professor, Josai International University)

Fictive Space :
for Architecture, Literature and Film

by TAKAYUKI TAKI SUZUKI

©Takayuki Suzuki, 2017

Published by RONSO Publishing, Co., Ltd.

Kitai Building, 2-23, Jinbocho, Kanda, Chiyoda-ku, Tokyo.
101-0051 Japan.
Tel. +81-3-3264-5254 Fax. +81-3-3264-5232
Web. http://www.ronso.co.jp/

Book Design : Kano Nagai
Printed by Chuo Seihan Printing Co., Ltd.

表現空間論

建築／小説／映画の可能性

2017年11月25日　初版第一刷印刷
2017年12月1日　初版第一刷発行

著　者̶̶̶̶鈴木隆之

発行者̶̶̶̶森下紀夫

発行所̶̶̶̶論 創 社
〒101−0051
東京都千代田区神田神保町2−23　北井ビル
tel. 03 (3264) 5254　fax. 03 (3264) 5232
web. http://www.ronso.co.jp/
振替口座　00160−1−155266

装幀・組版̶̶̶永井佳乃
印刷・製本̶̶̶中央精版印刷

ISBN978-4-8460-1632-6
©2017 SUZUKI Takayuki, Printed in Japan

論創社

パーフェクト・ワールド

The Perfect World by Suzuki Takayuki

鈴木隆之

群像新人賞受賞作家による近未来SF超大作

ある日、NASAは巨大隕石落下の可能性を全世界に配信する。次々と地球を襲う災害、災厄。世界中の人々が終末的な危機感を抱えるなか、少数のエリートたちで構成される〈賢人組織49人委員会〉による人類の地球外移住プロジェクトが発足した。果たして、人類は生き延びることができるのか──？

本体2000円

好評発売中